Imagine, Inquire, and Create

Other Books by the Authors

Activating Assessment for All Students: Differentiated Instruction and Information Methods in Math and Science, 2nd Edition

Activating Assessment for All Students: Innovative Activities, Lesson Plans, and Informative Assessment

Demystify Math, Science, and Technology: Creativity, Innovation, and Problem-Solving

Demystify Math, Science, and Technology: Creativity, Innovation, and Problem-Solving, 2nd Edition

Helping Students Who Struggle with Math and Science: A Collaborative Approach for Elementary and Middle Schools

Shaping the Future with Math, Science, and Technology: Solutions and Lesson Plans to Prepare Tomorrows Innovators

Teaching Math, Science, and Technology in Schools Today: Guidelines for Engaging Both Eager and Reluctant Learners, 2nd Edition

Tomorrow's Innovators: Essential Skills for a Changing World

Imagine, Inquire, and Create

A STEM-Inspired Approach to Cross-Curricular Teaching

Second Edition

Dennis Adams and Mary Hamm

ROWMAN & LITTLEFIELD
Lanham • Boulder • New York • London

Published by Rowman & Littlefield
A wholly owned subsidiary of The Rowman & Littlefield Publishing Group, Inc.
4501 Forbes Boulevard, Suite 200, Lanham, Maryland 20706
www.rowman.com

Unit A, Whitacre Mews, 26-34 Stannary Street, London SE11 4AB

British Library Cataloguing in Publication Information Available

Library of Congress Cataloging-in-Publication Data
Adams, Dennis, 1947– author.
Imagine, inquire, and create : a STEM-inspired approach to cross-curricular teaching / Dennis Adams and Mary Hamm. — Second edition.
    pages cm
Includes bibliographical references.
ISBN 978-1-4758-2176-5 (cloth : alk. paper) — ISBN 978-1-4758-2177-2 (pbk. : alk. paper) — ISBN 978-1-4758-2178-9 (electronic)
1. Science—Study and teaching—United States. 2. Technology—Study and teaching—United States. 3. Engineering—Study and teaching—United States. 4. Mathematics—Study and teaching—United States. 5. Interdisciplinary approach in education—United States. 6. Creative ability in science. 7. Creative ability in technology. 8. Creative teaching. I. Hamm, Mary, author. II. Title.
Q181.A288 2015
507.1'273—dc23   2015024386

Printed in the United States of America

Contents

Preface

Drew Gilpin Faust, president of Harvard University, suggests that the STEM subjects have a natural connection with subjects across the curriculum: "A liberal arts education is one that embraces—indeed requires—broad learning across the fields of natural and social sciences and humanities. Its goal is to create citizens equipped with habits of mind and analytic capacities to shape human experience within the context of the natural realities and technological forces—and opportunities—we confront. . . . Liberal arts learning contrasts itself not with STEM fields, which it encompasses, but with purely vocational education."

This book focuses on approaches and methods for infusing twenty-first-century skills into basic subject matter lessons. The basic assumption is that all students must be educated to the point where they can deal with the nature of the problems and the possibilities found in a brave new world.

As teachers work to prepare tomorrow's innovators, it is important for them to recognize the fact that others influence every creator in both time and space. Just about every imaginative new idea or product builds on the concepts, tools, and models of many people. So it is important for students to explore what others have done as they collaborate to discover and create new things.

The old foundations of reading, writing, and mathematics—and the new basics of science, technology, and the arts—are viewed as being at the core of schooling. Creative thinking, collaborative learning, technological wisdom, adaptability, and innovation are all part of the mix. Attention is also given to how elements of the STEM subjects can be integrated across the curriculum.

In any era, transforming a classroom or school into a contemporary learning environment requires paying attention to consistent classroom routines, using assessment data for improvement, and having a coherent organizational structure. It is our hope that by connecting the best ideas of yesterday and today, it will be possible to build a bridge to the essential skills of the future.

Broad cultural, social, technological, and educational trends are challenging old assumptions and inviting new dreams. As changes take place, there is a natural tension between what we know and what we can imagine. Recognizing that reality requires exploring topics related to teacher professional development, the cognitive nature of learning, and the pedagogical implications of technology.

In an increasingly globalized world, the next generation has to be more savvy about what is going on around the world. To make this happen, school culture and lessons have to be developed in a way that pay closer attention to an interconnected world. To be successful in such an environment requires updating our classrooms in ways that breathe new life into teaching and learning.

Whether it is the challenges associated with globalization, instructional reform, and new media, there is always the danger of change biting back. Technology is a good example of an area where we have to apply a little critical thinking. Although it's not going to take over the world anytime soon, it is bound change us all in unpredictable ways.

It's a complicated and uncertain time, with at least some basic technology present in every classroom. The question is how much *digital* technology should students at different grade levels use.

Is it wise to use digital devices if they take time away from the hands-on exploration and collaborative problem solving that children need? To answer these and other questions requires thinking about the benefits, the costs, and the age of learners before investing in expensive educational tools and materials.

It is probably not wise to use digital devices if they take much time away from the hands-on exploration and collaborative problem solving that children need. But no matter what happens in the classroom, students will be spending many hours each day in front of a screen. That can be helpful and/or it can get in the way of deep learning. One of the problems: the Web has made it possible to live in a "filter bubble" that lets in only information with which you already agree.

Uncertainty is as inevitable at home and at school as it is on the frontiers of knowledge. Reflection, discussion, and cultivating the disposition for creative and critical thinking can always inform and enrich teaching and learning. Remember, change really does favor the prepared mind.

In times of rapid change, there tends to be a power struggle between what we know and what we can imagine. When schools feel the pressure to change the habit of the familiar, it is tempting to resist and simply continue with day-to-day routines. So it is important to recognize that there are some very negative consequences attached to succumbing to inertia, indifference, and distraction.

We view learning as a continuum—a lifelong awakening to the complexities of the world. There are no "silver bullet" solutions to educational problems. We certainly can't fire our way to better schools. But we can identify and respect the complexity of the problems that have to be solved.

Schools can make a big difference, but they can't do it alone. For students to be successful, schools and community-based support have to be wrapped around each other in a way that supplies a good educational foundation and sustained support.

It may not be possible to guarantee every child a wonderful home life, but working together, it should be possible to provide a high-quality education for all young people.

Education can be a powerful instrument for social progress in an environment where teachers have the opportunity to forge the future they imagine.

In spite of all the obstacles that may get in the way, teachers can make a huge difference in the lives of many students. Of course, no one is certain that great teachers, technological marvels, or anything else will result in a more prosperous and just society where all youngsters can thrive. But if there is enough imagination, compassion, courage, and resources, it is possible to achieve the goal of educating all children to their full potential.

With or without outside obstacles, the teacher is the biggest single determinant of how well students move along the road to a deep understanding of whatever subject is being studied. The key to quality learning in the classroom: teachers who clearly understand the subjects they teach and are fully aware of the characteristics of effective instruction.

We can't predict the future, but it is possible to think about the different terrains where we may find ourselves living, learning, and working. Fortunately, certain guidelines and basic pedagogical principles will not disappear. For example, in any conceivable future, the curriculum has to be meaningful, make connections, emphasize responsibility, and reflect human values.

Imagine, Inquire, and Create! A STEM-Inspired Approach to Cross-Curricular Teaching suggests some possible routes that can be taken today and explores conceptual principles and practical approaches that have meaning for tomorrow's schools. Although attention is paid to modern realities, plenty of room is left for idealism, hope, and practical ideas that can help us develop schools worthy of our children.

We can anticipate constant waves of change flowing across any structure that gets built. Still, the need to prepare for an uncertain future is clear. The days of fairly stationary educational goals are over; hitting moving targets is part of today's reality. One of the few permanent things now is change itself.

Nothing great was ever achieved without enthusiasm.

—Emerson

Chapter 1

Introduction

Essential Skills in a Changing World

Innovation lies at the intersection of learning, imagination and reality.
What a learner believes is possible shapes the range of possibilities.

—Carol Dweck

In the last few decades, we have seen major changes in academic subjects, the global economy, and the nature of human interaction. At the same time, educators and policymakers have been creating new standards and methods for encouraging a climate of achievement and creativity in the classroom.

The long health of our society and economy depends on creating even more innovation. For future innovators to get it right requires more than the STEM subjects of science, technology, engineering, and mathematics. Reading, writing, literature, and the arts are examples of other subjects that contribute to building the essential skills needed to shape the future.

Developing the imaginative and inventive capacities of young people requires tapping the creative possibilities found in subjects across the curriculum. Creating tomorrow's innovators requires paying attention to preparing students who can work collaboratively, think critically, and communicate well with peers in the classroom and around the world.

Opening doors to inventive success has a lot to do with what happens in the space between group members. In many ways, the whole is greater than the sum of its parts.

Informed teamwork and discipline have more to do with innovation than individual flashes of imagination. Lightning bolts only hit once or twice. Genius may help, but being able to work with others to solve challenging problems seems to matter more than IQ.

Some of us may be more creative than others, but *everyone* can make creative contributions. The boundary encompasses our imagination and the natural laws of the universe.

A great deal of attention has to be paid to technology because it has the potential to be both wonderful and horrifying at the same time. They are the basis of National Security Agency (NSA) spying, drones that kill, and the privatization of biological life. Still, the potential is there for building a better world. We have to make sure that these products of science serve good futures (Brattgon, 2015).

In today's world, societal changes and technological breakthroughs are reaching a critical mass. In fact, the speed of today's changes has a lot to do with pressures to quicken the pace of educational renewal.

When it comes to innovation, the Internet and social networks seem to have canceled out some of the historical advantages of physical proximity. But the results may not be applicable at school. The research on the usefulness of digital technology in the classroom has come up with mixed results—especially at the primary level. Still, it is becoming increasingly clear that *active learning* and modern technology have the potential to enhance teaching and learning.

New ideas and products often involve taking the tools, concepts, and understandings available today and mixing them together in a way that creates something new. Inventive new concepts and imaginative possibilities often depend on networks of knowledge (Johnson, 2014).

You can be cautious about the role of technology without diminishing its importance. Understanding what's going on and being able to think critically matter more than getting caught up in the rush to get the latest gadgets.

Academic success depends more than ever on human nature and teacher ingenuity. What matters most in the classroom is teamwork, solving problems, and being able to come up with new ideas.

Is there a fixed reality apart from human observations—or are there infinite possibilities?

INNOVATION AND AN UNCERTAIN FUTURE

Innovative ideas or products are rarely dreamed up by someone working in isolation. Teamwork and the ability of all concerned to respond to a rapidly changing world are two of the keys to success. When it comes to individual teachers in the classroom, turning imaginative possibilities into helpful realities depends on preparation, peer collaboration, educational vision, and a well-designed curriculum.

The effectiveness of new educational approaches has a lot to do with the strength of people behind change and the strength of the school culture

(Gruenert & Whitaker, 2015). Consider arts education where new conceptual challenges and techniques abound. Like it or hate it, the Web does allow you to tour the best museums on the planet.

Advances in digital technology and the Internet have created new kinds of art possibilities that can help make good art or ruin the entire process. Man Ray, Alexander Calder, and Igor Stravinsky all used the new technologies of their time to conceptualize new forms of visual art and music. The difference is that with today's technology, just about anyone with a computer can hammer out an art print or a musical composition. How good are you at sorting out the good from the horrible?

Take the example of music. Today's technology is so powerful that students who don't know anything about scales—or much else musically—can use devices and apps like the Native Instrument Machine to make original compositions. For children, it may be fun and informative. Still, melodies, timing, and lyrics and just about everything else can be worked out by the computer as students bang away on the keyboard.

Teachers and students have to figure out when it is best to use basic technology (like paint and canvas) and when it is best to use digital tools as assistants in the creative process. There is no reason why anyone has to rush headlong into the new digital age. But no matter how you approach it, neither teaching nor learning should be a passive or a solitary experience in front of a screen.

Neither teachers nor the arts are in danger of being replaced by new forms of technology—or anything else. Digital technology is, at best, a complement (not a replacement) for traditional art, teacher innovation, and student engagement. Science simulations, virtual museum visits, and word processing are one thing, but if tech tools aren't well suited to the task, then they may not be worth the time or the cost.

There is at least some truth to the idea that you should be careful about how you interpret the world because that interpretation may alter your perception of reality. A good example is how one approach to increasing economic productivity has changed things. Now, artificial intelligence, advanced robotics, and a host of other innovations are replacing jobs higher and higher up the skills ladder (Brynjolfsson & McAfee, 2014).

Have we reached a stage where the increases in productivity increase the wealth of fewer and fewer people? Does the wage gap have a lot to do with the education gap?

Knowledge in the service of creativity may open up some positive long-term possibilities. For example, as part of hands-on lessons—from the arts to engineering—students can be encouraged to take virtual tours of museums, musical and theatrical productions, and science simulations (Suggestion: in the classroom, a few online hints are fine for developing questions, but viewing longer segments is best done as homework).

Networking possibilities are expanding rapidly; today's technologies support global observation, interaction, and learning as never before. It's a new world order. Still, the shape of a nation's future depends more on the quality of its educational system than on new media possibilities.

Quality instruction always comes down to teachers and their understanding of the characteristics of effective instruction (pedagogy). Still, as students move into the upper elementary grades, combining new information distribution possibilities with the more personal collaborative aspects of interactive face-to-face learning can stimulate aesthetic learning environments.

The more the STEM subjects and their associates advance our mastery of the natural world, the more difficulty we seem to have with things that are difficult to understand or control. As science and its technological tools advance, there seems to be less of a disposition to deal with the unknown. Does not knowing what will happen tomorrow create more fear than ever?

In a world of uncertain challenges, good preparation includes developing an analytic spirit, learning to deal with ambiguity, and cultivating the capacity for questioning and judgment. The capacity of teachers and students to deal with change, learn from it, and help each other manage the surrounding uncertainty is critical to the future development of our society.

Change is influenced by the intellectual energy of a civilization, and it favors the prepared mind. To prepare students who can be successful in an unknowable future requires teachers who can help students collaboratively perceive, analyze, interpret, and discover a whole new range of meanings (Beghetto et al., 2014).

SOCIAL REALITIES IN THE AGE OF INFORMATION

When all students have access to computers and other digital devices, the learning gap between students may actually increase. Whether it is on or off campus, after some initial enthusiasm, students who are having academic difficulty tend to waste more time than students who are doing well (Pinker, 2014).

Is digital technology a useful tool, a distraction, or both? A lot depends on how tech tools are used and how students are taught to understand and create with the most powerful media available. If children spend nearly half their waking hours in front of a screen (without adult supervision), bad things tend to happen. Still, when technology is used well, it can support creativity, collaboration, and curriculum standards in ways that reinforce all three.

The interaction of events and technological trends requires new definitions and new approaches to teaching and learning. Information economies require higher levels and more frequent education for everyone. There is a convergence in knowledge, producing possibilities involving publishers, schools, the Internet, television, libraries, universities, and museums.

We face a future in which human communication, interaction, and learning are no longer bound by time, space, and form. Fortunately, everything we know and value won't fade into oblivion. In any conceivable future, children will have to learn how to read, write, and do mathematics. Also, learners will have to develop the thinking skills needed to sort through today's avalanche of information and take an informed position on a wide range of issues.

Any future effective educational model will be influenced by the research on instruction, new understandings about the social nature of learning, and advancing technological possibilities. Like it or not, educators will bear some of the responsibility for arranging new instructional models in a way that helps produce citizens who can live and work productively in an increasingly complex world.

Every high-quality educational future requires putting more resources into focused learning opportunities for teachers. It takes well-educated teachers to help students learn how to connect to wider and wider circles of knowledge and social issues. To be successful, any model of quality schooling has to include perpetual staff development and school-embedded learning.

The world outside the classroom is changing more rapidly than ever. Everyday reality intrudes into schools like never before. In today's social milieu, the schools are sometimes the child's only venue for socially and intellectually stimulating work. Giving children an education sufficient for healthy and productive lives is more important than ever.

Under the right circumstances, everyone is capable of coming up with new and innovative ideas. Generating imaginative new ideas requires putting up with multiple failures and taking thousands of steps to get it right. It also requires working in an endless loop of problems and solutions. To paraphrase Margaret Mead, a clear understanding of a problem prefigures its lines of solution.

Every child should be able to use all the tools available to explore material in a manner that sparks curiosity, encourages collaborative inquiry, and extends learning possibilities. Literacy, for example, is often viewed as more than reading the printed word. Adding science and the arts to the mix are but two examples of how students can be motivated to go beyond words to improve their work across the curriculum (Marshall & Donahue, 2014).

Question: Are the uncertainties we find around us simply a reflection of our imperfect knowledge of human nature and the natural world?

Some things are quite clear. For example, we know that the social nature of language and creative development are so interconnected that it is hard to separate one from the other. Across the curriculum, when new things materialize, their usefulness depends on whether or not they empower us to collaboratively reach further in the world.

To deal with real-world problems and stay relevant, teachers need to know about what's going on in various subject fields. And they need to work together (professional development) to translate current events for their classes. It may take more than what teachers can do alone to generate adequate resources for integrating the most powerful approaches and methods into day-to-day lessons. Both the pedagogical and funding pieces have to be in place to enable major changes to emerge smoothly.

To paraphrase Goethe:

What you know or dream you can begin.
Boldness has genius, power, and magic in it.
Engage, then the mind grows heated —
Begin it, and the work can be completed!

DO YOUR BEST TODAY; DO BETTER TOMORROW

Schools can become a community of learners by creating a caring atmosphere, attending to student interests, and promoting meaningful learning. That's easy enough to say, but it's often hard to do. It certainly helps when the school culture values personal commitment and academic achievement.

To make sure that good things happen sometimes requires breaking down barriers to learning and moving students in the direction of academic success. It also requires opportunities for students to be active participants in their own learning.

Teachers need consistent societal and administrative support. Blaming teachers for most of the bad things that happen at school is counterproductive. After all, in one way or another, we are all involved in the education of children. So all of us must do what we can—taking every opportunity to recognize the impact and positive influence that teachers can have on children's lives.

What does it take to become a good teacher? First of all, prospective teachers need to develop the intellectual tools learned in the arts and sciences. Equally important, they need to acquire the foundational skills that relate to strategic learning and pedagogical methods.

Even the best college graduates flounder if they start teaching without a thorough knowledge of the characteristics of effective instruction. Another factor in learning to be a successful teacher: early fieldwork experiences in different communities and in different school settings.

The research suggests that the most effective teachers are enthusiastic about their work and have high expectations for their students. This involves respecting students' creative potential and developing professionally appropriate personal connections. No one has to invade privacy to make good things happen.

For teachers: it is probably best not to give out your phone number or home email address because you need time away from schoolwork. Still, you need to recognize the fact that interpersonal relationships that develop over matters of content are at the heart of schooling.

Schools that involve teachers in participatory decision making and collaborative strategies for addressing school problems will reinforce a teacher's commitment to the profession. Effective staff development programs have taken this into account as they address the challenge of sustaining the long-term commitment of dedicated and committed teachers.

Through active participation in staff development programs, teachers can work in association with peers and "experts" to grow professionally and personally. Also, well-chosen university classes and professional conferences can certainly help.

By collaborating with a wide range of others to reach common goals, teachers are more likely to appreciate new instructional ideas and respect other professionals (Pahomov, 2014). Positive attitudes make a big difference. When teachers possess a positive attitude toward professional development and their own teaching, they will continue to be lifelong learners.

It does, after all, take time to become a really good teacher. A good motto: do your best today; do better tomorrow.

BECOMING A MORE EFFECTIVE TEACHER

Experienced teachers understand that teaching is a complex undertaking that requires time. Conditions may be difficult, but effective teachers accept and enjoy the challenges. They know that they make a difference in students' lives.

Many teachers describe success in personal terms and view it as related to being personally durable and capable. Knowing the child and understanding the community are frequently mentioned as important. Most teachers who have elected to remain in their schools for more than three years feel in control of their environment and believe teaching is a rich and rewarding experience.

Effective teachers are more likely to believe that:

- Creating a feeling of excitement about the subject matter or skill being taught is important.
- Children can always learn more and that the teachers' effort and energy are instrumental in students' learning.

- Providing children the opportunity for active participatory experiences is a powerful incentive for learning.
- It is important to reflect a strong sense of personal caring about students and adjust instruction to their needs.
- Children try hardest when they are fairly certain of success, but not absolutely positive.
- Students learn most from teachers who believe that the level of student effort can predict achievement.
- Young people learn most when their questions and learning activities are connected with big ideas, key concepts, and their intellectual curiosity.

Although there are many approaches to good teaching, it is our belief that effective teachers often share some of the same characteristics.

Activity: Take a few minutes and write down a few of the teaching characteristics of your favorite teacher. Share with another person, a small group, or with the whole class. What are the similarities and differences between the above list and your favorite teacher? See if you can change a point or add an important characteristic to the above list. Would you take something out? Remember, no human teacher is going to have *all* the "right" characteristics.

CONFIRMING THE IDEALS OF PUBLIC EDUCATION

Global competition is one thing, the future of our democracy is quite another. They do, however, have at least one thing in common: both depend on the revitalization of the public schools (Darling-Hammond, 2010).

No matter what happens just over the horizon, the majority of American children will continue to be educated in the public schools, making choices about life and connecting to youngsters from different backgrounds. It is also where images are formed of what it means to be a good person, have a good life, and live in a good society.

The interpreting and reinterpreting of the ideals of universal public education will be with us throughout the twenty-first century. Small-scale private sector experiments are fine, but to reach the majority of students, innovations must be transferred successfully to the public sector.

In the workplace or in school, specific skill and general intellectual development activities completed in small groups can make learning more lively and interesting for everyone. The best schools are constantly building on the latest research-based techniques, while continuously recycling the most successful practices of the past.

Fortunately, many of the basic pedagogical principles remain fairly constant. Whether it's yesterday, today, or tomorrow, effective teachers have been and will continue to be teaching for understanding.

In any conceivable future, educators will be designing activities that place an emphasis on reasoning, collaboration, and communication (Opitz & Ford, 2014). Another consistent educational goal: the creation of learning communities that encourage students to become active and collaborative participants in the construction of meaning.

Some schools really have their act together. But there is general agreement that in at least a few schools, students are made to feel unwelcome, intellectually inadequate, uncomfortable, and bored. At the earliest opportunity, they drop out. For some who stay, schools may offer little encouragement for those who have talents extending beyond the ability to manipulate words and numbers.

Figuring out what to keep the same and what to change isn't easy. Yes, transforming our schools will occasionally require dealing with state and district systems that are hostile to change. But top-down mandates usually do more harm than good.

We all share in the responsibility for the education of children, so it takes community engagement to turn around some schools and some students. In spite of the grim social realities that weigh heavily on the shoulders of disadvantaged students, the right kind of adult support can make a permanent difference.

Large-scale educational change requires a sustained public commitment. Once this is in place, we must involve a widespread cadre of public school educators who are willing to implement high-quality approaches in their schools. The overall goal should be nothing less than making sure that all of our schools shine when compared to schools around the world.

Ideally, curriculum designs should build on Western traditions while valuing values and cultures from around the world. This has to happen while schools carry out rigorous self-examinations, incorporate vigorous innovations, and develop a commitment to greater effectiveness.

EDUCATION, CULTURE, AND LEADERSHIP

Culture can be viewed as a coherent system of attitudes, values, and institutions that influence both individual and group behavior. The idea of culture has become evermore elastic and blurred by modern communications, swift transport, and the breakdown of some traditional societies.

In some regions of the world, the fabric of civil society is unraveling—making anarchy more common than a coherent ideology. In other areas, the national identity and cohesion are strong. But no matter how tight the national structure, we live in a connected world where education is not limited to school experiences alone.

Technologies such as computers, satellites, and the Internet are able to weave the world together as never before. Like books, wiz-bang technologies can be used in smart ways to support learning, or you can do time-burning, dull things with it.

As far as academic achievement is concerned, the important thing is figuring out how student performance can be improved—while providing greater equity and better preparing students for an imaginative life in tomorrow's world.

Cultures that nurture the human creative capacity across age groups usually do better than those that don't. When education is thought of as a continuum from prenatal care through adult life, it is bound to have a more powerful effect. Learning is now much more than something that happens to the young; today, lifelong learning is a fact of life.

At any level, peer culture and the media can get in the way, but parents are a key ingredient in a child's education. Academic achievement is strongly influenced by the level of insistence on the part of parents that children take their studies seriously. In today's world, some parents may not be able to help much. They need social support networks and assistance in learning about how child rearing affects schoolwork.

Fundamental change in schools requires fundamental changes in communities and the larger society. Hard questions must be asked and the uncomfortable issues dealt with. For schools to make a major impact on childhood difficulties requires parallel changes in cultural beliefs, social incentives, the status of teachers, and basic notions about schooling.

Limiting the educational focus to concerns like national testing and school choice avoids the more crucial issues of moral numbness, individualism degenerating into greed, spiritual alienation, social injustice, or the diminishing prospects for a healthy future. For too long, many have not worried enough about future generations, or obligations that different age groups have to each other.

When it comes to improving the schools, it isn't just money; it's values, willingness to sacrifice, and the ability to look at children and young adults in their totality. Also, to deal with many of the issues that are most important to a child's future, educators will have to be ready to teach in ways that haven't been fully conceived of yet.

School culture must encourage teachers to collaboratively approach new ways of thinking and turn possibilities into reality. It may not be possible to change yesterday's mistakes, but it is possible to make a positive influence on the future. High-quality teachers and informed parents are the key.

But it also takes leadership that is willing to address the issues of our time in a bold manner—to inspire, instill trust, and carry out carefully conceived plans.

As far as school principals are concerned, success is often attributed to having latitude in curricular and spending decisions. Other positive factors include having tangible goals, careful teacher recruitment, and parent outreach programs.

Strong leaders don't just reflect on the health or ailment of a society—they help create them. At the school district level, long-term leadership with high expectations is important. In the best schools, the attitude is, "We can teach anybody to learn."

SAMPLE ACTIVITIES FOR ALL STUDENTS

Imaginative new ideas and products are rarely completely original. In fact, innovation is often the result of a step-by-step process that builds on ideas that are at least partly developed by others. The team that puts the puzzle together in a unique way—*and acts on the results*—usually gets the credit.

This STEM lesson contains elements from many sources, including ideas from Atlantic Canada's Science curriculum that deals with sound, engineering, and music.

Procedure: Divide the class into groups of two or three. Have one small-group practice a song using lyrics that are printed on paper. Practice when no one but the singers are in the room; no memorization. If you can play the guitar (or if there is a piano in the room), you can do it. If not, see if anyone in the room can play guitar—be sure that they are in the practice group. If no one can play anything, just have the song playing in the background as three or four students sing.

Instrument Building Activity (after the song): The group starts by putting their design for an instrument on paper.

Each group of two or three gets:

Scissors and balloons
Duct tape and masking tape of different colors and designs
Different kinds of string, sewing thread, rubber bands, and plastic cups
A box about 12″ and 9″ in size and about 3″ deep (We got ours from Staples where they use a good-size box whenever you get something copied.)

Give students time to build and try out their instrument.

Do the same song you used to start the lesson; each group should use their
   instrument as the song is sung by the entire class. Do the same thing a
   second time if you think that is appropriate.
How many different sounds can your instrument make?
Explore the science of sound.

A STEM lesson designed by Peter Cudmore

*Activity: The Super Creature: Structural Features of an Animal That Enables
Them to Survive in Their Habitat*

This lesson is intended for grades three and up. It is designed to encourage students to use their knowledge of science and math to engineer features
needed for an animal to survive in multiple habitats.

Objectives:

1. Students will compare the external features of several organisms and relate
   these features to the basic survival of the animal in their natural habitat.
2. Students will predict the structural adaptations needed for an animal to live
   in a particular habitat, real or imagined.
3. Students will work in groups of three or four to choose an animal they
   wish to adopt.
4. Students will draw and present their evolved organism's features and how
   it can live in three of the six given habitats.

Materials: Markers of different colors, pencils, butcher paper (2.5 by 4 feet)
and any item students have to manipulate their work.

Procedures:

1. The teacher will ask for examples of special features that help animals
   survive and attain their basic needs (food, water, shelter, and air).
2. Further examples of special features will be shown using pictures and
   characteristics explained by the teacher.
3. The teacher will describe the task of building an animal with special features that allow it to adapt to at least three different habitats. The teacher
   will give out six different habitats with pictures and a written description
   of each.
4. Students will be divided into groups of three or four to collect materials to
   complete their project.
5. Students work in their groups to create adaptations for their chosen animal. Adaptations must be noted and labeled. These evolved animals will
   be presented to the class.

Evaluation: Together, groups will present their animal and how it can survive in three of the six given habitats. Students must explain why each new adaptation will benefit their organism.

A Friction Lesson with Sara MacKay

Lesson Title: *Fantastic Friction*

This experience is designed to help children collaboratively explore the force of *friction*—the force that is created whenever two surfaces move or try to move across each other. The amount of friction depends on the texture of both surfaces and the amount of contact force that is pushing the two surfaces together. Students will have the opportunity to develop a sense of space, orientation, perspective, and relationship between different objects and materials.

Lesson Goals:

• To teach students that motion relies on the "rolling resistance" of a specific surface
• To help students understand that:
  ○ friction always opposes the motion or attempted motion of one surface across another surface.
  ○ friction is dependent on the texture of both surfaces.
  ○ friction is also dependent on the amount of contact force pushing the two surfaces together.

Procedures: Introduce the lesson with a *Bill Nye the Science Guy* video, *Friction*. You may want to view most of the video in class—or view a few clips with the entire class and let the students know where they can see the whole segment as homework. Either way, this approach works for visual and oral learners as children listen, watch, and discuss. After the video, ask the children for some important words to define and discuss. Examples include *rub*, *float*, *stick*, *faster*, *slower*, and *stop* (If you can't get the video for the classroom, just cover the words and ideas yourself).

Activity: In groups—or in the whole class—it is possible to do an experiment involving a ramp, toy cars, and four different surface materials. The basic idea is to test different surface materials to make predictions about which will produce the most and the least amount of friction. Try to draw some scientific conclusions from the observations.

You need a wooden ramp about eight inches wide and about forty inches long. Try to get it at about a forty-five-degree angle. Place four different types of surface materials at the bottom of the ramp, each with a different level of friction. Make predictions about how far a toy car might go.

As a car exits down the ramp, measure the distance the car goes on different surface materials. Mark where the car stops on each material and decide as a group or as a class which material produces the most and the least amount of friction. Students compare predictions with what actually happens.

Materials:

Wooden ramp
Toy cars
Piece of carpet
Piece of plastic
Piece of velcro
Piece of hardwood
Metric and yard stick
Stickers

Assessment: Students will each be given a worksheet to record their estimations and eventual findings after the experiment. Next, they will compare their estimations and their findings and give a conclusion. Look for key words such as *faster*, *slower*, *fastest*, *slowest*, and more.

Finish with an overview of the activity as a class, and reflect on the answers together.

Curriculum Standards and Outcomes

- Making predictions about how various factors will affect the motion of an object
- Using terms like *faster* and *slower* and tools such as rulers, string, and stopwatches to test predictions
- Drawing simple conclusions about the factors that affect movement based on their investigation.

Challenges are more than puzzles to be solved. When you start, some of the pieces may not even be on the table. In the process of working toward solving a problem, new things come up and change things. So it's best to leave room for the unexpected.

SCIENTIFIC AND TECHNOLOGICAL ACCELERATION

Expressions of scientific knowledge and better technology are now global in its effect. Science and its technological tools have directly accounted for fundamental changes in the world economy, and at the same time, they have tied the world together by nearly instantaneous communication.

From genetic engineering to the Internet, technologies and their scientific associates are now in a position to direct and manipulate the world more than ever. As far as the future is concerned, the best we can do is get a dim glimpse of the world ahead by looking around us now.

Genetics, robotics, and nanotechnologies are just three of the newer technologies that pose a potential risk to the physical world. The possibility of people able to order out for private futures is one ethical problem. Machines that can self-replicate themselves is another challenge. From the genetic shaping of individuals to digital experiences bought off the shelf, it is becoming easier to create natural facts (like new species or molecules).

What are the consequences of giving more and more of our lives over to computer-based algorithms?

Developing a moral compass is more important than ever. John Goodlad, for example, has pointed out that since schools are moral enterprises, they are central to the future of our democracy. Social development and good citizenship are part of today's academic menu. New media can help and/or hurt the process.

The Internet and its "clouds" (like Apple's iCloud) are examples of how, right or wrong, the collective unconscious is a powerful part of moral development. The *cloud*, by the way, may be thought of as distant computers full of data that can be accessed from any Internet connection.

The dynamic and compelling force of information and communication technology is becoming more effective at creating virtual realities. These made-to-order worlds are bound to take time away from face-to-face human interaction and ordinary sensory experiences. So be sure to leave space for human interaction.

The optimistic and self-congratulatory high-technology industry may have to step back from their chaotic advance into an uncertain technological future and debate the issues surrounding the inherently negative possibilities of rapidly evolving technologies (Catmull, 2014).

Schools can temper some of the harsh edges of digital technology by becoming good role models for connecting the social aspects of learning with broader online communities. Remember, all instruction works best when it is student centered and designed to facilitate instruction through interactive mediation processes.

The revolution in the provision of information is a huge educational and cultural change that requires new ways of thinking and learning. To use new media and their applications is to extend the idea of what is possible—altering the way people think and the way they act. For a jump of comparable importance, you have to go back to the transformation of culture, thinking, and learning that was caused by the introduction of the printing press.

With or without a host of digital devices, it is important that teachers recognize today's realities and become actively involved in enriching learners' lives. Large or small, educational changes require teachers who are directly involved in shaping the decisions that affect their school's future.

THE INTERSECTION OF TRENDS, EVENTS, AND LEARNING

To have a positive effect on learning, any new idea, approach, or product has to avoid getting in the way of building genuine face-to-face interaction with others. That is because genuine learning depends on personal interaction among students and ideas in an aesthetically and intellectually stimulating environment.

Technology, economics, education, and culture are increasingly tied together. Major social and technological advances have moved rapidly—tying humanity together with a new immediacy and intimacy. More than ever, global change is driven by new ideas and media innovations that have taken on a speed of their own. What might get in the way of schools adjusting to these changes?

Test taking and test preparation are but one example of how efforts to improve the schools can sometimes have the opposite effect. Increasingly, teachers and students are being coerced into spending a lot of time and effort on out-of-context tests. Would it be better to spend the time with more stimulating information and more imaginative activities?

The word *inertia* is often associated with attempts to change the curriculum. Teacher attitudes, assessment practices, the need to reeducate students, and traditional ways of doing things can all get in the way of initiating a new curriculum while operating an old system. Still, some schools have worked their way around these obstacles.

In the classroom, students learn best when there is opportunity for social interaction that encourages them to collaboratively create and communicate meaning. This can be done with an array of old and new media that provide information, stories, and folklore in a way that contributes to a shared intellectual curiosity.

We are still learning how to capitalize on schools' social character to contribute to healthy educational growth. As successful teachers know, not staying up to date is to fall behind. Therefore, one of the most important features of a successful educational system is providing the capacity for self-renewal and continuous change.

Although teaching and learning have taken on new dimensions, some schools have not changed as much as the world around them. Unlike the tech industry, for example, innovative thinking and novel ideas have often been viewed as risky in the educational field. This is in spite of the fact that purposeful risk can actually increase teacher innovation, get students more engaged, and help all concerned do a better job of dealing with the unknown (Moss & Brookhart, 2015).

In a world in which there are fewer certainties, there is more demand for high levels of education and competency. Of course, there are some speed bumps on the way to imaginative new practices and future possibilities. Among the challenges: providing high-quality teacher education, using assessment practices that actually improve learning, and putting new arrangements in place while operating under the old system.

SUMMARY, CONCLUSION, AND LOOKING AHEAD

Both innovation and learning are more powerful when done in association with others. From Edison to Jobs, bringing together creative teams was in some ways a greater achievement than the products of any individual's imagination.

Positive educational change has usually been centered on collaborative teachers and individual schools. Experts and professors can help. But a note of caution: passing legislative bills and drafting school district policies are not going to make all that much difference if teachers don't buy into it.

If you are reading this book, you are most likely committed to designing engaging learning experiences that can meet the needs of all students. The degree to which you choose to make use of new media is a professional and situational choice. But no matter how much use you make of digital technology, it *is* important to be aware of what it can and can't do.

Ask yourself at least two questions: How might digital devices and their applications help accomplish instructional goals? What are the existing possibilities and dangers found in the STEM subjects? Whatever your answers, there is no escape from the mysterious nature of our innovation-driven world.

Whether it is science, technology, engineering, or mathematics, new perspectives can be opened, illusions magnified, and obstacles to our aspirations revealed. Any of the STEM fields can be dangerous if left in the shadows (Wagner, 2012). A good example is the Internet, where thoughtful quality is hard to find and lunatics are numerous. Books and newspapers (with well-informed writers and editors) are one thing, but being able to sort through an unfiltered glut of online information is quite another.

Whether it's high tech or low tech, it is important that everyone in the school community should at least be aware of both intellectual and technical tools in their most powerful forms. It is important to recognize the fact that many subjects are getting so complex that their consequences are getting harder and harder to foresee.

When it comes to quality teaching, it all depends on teachers being up to date with the subject matter *and* being familiar with the art and science of teaching (pedagogy). So it should come as no surprise to find out that integrating curricular reform with professional development is one of the keys to successful educational change.

There are solid examples of successful practices and positive educational change around the country. Unfortunately, things that work well in one school may not work so well in another. So it is up to educators to sort through, select, and adapt the best practices for different school situations. Administrators and policymakers need to provide the resources that allow new ideas to blossom.

In an interconnected world, it is up to teachers to conceptualize and construct learning environments that reflect their best hopes, dreams, and values. The next step is for educators and students to symbolically link arms and reach past today's obstacles.

An explosion of new tech tools, exciting discoveries, and subject matter standards have taken on an unsettling momentum of their own. In some ways, this makes it harder than ever to control what is happening. Still, if you are well informed, you may be able to influence the trajectory of new ideas, approaches, and discoveries.

Few of us will reach the heights of creativity and invention. You may not, for example, be able to become a Nobel Prize–winning scientist. But it is possible and necessary for you to achieve a level of scientific literacy that allows you to have some idea of what is going on in the world. Good citizenship requires knowledgeable citizens.

Don't stop believing that you can make a difference. We can all create, and we can all work to avoid dumbing down the future with shallow thinking. How? In part, by helping to increase the level of general understanding about the complexities surrounding the systems in which we are embedded. Or, as Benjamin Bratton put it in a TED talk, *more Copernicus, less Tony Robbins.*

The future is not some place we are going, but one we are creating.
The paths are not just found, but made.
And the activity of making them changes both the maker and the destination.

                                        (Paraphrasing John Schaar)

REFERENCES

Beghetto, R., Kaufman, J., & Baer, J. (2014). *Teaching for creativity in the Common Core classroom.* New York: Teachers College Press.

Bratton, B. (2015). *The stack: On software and sovereignty.* Cambridge, MA: MIT Press.

Brynjolfsson, E., & McAfee, A. (2014). *The second machine age: Work, progress, and prosperity in a time of brilliant technologies.* New York: W. W. Norton & Company.

Caine, R., & Caine, G. (2011). *Natural learning for a connected world: Education, technology, and the human brain.* New York: Teachers College Press.

Catmull, E. (2014). *Creativity, Inc.: Overcoming the unseen forces that stand in the way of innovation.* New York: Random House.

Darling-Hammond, L. (2010). *The flat world and education: How America's commitment to equity will determine our future.* New York: Teachers College Press.

Dweck, C. S. (2012). *Mindset: How you can fulfill your potential.* London, UK: Constable & Robinson.

Gruenert, S., & Whitaker, T. (2015). *School culture rewired: How to define, assess, and transform it.* Alexandria, VA: ASCD.

Johnson, S. (2014). *How we got to now: Six innovations that made the modern world.* New York: Riverhead Books (Penguin Group).

Jorgenson, O. et al. (2014). *Doing good science in middle school, expanded 2nd edition: A practical STEM guide.* Arlington, VA: National Science Teachers Association (NSTA).

Marshall, J., & Donahue, D. (2014). *Art-centered learning across the curriculum.* New York: Teachers College Press.

Moss, C., & Brookhart, S. (2015). *Formative classroom walkthroughs: How students and teachers collaborate to raise student achievement.* Alexandria, VA: ASCD.

Opitz, M., & Ford, M. (2014). *Classroom catalysts: 15 efficient practices that accelerate readers' learning.* Portsmouth, NH: Heinemann.

Pahomov, L. (2014). *Authentic learning in the digital age.* Alexandria, VA: ASCD.

Pinker, S. (2014). *The village effect: How face-to-face contact can make us healthier, happier, and smarter.* New York: Spiegel & Grau.

Wagner, T. (2012). *Creating innovators: The making of young people who will change the world.* New York: Scribner.

Chapter 2

Thinking and Learning

STEM in a Technologically Intensive World

*Out of the questions of students come most of the creative ideas
and discoveries.*

—Ellen Langer

STEM instruction is an interdisciplinary approach to teaching science, technology, engineering, and mathematics. It builds on the idea that learning STEM subjects should be integrated and applied to real-world problems. By building on relevance and combining two or more of these subjects, students are more likely to ask good questions and see the relationships among subjects.

The ability to deal with the convergence of thinking and technological tools is one of the keys to the twenty-first century. Take the Internet as an example. It can help us extend our imaginations and our connection to others. But the Internet can also be the biggest distraction to come along since television. The difference between useful and useless has a lot to do with learning how to use digital technologies and their associates with a measure of wisdom.

Digital technologies are constantly getting faster and denser with information. By becoming better at representing the real (physical) world, technology opens up new dimensions. At the same time, it can close down possibilities by encouraging shallow thinking and diminishing social skills.

Clearly, our devices and their associates are becoming ever more powerful forces for contracting *and* expanding human potential.

With or without digital technology, most educators favor paying close attention to thinking and reasoning. As far as thoughtful behavior is concerned, it is time to think about where technology belongs and putting it in its place. In spite of the negatives, it is still possible that as technology continues to improve, the benefits of our new media tools can be shaped in a way that outweighs the drawbacks.

New technologies affect nearly every aspect of our life and require new ways of thinking. When used in an informed and disciplined way, they open up the possibility of imaginative solutions and alternative paths to the future. So it is little wonder that educational systems around the world look for ways to produce more thoughtful innovators and informed knowledge workers.

A good metaphor for how to teach thinking skills might be found in the difference between a sponge and panning for gold. The sponge approach emphasizes fairly passive knowledge acquisition; the panning for gold approach stresses active interaction with knowledge as it is being acquired (Dede & Richards, 2012).

Whatever combination of approaches you take as a teacher, developing the ability to think clearly, creatively, and critically is an important part of education today.

CREATIVE AND CRITICAL THINKING

Here, creative and critical thinking are viewed as overlapping concepts. Creative thinking tends to look at problems or situations from an imaginative perspective and suggest fresh solutions. Students might be stimulated by methods ranging from brainstorming to the step-by-step processes of lateral thinking (O'Toole & Beckett, 2009).

Critical thinking often involves a persistent effort to examine information in light of reliable evidence. Along with carefully selected information, creative and critical reasoning can reinforce each other. Thinking transforms the information gathered by our digital devices, and that information invites thinking (Howie, 2011).

Developing approaches that extend students' thinking skills across the curriculum is a strategy that is widely supported. Both the concept and the teaching strategies associated with thinking skills can be found in just about every curriculum. Better yet, most teachers are building at least some pieces of the thinking skills puzzle into their day-to-day work.

YESTERDAY, TODAY, AND TOMORROW

We have always known that new technologies produce problems—it's just that it's hard to figure out in advance what those problems will be. Technological devices have always been part of the equation; it's just that texting, instant messaging, iPhoning, tweeting, and the like have changed thinking in unexpected ways. Today's media, for example, have helped move thinking from a relatively calm and focused process into something that needs to take in and dole out information in short, disjointed, and overlapping bursts (Carr, 2010).

Our mobile Internet age has produced some *digital natives* who expect continuous connection and feel uneasy when expected to think in the few moments they are truly alone (Turkle, 2011). It is little wonder that many students today have more trouble concentrating or thinking intelligently when they spend so much time skimming one surface after another to the point of distraction.

The educational path that was developed in the early twentieth century stressed the behaviorist view of learning. What could be seen as behavior? Learning was looked at as changed behavior. Lacking the knowledge of what goes on inside the thinking process, the behaviorists measured behaviors and learned to alter them with behavior reinforcers (rewarding positive behaviors, punishing negative actions).

As behaviorism faded from the scene, cognitive science moved in to fill the void. Most educators welcomed the change. Cognition may be thought of as the process of knowing. Cognitive science included a wide range of human activities: critical thinking, making judgments, decision making, and creative thinking. Cognitive science also moved the ball in the direction of constructivism. The basic idea was that the thinking individual does not simply take in knowledge but is actively involved in constructing that knowledge.

In the classroom, good teaching encourages students to actively construct knowledge within lessons that have clear goals, allow for guided practice, and provide ongoing assessment. Also, leaving some room for student choice amplifies critical and creative thinking.

MEANINGFUL CRITICAL AND CREATIVE THINKING

The thinking of every child can be enhanced if the learning is *challenging*; this means that in addition to providing proof of new facts and experiences, there must also be *group feedback*. Challenges can be as simple as presenting original content, including journal writing and hands-on materials. It's important to often change teaching strategies, to apply computer programs, have students work in groups, give students choice when doing projects, and take field trips.

Student feedback should not be overlooked. This builds confidence, reduces stress, and increases thinking's coping abilities. Students' peers are the greatest stimulus in the classroom. Collaborative groups provide students with a sense of feeling valued and cared for.

Thinking is a search for meaning, a purposeful quest for understanding and clarity. This journey often provides new points of view and solutions to problems. Thinking is intentional, purposeful, and deliberate. Individuals can be resourceful and adventuresome. Stimulating their students' critical and creative imagination is one of the most important teaching challenges teachers face today.

Thinking is built on personal experiences. It is also influenced by emotions, culture, home environment, and educational possibilities. Critical and creative-thinking experiences express original ideas and solutions. They have a conscious and mental focus. The playful spirit of *creative thinking* can occur while daydreaming, fantasizing, or just having an idea while taking a hike along a trail. Creative thinking extends art and beauty as it reaches beyond the adequate to try elegant solutions.

Critical thinking is constructing meaning by observing, interpreting, analyzing, and manipulating information in response to a problem. Clarifying and solving problems, pondering alternatives, strategically planning, and analyzing the results are all activities that support critical thinking. *Creative thinking* is flowing, flexible, novel, and detailed. Creative-thinking skills try to create novel expressions, unique conceptions, and original approaches. The mental power to see things in an unusual and imaginative way is linked with problem solving and is part of critical thinking.

As teachers encourage the original ideas developed by children, it is important to remember that people who are flexible, open, unique, and actively productive will solve many problems of the future. Critical and creative thinking means being able to choose alternative explanations and show intellectual curiosity in a manner that is flexible and unique.

Critical-thinking lessons might include having students analyze the hidden assumptions that produce meanings and different results of data or information. Such intellectually demanding thinking helps students identify, clarify, and solve problems. The questions explored can be as general as "Can we be certain about the knowledge of this subject?" Questions can be as simple as "How was that done?" or "What does that mean?"

T. S. Eliot maintained that genuine poetry communicates before it's understood. The wording may be changed. Students are never too young to analyze the underlying assumptions that influence meaning. And they are never too young to question the explanations of findings and participate in the act of knowledge creation. We listen to what David Whyte said: ". . . the eddies and swells of everyday experience." He uses poetry to finish his point: "I turned my face for a moment and it became my life."

TEACHING, LEARNING, AND THINKING HABITS

Understanding the relationship between theory, research, and practice is the foundation of pedagogical knowledge. The content standards build on this cycle to give a coherent, professionally defensible conception of how a subject can be framed for instruction. They do not put forward one best way to teach subject matter *or* thinking skills. Instead, all the standards projects have left room for interpretation.

A good place to start with students centers on real-life experiences that evoke personal meaning. Across all subjects, high-quality lessons often begin with real materials and make use of interactive learning in a way that allows students to explore the many dimensions of thoughtfulness, subject matter, and real-world applications. The basic idea is to help students form a new set of expectations and to create a new sense of understanding. Asking the right questions certainly helps (Browne & Keeley, 2009).

We all make sense of something by connecting to a set of personal, everyday experiences. So good teachers have always connected educational goals to practical problem solving and students' life experiences. This way, thinking skills are introduced into the curriculum so that students are intensely involved in reasoning, elaboration, forming hypotheses, and problem solving. New ideas of literacy will have to move beyond disciplinary boundaries.

Evolving mature thinkers who are able to acquire and use knowledge involves educating minds rather than training memories. Often, the acquisition of advanced thinking skills is well structured and planned; other times it's a chance encounter. Raising thoughtful questions about what's being viewed, heard, or read is a dimension of thinking that makes a meaningful contribution. When encouraged to think intelligently, students often come up with good decisions and elegant solutions. As all of these elements come together, they shape the core of effective thinking and learning.

Using new methods for teaching mathematics, science, the arts, and language arts depends on reflective teachers. This means that both beginning and veteran teachers should take courses in learning math and science through inquiry and learn to apply the arts and language arts concepts within a context similar to the one they will arrange for their students. The result enlarges horizons and organizational possibilities.

Creative and critical thinking are natural human processes that can be extended by awareness and practice. Both critical and creative thinking use specific core thinking skills. Classroom instructional practice in the development of these skills might include the following:

1. Be accurate, clear, open minded, and sensitive to others; defend a position.
2. Engage in difficult problems, extend the limits of your knowledge, find new ways to look at situations outside conventional boundaries, dare to imagine, innovate, and trust.
3. Listen with understanding when listening to another person and try to understand their point of view. This is one of the highest forms of communication.

4. Be aware of your thinking: be sensitive to feedback, plan, and evaluate your actions. Take your time, remain calm, and think before you act.
5. Be attentive. This includes skills such as observing, getting information, forming questions, and using inquiry.
6. Pose clear questions in easy-to-understand language.
7. Remain open to continuous learning.
8. Analyze and form hunches. Analysis is at the heart of critical and creative thinking. This includes recognizing and articulating attributes, focusing on details and structure, identifying relationships and patterns, and finding errors.
9. Use models and metaphors. Higher-order thinking includes activities such as making comparisons, using metaphors, producing analogies, and providing explanations.
10. Gather data and assess and evaluate ideas. This establishes criteria or verifies data.
11. Take risks. Elegant solutions oftentimes demand risk taking and thinking independently.
12. Search out humor. This frees creativity and stimulates higher-thinking skills. People who initiate humor are verbally playful when interacting with others; they thrive on being able to laugh at situations and themselves.
13. Every inquiry, if explored with enthusiasm and with care, will use some of these core thinking skills (Jacobs, 2004).

ILLUMINATING LEARNING BY TEACHING
FOR THOUGHTFULNESS

The multidimensional search for meaning is made at least a little easier when there is a supportive group climate for generating questions and investigating possibilities. Critical-thinking questions may also come into play after solutions are put forward. Ask students to analyze problems they have solved. As they examine how underlying assumptions influence interpretations, children can be pulled more deeply into a topic. And by evaluating their findings on the basis of logic, they invite other possibilities.

To have power over the story that dominates one's life in these technologically intensive times means having the power to retell it, deconstruct it, joke about it, and change it as times change. Without this power, it is more difficult to think and act on new thoughts and open the doors to deep thinking.

The old view of teaching as the transmission of content has been expanded to include new intellectual tools and new ways of helping students thoughtfully construct knowledge on their own and with peers. Teachers who invite thoughtfulness understand that knowledge is to be shared or developed rather than held by the authority. They arrange instruction so that children construct concepts and develop their thinking skills. As a result, everyone involved becomes an active constructor of knowledge and more capable of making thoughtful decisions in the future.

Recognizing the development of thinking skills is a good first step toward its application and assessment. Beyond specific teaching strategies, the climate of the classroom and the behavior of the teacher are very important. Teachers need to model critical-thinking behaviors—setting the tone, atmosphere, and environment for learning. Being able to collaborate with other teachers can make a formative contribution to how the teacher might better see and construct individual classroom reality.

In collaborative problem solving, teachers can help each other in the clarification of goals. They also share the products of their joint imaginations. Thus, perceptions are changed, ideas flow, and practice can be meaningfully strengthened, deepened, and extended. Like their students, teachers can become active constructors of knowledge.

A curriculum that ignores the powerful ideas of its charges will miss many opportunities for illuminating knowledge. To teach content without regard for self-connected thinking prevents subject matter knowledge from being transformed in the student's mind. If the curriculum is to be viewed as enhancing *being and opening to the unfamiliar*—rather than merely imparting knowledge and skills—then reasoned decision making is part of the process.

Taking student thinking seriously is more likely to be successful in cultivating thoughtfulness and subject matter competence. Respecting unique thought patterns can also be viewed as a commitment to caring communication and openness.

Encouraging fresh ideas or opposing views is often difficult for administrators. All of us need the occasional push or encouragement to get out of a rut. Breaking out of established patterns can be done collectively or individually. But it takes those most directly involved to make it happen.

JOURNEYS OF DISCOVERY

It is important for all of us to develop our own reflection and inquiry skills—becoming students of our own thinking. For example, when a teacher decides to participate with students in learning to think on a daily basis, they nourish human possibilities. Can teachers make a difference? Absolutely. The idea is to connect willing teachers with innovative methods and materials so that they can build learning environments that are sensitive to students' growing abilities to think for themselves.

The Common Core suggests that there are certain student thinking skills that are needed across the curriculum (Bellanca et al., 2012). By promoting thoughtful learning across the full spectrum of personalities, cultures, and ways of knowing, teachers can make a tremendous difference and perform a unique service for the future.

When the ideal and the actual are linked, the result can produce a dynamic, productive, and resilient form of learning. What we know about teaching and thinking is increasingly being put into practice in model classrooms and schools. These exemplary programs recognize that powerful inquiry can help students make personal and group discoveries that change thinking. Good thinking skills can turn an unexamined belief into a reasoned one.

By nurturing informed thinking and awareness, we can all learn how to actively apply knowledge, solve problems, and enhance conceptual understanding across social boundaries. As children use reason and logic to change their own theories and beliefs, they grow in ways that are personally meaningful. Understanding the essence of contradictory points of view means understanding some of the universal truths that speak to everyone. A diversity of new voices can add vigor to understanding the world and our place in it.

As students learn about the perspectives of other cultures—including social and historical backgrounds—they can explore where stereotypes come from. With a little homework, each student can design a large graphic family tree to share. This way, each student's cultural background can be a valuable tool for learning about themselves and how their communities connect to others around the world.

With the globalization of media and business, it becomes ever more important to see how events in the United States affect people in other countries—and vice versa. Gaining a global perspective means developing a more integrative understanding of the human community and overlapping cultural experiences. As teachers learn to thoughtfully view the world from multiple perspectives, the way is cleared for them to become more sensitive to variation and more capable of reaching diverse learners.

DISCOVERING RELATIONSHIPS AND INVENTING NEW PERSPECTIVES

Recognizing the fact that thinking skills are key to successful learning doesn't come as a surprise to most teachers. In science, for example, you formulate hypotheses, organize experiments, collect data, analyze and interpret the findings, and solve problems. As scholars who are doing original work in any field will tell you, the reality is far less clear-cut and tidy.

There are many false starts and detours as they work through alternatives to discover relationships and invent new perspectives. What makes it satisfying for many scholars is the sheer power of searching at the frontiers of knowledge. This passion for inquiry and reaching outward into the unknown outward (for new experiences) is just as important for children.

Critical and creative thinkers tend to be reflective, flexible, and curious; they think problems through and consider original solutions. They pose and expand on new questions. The research evidence suggests that providing students with multiple perspectives and entry points into subject matter increases thinking and learning (Willis, 2006).

As Common Core and each of the standards projects point out in their own way, notions about how students learn a subject need to be pluralized. Almost any important concept can be approached from multiple entry points—emphasizing understanding and making meaningful interdisciplinary connections.

Today's schools are incorporating frameworks for literacy and learning that build on the multiple ways of thinking and representing knowledge. By organizing lessons that respect multiple entry points to knowledge, teachers can enhance thoughtfulness and make the classroom a rich environment for inquiry. By fusing the personalization of learning to achieving an attainable level of literacy across the curriculum, teachers can lay a powerful foundation for learning.

We now have diverse models of thoughtful schooling to choose from. If many of today's dreams, possibilities, and admired efforts are going to be put into widespread practice, then we all must be more courageous in helping move good practice from the educational margins and into the schools.

A child's thinking ability evolves through a dynamic of personal abilities, social values, academic subjects, and out-of-school experiences. Although teachers are usually the ones held accountable, everyone is involved (directly or indirectly) in the education of children.

Revitalizing the educational process means recognizing the incomplete models of how the world works that children bring to school with them. From birth, children are busy making sense of their environment. They do this by curiously grappling with the confusing learning ways of understanding, developing schemes for thinking, and finding meaning.

Discipline and imaginative thought may seem antithetical, but discipline without thoughtfulness is sterile—and creative energy without discipline aborts its image.

As they begin school, children can tell stories, sing songs, and use their own processes of reasoning and intuiting to understand their surroundings. They have already developed a rich body of knowledge about the world around them by the time they reach first grade.

This natural learning process can be extended in school when a teacher is committed to critical thinking throughout the year. It is important to pay attention and work with students' natural rhythms, but it takes learning-centered instruction to continue the process of developing mature thinkers. Cognitive science was partly responsible, as well as perspectives on multiple intelligence.

TOWARD A NEW VISION OF INTELLIGENCE (MULTIPLE INTELLIGENCES [MI])

Learning has a lot to do with finding your own gifts (Armstrong, 2009). To make learning more accessible to children means respecting multiple ways of making meaning.

The brain has a multiplicity of functions and voices that speak independently and distinctly for different individuals. Howard Gardner's framework for multiple entry points to knowledge has made an impact on the content standards. There are many differences, but each set of content standards is built on a belief in the uniqueness of each child and the view that this can be fused with a commitment to achieving worthwhile goals.

Lessons built on Gardner's ideas proved helpful in providing alternative paths for learning.

Multiple Intelligences

1. Linguistic intelligence: the capacity to use language to express ideas, excite, convince, and convey information—speaking, writing, and reading.
2. Logical-mathematical intelligence: the ability to explore patterns and relationships by manipulating objects or symbols in an orderly manner.
3. Musical intelligence: the capacity to think in music; the ability to perform, compose, or enjoy a musical piece—rhythm, beat, tune, melody, and singing.
4. Spatial intelligence: the ability to understand and mentally manipulate a form or object in a visual or spatial display—maps, drawings, and media.
5. Bodily-kinesthetic intelligence: the ability to use motor skills in sports, performing arts, or art productions, particularly dance or acting.
6. Interpersonal intelligence: the ability to work in groups—interacting, sharing, leading, following, and reaching out to others.
7. Intrapersonal intelligence: the ability to understand one's inner feelings, dreams, and ideas—introspection, meditation, reflection, and self-assessment.
8. Naturalist intelligence: the ability to discriminate among living things (plants, animals) as well as sensitivity to the natural world (Gardner, 1993).

Gardner defines intelligence as the ability to solve problems, generate new problems, and do things that are valued within one's own culture. MI theory suggests that these eight "intelligences" work together in complex ways. Most people can develop an adequate level of competency in all of them. And there are many ways to be "intelligent" within each category.

Will the "intelligences" that were so important in the twentieth century be as central to the twenty-first?

Is it possible to take issue with Gardner's approach on several points, like not fully addressing spiritual and artistic modes of thought? Although it is a distortion of MI theory, for some, it's a short leap from preferred ways of learning to learning styles. Still, there is general agreement on a central point: *Intelligence is not a single capacity that every human being possesses to a greater or lesser extent.*

There *are* multiple ways of knowing and learning. And whether or not we subscribe to MI theory, methods of instruction should reflect different ways of knowing. Working out the ecology of teaching for thoughtfulness requires taking risks with a wide range of bold and explicit insights.

Suggestions for Using Multiple Intelligence Activities

1. Put Multiple Intelligence theory into action. Some possibilities:

linguistic intelligence
write an article
develop a newscast
make a plan
describe a procedure
write a letter
conduct an interview
write a play
interpret a text or piece of writing

musical intelligence
sing a rap song
give a musical presentation
explain music similarities
play a musical instrument
demonstrate rhythmic patterns

logical-mathematical intelligence
design and conduct an experiment
describe patterns
make up analogies to explain
solve a problem

spatial intelligence
illustrate, draw, paint, sketch
create a slide show, videotape
chart, map, or graph
create a piece of art

bodily-kinesthetic intelligence
use creative movement
design task or puzzle cards
build or construct something
bring hands-on materials to demonstrate

interpersonal intelligence
conduct a meeting
participate in a service project
teach someone
use technology to explain

| use the body to persuade, console, or support others | advise a friend or fictional character |

naturalist intelligence	*intrapersonal intelligence*
prepare an observation notebook	write a journal entry
describe changes in the environment	describe one of your values
care for pets, wildlife, gardens, or parks	assess your work
use binoculars, telescopes, or microscopes	set and pursue a goal
photograph natural objects	reflect on or act out emotions

2. Build on students' interests.
   When students do research either individually or with a group, allow them to choose a project that appeals to them. Students should also choose the best way for communicating their understanding of the topic. In this way, students discover more about their interests, concerns, learning styles, and intelligences.
3. Plan interesting lessons. There are many ways to plan interesting lessons.

Lesson Planning

1. Set the tone of the lesson. Focus student attention and relate the lesson to what students have done before. Stimulate interest.
2. Present the objectives and purpose of the lesson. What are students supposed to learn? Why is it important?
3. Provide background information: What information is available? Resources such as books, journals, videos, pictures, maps, charts, teacher lectures, class discussions, or seatwork should be listed.
4. Define procedures: What are students supposed to do? This includes examples and demonstrations as well as working directions.
5. Monitor students' understanding. During the lesson, the teacher should check students' understanding and adjust the lesson if necessary. Teachers should invite questions and ask for clarification. A continuous feedback process should be in place.
6. Provide guided practice experiences. Students should have a chance to use the new knowledge presented under direct teacher supervision.
7. It is equally important that students get opportunities for independent practice where students can use their new knowledge and skills.
8. Evaluating and assessing students' work are necessary to show that students have demonstrated an understanding of significant concepts. Paper-and-pencil tests do not adequately measure students' critical and creative thinking. Observing students' behavior and their interaction with

the teacher and peers are often more effective and revealing. Portfolios represent the cutting edge of more authentic and meaningful assessment. They are powerful assessment tools that require students to select, collect, and reflect on what they are creating and accomplishing.

A Sample MI Lesson Plan

Lesson Title: How Intelligence Cells Work

Students should develop understandings of personal health, changes in environments, and local challenges in science and technology. The human body and the brain are fascinating areas of study. The brain, like the rest of the body, is composed of cells, but brain cells are different from other cells (Beghetto, Kaufman, & Baer, 2015). This lesson focuses on the science standards of inquiry, life science, science and technology, and personal and social perspectives.

Lesson Goals: The basic goal is to provide a dynamic experience with each of the eight "intelligences" and to map out a group on construction paper.

Procedures:

1. Divide the class into groups. Assign a specific intelligence to a group.
2. Allow students time to prepare an activity that addresses their intelligence. Each small group will give a three-minute presentation (with a large map) to the entire class.

Objective: To introduce students to the terminology of intelligence and how intelligence functions, specifically the function of intelligence cells.

Grade level: With modifications, K–8.

Materials: paper, pens, markers.

Intelligence (thinking) "Recipe"

Combine five cups of instant potato flakes, five cups of hot water, two cups sand, pour into a one-gallon ziploc bag. Combine all ingredients; mix thoroughly. It should weigh about three pounds and have the consistency of a real part of our thinking process in our head.

Background Information: No one understands exactly how thinking works. But scientists know the answer lies within the billions of tiny cells, called nerve cells, which make up the thinking process. All of the body's feelings and thoughts are caused by the electrical and chemical signals passing from one neuron to the next. A nerve cell looks like a tiny octopus, but with many more tentacles (some have several thousand). Nerve cells carry signals throughout our thinking process that allows us to move, hear, see, taste, smell, remember, feel, and think.

Procedure:

1. Make a model of the thinking process to show to the class. The teacher displays the thinking process and says, "The smell of a flower, the memory of a walk in the park, the pain of stepping on a nail—these experiences are made possible by the three pounds of tissue in our heads—'OUR THINKING PROCESS!'"
2. Show a picture of the nerve cell and mention its various parts.
3. Have students label the parts of the cell and color them if desired.

Activity 1, Message Transmission: Explaining how thinking (nerve) cells work.

A message traveling in the nervous system of our intelligence can go two hundred miles per hour (mph). These signals are transmitted from intelligence cell to cell across a connection. To understand this system, have students act out the thinking cell process.

1. Instruct students to get into groups of five. Each group should choose a group leader.
2. Direct students to stand up and form a circle. Each person is going to be an intelligence or a thinking cell. Students should be an arms' length away from the next person.
3. When the group leader says "Go," have one person from the group start the signal transmission by slapping the hand of the adjacent person. The second person then slaps the hand of the next, and so on until the signal goes all the way around the circle and the transmission is complete.

Explanation: The hand that receives the slap is the branching part of the nerve cell. The middle part of the student's body is the "cell body." The arm that gives the slap to the next person is the "nerve cell," and the hand that gives the slap is the "nerve cell" terminal. In between the hands of two people is the "nerve connector."

Inquiry Questions: As the activity progresses, questions will arise: What are parts of a thinking nerve cell? A tiny nerve cell is one of billions that make up the thinking process. A nerve cell has three basic parts: the *nerve cell*, the *cell body*, and the *nerve cell connector*. Have students make a simple model by using their hand and spreading their fingers wide. The hand represents the "cell body," the fingers represent the part that brings information to the cell body, and the arm represents the "cell connecter" that takes information away from the cell body. Just as students wiggle their fingers, the nerve cells are constantly moving as they seek information. If an intelligence cell needs to send a message to another cell, the message is sent out through the nerve cell. The wrist and forearm represent the cell body. When a cell sends information down its cell body to communicate with another nerve cell, it never actually touches the other cell. The message goes from the nerve cell of the sending cell to another nerve cell by "swimming" through the space called the "cell connector." Neuroscientists define *learning* as *two nerve cells communicating with each other.* They say that nerve cells have "learned" when one cell sends a message to another cell.

Activity 2, Connect the Dots: This activity will show the complexity of connections of the thinking process.

1. Have students draw ten dots on one side of a sheet of typing paper and ten dots on the other side of the paper.
2. Tell students to imagine these dots represent nerve cells; assume each cell makes connections with the ten dots on the other side.
3. Then, connect each dot on side one with the dots on the other side. This is quite a simplification. Each nerve cell (dot) may actually make thousands of connections with other cells.

Another part of this activity is teaching intelligence songs to students:

"I've Been Working On My Thinking"
(sung to the tune of "I've Been Working on the Railroad")
I've been working on my thinking, All the live long day.
I've been working on my thinking, Just to make my genius play.
Can't you hear my thinking snapping? Impulses bouncing to and fro,
Can't you tell that I've been learning? See how much I know!

"Because I Can Think"
(sung to the tune, "Because I Can Think")
I can flex a muscle tightly, or tap my finger lightly,
It's because I can think,
I can swim in the river, though it's cold and makes me shiver,
Just because I can think.

I am really fascinated, to be coordinated,
It's because I can think.

I can see lots of faces, feel the pain of wearing braces
Just because I can think.

Oh, I appreciate the many things that I can do,
I can taste a chicken stew, or smell perfume, or touch the dew.

I am heavy with emotion, and often have the notion,
That life is never plain.
I have lots of personality, a sense of true reality,
Because I can think.

Multiple Intelligences Learning Activities

Linguistic—writing a reflection about the activity, researching how a nerve
    cell works, keeping a study journal about how nerve cells work
Bodily/Kinesthetic—move like a nerve cell
Group drama—cell signal transmission
Visual/Spatial—mapping the connections of our thinking process (connect
    the dots)
Musical—singing songs about nerve cells, tapping out rhythms to the song
    "Because I Can Think"
Naturalist—describing changes in your thinking environment illustrating a
    thinking connection
Interpersonal—participate in (act out) a group signal nerve cell transmission
    by observing/recording
Intrapersonal—reflecting on thinking, keeping a journal of how the brain
    works
Mathematical/Logical—calculating nerve cell connections

Evaluation: Each group will write a reflection on the activity. Journal reflections should tell what they learned about thinking and how that helped them understand how the thinking process works.

Examples of STEM Activities

Kindergarten and First Grade:

The research suggests that students do better with science, technology, engineering, and mathematics in the upper grades if they start with STEM activities early on (Honey & Kanter, 2013).

STEM content can be learned through investigation, play, and focused intentional teaching. Sometimes it's as simple as asking better questions.

Take the example of a STEM inquiry approach to the sand tables that are found in many K–1 classrooms:

Procedure: Children gather around a sand table and explore the sand and let some of the grains run through their hands. The teacher, then, provides some props: marbles, rulers, cups, and small boxes.

Possible Directions and Questions [Be sure that the students have time after each direction or question]:

- "Get a partner and a set of tools."
- "How can you make the marbles roll on the sand?"
- "What do you think makes your marble slow down or stop as you roll it across the sand?"
- See if the students come up with using the ruler. If not, give a few hints.
- "Why did it go faster on a ruler than in the sand?"

After the lesson is over, bring the whole class back together and briefly discuss the results.

There is general agreement that basic technology like rulers, blocks, and balance scales is fine for younger children. But when it comes to *digital* technology, the research is mixed. Still, you should know that there are online activities for the early grades.

An example of a website for student STEM activities at the K–3 level is *ScratchJr*, developed by MIT and Playful Inventions to bring STEM concepts to the early childhood level.

When creativity, critical thinking, and innovation are important, try not to tell students *how* to do things, tell them *what* to do, and let them surprise you with their ingenuity.

A Middle Grades and Up Example: The National Science Teachers Association (NSTA) suggests integrating the intellectual tools of STEM with subjects ranging from the language arts to social studies and the arts. One example: STEM with an Environmental Focus.

NSTA points to schools using an "E-STEM" procedure that emphasizes environmental issues and sustainability. One of their examples: a class where students collaboratively explore how the ecospheres (biosphere, lithosphere, hydrosphere, and anthrosphere) are made or modified by humans. NSTA reports that such an approach amplifies "student innovation and curiosity about real-world situations."

As teachers use STEM concepts across the curriculum, they are encouraged to create learning situations that incorporate prior knowledge, questioning, and problem solving. For more information, see *NSTA Reports*, February 2014.

* Everyone in this class will be asked to develop a lesson plan that integrates STEM tools with another subject.

> *Many of us use both basic and advanced technology without*
> *the slightest idea of why it works or how it came to be.*

—Johnson

A STEM Lesson Example for the Upper Grades

A Guide for Rebooting the World
Astrobiologist Lewis Dartnell suggests extending classroom STEM activities and thought experiments designed by the Nobel Prize–winning physicist Richard Feynman. The lesson example here builds on their work and explores how human knowledge is collectively distributed across the population.

This activity involves having students come up with a starter kit for rebuilding civilization after an extinction event. (It could be an asteroid hitting earth, a nuclear war, or an Ebola-like virus spreading around the world.)

Question: If all stored knowledge was destroyed, what key principles of STEM would be necessary to rebuild our world from scratch? * If you could pass along just one STEM idea that would be key to moving toward a better future, what would it be? One sentence only.

After a little explanation to the whole class, the students can write their sentence. Next, students work together in small groups, where they share their ideas. Have two or three of the original ideas included in the list.

Combine nine to eleven listed topics so that they are *not* written in order of "importance." After the groups have their final list, the ranking is done. * *Directions for a group of three or four: Discuss and decide what the rank order of importance should be* (The most important should be listed first and the least important last). After each group has done its ranking, the whole class discusses the group choices. The list could include:

- *Transform base substances*: Information about how to transform things like clay and iron into brick and steel.
- *Germ theory*: Contagious diseases are caused by small organisms that you can't see. What to do? Drinking water, for example, can be disinfected with diluted bleach; hands can be cleaned with soap.

- *Scientific method*: A great knowledge-generating approach for things in the past and yet to be discovered. It's a method of research in which a problem is identified, observations made, data gathered, and a hypothesis is tested.
- *Atomic theory*: All things are made of atoms. These little particles constantly move around—attracting each other when they are at some distance apart and repelling each other when tightly squeezed.
- *Mathematical algorithm*: Used in mathematics and computer science as a step-by-step procedure for solving computational problems. It's like a cooking recipe for mathematical calculation and problem solving.
- *Agriculture*: The ability to grow and stockpile food. Cereal crops like rice, wheat, and maize have sustained civilizations for thousands of years.
- *Engineering*: The application of scientific and mathematical principles to the design and solution of practical problems. Knowing how to design and build structures like bridges, buildings, and roads.

* After the group choices are made, bring the whole class back together and have each group present and defend their list.

For reference, consult a 2014 book on the subject: *The Knowledge: How to Rebuild our World from Scratch* by Lewis Dartnell (New York: Penguin Press, 2014).

> *The years doors open like those of language to the unknown.*
> *Last night you told me to think up signs*
> *Sketch a landscape on the double page of day and paper.*
> *Tomorrow we shall have to invent once again the realities of this*
> *world.*
>
> —Elizabeth Bishop

BRAIN RESEARCH AND LEARNING

Human intelligence, across all age groups, is malleable and stable enough for learning to occur and solidify into wisdom. Thousands of new nerve cells form every day and migrate into areas that influence thinking and decision making. If a steady stream of new thinking cells is continually arriving to be integrated into new circuitry, then our thinking is even more malleable than had been thought in the past. Research now suggests that the thinking process remains remarkably plastic, and we retain the ability to learn throughout our lives (Jossey-Bass Publishers, 2008).

Brain researchers have found that a small, well-connected region of our thinking process is in charge of organizing and coordinating information, acting like a global workspace for solving problems. Neuroscientists also emphasize that thinking is extremely plastic and dynamic, very responsive to experience, and is an "ever-changing place" (Schank, 2011).

INTELLECTUAL TOOLS OF THE FUTURE

Since it is so difficult to figure out what knowledge will be crucial to students in the future, it makes sense to pay more attention to the *intellectual tools* that will be required *in any future*. This suggests focusing on how models of critical thought can be used differently, at different times, and in different situations. The idea is to put more emphasis on concepts with high generalizability—like collaborative problem solving, reflection, perceptive thinking, self-direction, and the motivation needed for lifelong learning. A more thoughtful and personalized brand of learning is the goal.

Information isn't a substitute for thinking. But information and thinking are not antithetical. At higher levels, thinking requires quickly sorting through a wealth of information to be effective. There will never be enough time to teach all the information that we feel is useful. But time must be taken to be sure that student thinking can transform knowledge in a way that makes it transferable to the outside world. When there is time for inquiry and reflection, covering less can actually help students learn more deeply.

Within this context, the following thinking skills can be taught directly:

- generating multiple ideas about a topic
- figuring out meaning from context
- understanding analogy
- detecting reasoning fallacies

Topical knowledge (content facts), procedural knowledge (how to study and learn), and self-knowledge are all part of critical thinking. All of these thinking skills are learned through interaction with the environment, the media, peers, and the school curriculum. Some students pick it up naturally, while others learn reasoning skills with difficulty.

Whether it is easy or hard for those involved, education in the twenty-first century is paying more attention to unleashing the creative thinking spirit of future innovators.

PROVIDING ACCESS TO THE THOUGHTFUL LIFE

Children can demonstrate what their reasoning ability is in a number of ways: think-out-louds, videos, performances, photo-collage, stories for the newspaper, websites on the Internet, or multimedia projects that can be shared with other students and members of the community. We are already seeing glimmers of a computer-based medium that is broadly expressive and capable of capturing many aspects of human consciousness. As the twenty-first century progresses, the whole spectrum of expression is being altered.

Communication and information technology sometimes complement and sometimes supersede previous media. Still, the basic learning process and the essence of any curriculum will continue to involve ways of engaging students in thought that matters and sharing what they find—information/knowledge/wisdom. Wisdom gives you the power to change the shape of ideas.

By giving students the truth of others, teachers can make it possible for them to discover their own. Feeling and meaning can be turned inside out as students learn how to construct their own knowledge and absorb new learning experiences in ways that make sense to them. This extends to anticipating and exploring (from many angles) the depths that await us under the surface of things, whatever those things may be.

New technologies can stimulate *or* get in the way of thoughtful behavior; each technology accelerates opportunities for change within and outside of itself. Since information now arrives so fast, it leaves little time or mental space for processing, reflecting, or thinking through implications. But no matter what we do, walking down certain high-tech paths is difficult to postpone and nearly impossible to avoid.

With the assistance of digital technology, we are living through the largest increases in expressive/thinking capacity in human history. Artificial intelligence, for example, is getting better at extending human thinking and intelligence. It can act as a supplement to human thought in areas ranging from medical problems to making suggestions about what book we may want to read. When combined with other technologies, like the Internet, the arena in which thinking resonates is vastly expanded.

There is no reason for educators to wait around in hope of someone else to make the kind of instructional changes they want. A better approach is for every informed teacher and every informed citizen to push for changes in their domain of influence.

SUMMARY, CONCLUSION, AND LOOKING TO THE FUTURE

In many ways, a wide range of technology expands the traits found in our minds. We also know that every new idea or technology has unexpected consequences for thinking, but it's hard to get specific about what they are going to be. The characteristics of technology matter, but it is even more important to consider the context in which technology is used. Like people, our wiz-bang gadgets have multiple selves that emerge (or don't) based on context.

The creation of something new often goes against traditional approaches and the authority of the present. Likewise, creative and critical thinking (like innovation) are, by their very nature, subversive and outside the specified lines of behavior. Still, the ability to think critically and act creatively is an essential part of today's educational package (Kelley & Kelley, 2013).

Fostering the critical and creative imagination is one of the most important recommendations found in the new subject matter standards. Each set of content standards has its own way of suggesting how students may be helped to move beyond literal meanings to critically interpret what they read, view, or create. More than simply recording facts, "writing" with various media is viewed as a special vehicle for analyzing, interpreting, and explaining.

Education is fluid and organic. Practice is enriched by theory. Theory is transformed in the light of practice—and research plays a clarifying role in this complementary process. The standards are grounded in a framework that relies on all three. As far as creative and critical thinking is concerned, they are woven into each set of standards, and therefore, extend across the curriculum.

As far as instruction is concerned, it is important for teachers to tune in to what students are doing in a way that helps them recognize interests and patterns of thinking so that lessons can be adjusted. Remember, thinking skills are part of a process that builds on previous experience to help us go about building knowledge and understanding (Leicester, 2010).

Learning in a socially connected world changes both *what* and *how* we think. So it is little wonder that the social side of expanding our reality (thinking) has an increasingly crucial role to play in schooling.

The future is not just something that is just going to automatically happen to us. It is something we can think about, revise, edit, and try to shape. To optimize the possibilities, our thought processes have to be flexible enough to accommodate change as new information, research, and concerns spring to life.

As new ideas come up and connections are made across subjects and everyday life, we are never finished with learning how to get things done. Like this last line in an Octavio Paz poem: "Tomorrow we shall have to invent, once again, the reality of this world."

REFERENCES

Armstrong, T. (2009). *Multiple intelligences in the classroom.* Third Edition. Alexandria, VA: Association for Supervision and Curriculum Development.

Beghetto, R. A., Kaufman, J. C., & Baer, J. (2015). *Teaching for creativity in the Common Core classroom.* New York: Teachers College Press.

Bellanca, J., Fogarty, R., & Pete, B. (2012). *How to teach thinking skills within the Common Core: 7 key student proficiencies of the new national standards.* Bloomington, IN: Solution Tree.

Berry, B. (2011). *Teaching 2030: What we must do for our students and our public schools.* New York: Teachers College Press.

Browne, M. N., & Keeley, S. M. (2009). *Asking the right questions: A guide to critical thinking.* Eighth Edition. Upper Saddle River, NJ: Prentice Hall.

Carr, N. (2010). *The shallows: What the Internet is doing to our brains.* New York: W. W. Norton & Co.

Dartnell, L. (2014). *The knowledge: How to rebuild our world from scratch.* New York: Penguin Group (USA).

Dede, C., & Richards, J. (2012). *Digital teaching platforms: Customizing classroom learning for each student.* New York: Teachers College Press.

Gardner, H. (1993). *Frames of mind.* New York: Basic Books.

Gladwell, M. (2005). *Blink: The power of thinking without thinking.* New York: Little Brown and Company.

Honey, M., & Kanter, D. E. (Eds.). (2013). *Design, make, play: Growing the next generation of STEM innovators.* New York: Routledge.

Howie, D. (2011). *Teaching students thinking skills and strategies.* London, UK: Jessica Kingsley Publishers.

Jacobs, H. H. (Ed.). (2004). *Getting results with curriculum mapping.* Alexandria, VA: Association for Supervision and Curriculum Development.

Jenson, E. (2005). *Teaching with the brain in mind.* Alexandria, VA: Association for Supervision and Curriculum Development (ASCD).

Johnson, S. (2014). *How we got to now.* New York: Penguin Group.

Jossey-Bass Publisher (Ed.). (2008). *Jossey-Bass reader on the brain and learning.* San Francisco, CA: Jossey-Bass Publishers.

Kelley, T., & Kelley, D. (2013). *Creative confidence: Unleashing the creative potential within us.* Crown Publishing [A division of Random House].

Langer, E. (1998). *The power of mindful learning.* Cambridge, MA: Da Capo Press (A division of Plemon).

Leicester, M. (2010). *Teaching critical thinking skills: Ideas in action.* London, UK: Continuum International Publishing Group.

Moomaw, S. (2013). *Teaching STEM in the early years: Activities for integrating science, technology, engineering, and mathematics.* St. Paul, MN: Redleaf Press.

Morozov, E. (2011). *The Net delusion: The dark side of Internet freedom.* New York: PublicAffairs.

O'Toole, J., & Beckett, D. (2009). *Educational research: Creative thinking and doing.* Oxford, UK: Oxford University Press.

Schank, R. (2011). *Teaching minds: How cognitive science can save our schools.* New York: Teachers College Press.

Turkle, S. (2011). *Alone together: Why we expect more from technology and less from each other.* New York: Basic Books.

Vasquez, J., Sneider, C., & Comer, M. (2013). *STEM lesson essentials: Integrating science, technology, engineering, and mathematics in grades 3–8.* Portsmouth, NH: Heinemann.

Whyte, D. (1994). *The heart aroused.* New York: Currency Doubleday.

Willis, J. (2006). *Research-based strategies to ignite student learning.* Alexandria, VA: Association for Supervision and Curriculum Development (ASCD).

Chapter 3

Collaborative Learning

A Role for Small Groups in Preparing Tomorrow's Innovators

There is much we can do alone. But together we can do so much more.

—Vygotsky

In one form or another, collaborative learning is one of the more important instructional tools to come along in the last thirty years. The idea of having students work together (in small groups) on the active construction of meaning rests on a solid database of research and practical experience. In addition, the content standards and Common Core projects recommend certain elements of collaborative or cooperative learning for reaching a diverse group of students.

In an interactive learning environment, students serve as learning resources for each other. Teamwork is viewed as one of the keys to accelerating students' imaginative development and academic achievement. The informal type of collaborative learning we discuss here builds on the social nature of learning and what we know about how students construct knowledge. The basic idea is to promote active learning in ways not possible with competitive or individualized learning models.

As far as preparing for innovation is concerned, it is important to recognize that it usually involves teamwork—and it usually moves along in small steps or in more risky transformational changes. Knowledge is a major innovation generator. But don't underestimate the element of chance—a random roll of the dice has a lot to do with outcomes. Since in many ways it is a new and useful method, product, and service, social networking may be viewed as a twenty-first-century example of innovation (Shih, 2011).

When it comes to collaboration and knowledge building in the classroom, the teacher organizes major parts of the curriculum around tasks, problems, and projects so that students can work together in small, mixed-ability groups. Lessons are designed with learning teams in mind so that students can combine their energies as they work toward a common goal. Positive interdependence amplifies student interaction by encouraging individuals to promote each other's productivity.

Whether formal or informal, collaborative learning is a proven way to make sure that all students are involved in learning the subject being studied. Along the road to academic achievement, student interaction can be improved by having group members reflect on how well they are functioning and thinking of ways to improve group work.

Collaborative learning is an educational approach that encourages students at various skill levels to work together, in small groups, to reach common goals. The basic idea is to move students from working alone to working in learning groups where they take responsibility for themselves and other group members.

Although the group "sinks or swims" together, individuals are held accountable because students receive information and feedback from peers and from their teacher. In a collaborative classroom, many activities are arranged in a way that allows for a merger of academic and social learning experiences.

By cooperating on academic tasks, it is our view that students can move toward becoming a community of learners, working together to enhance everyone's knowledge, proficiency, and enjoyment.

COLLABORATION AS AN APPROACH TO LEARNING

Collaborative learning might be viewed as both a personal teaching philosophy and a classroom technique. In collaborative lessons, there is respect for individual group members' abilities and contributions.

Group responsibility and individual accountability are key factors. There is also a sharing of authority and acceptance of responsibility among group members for the group actions. The group's results are based on consensus-building cooperation among group members.

Practitioners who build their own version of collaborative learning in the classroom sometimes view it as a way of living with and communicating with other people. The collaborative learning model sometimes allows students some say in forming friendships and interest groups. We often have the students turn in a confidential list of the four people that they would most like to work with. And we make the final choices.

The content standards in mathematics, science, language arts, and other subjects recommend having students collaborate as they go about doing some of their schoolwork. In addition, student talk is stressed as a way for working things out among group members (National Research Council). What is missing from the standards are specific activities and organizational techniques for making collaborative groups work in the classroom.

Collaborative learning builds on what teachers know about how students construct knowledge, promoting active learning in a way not possible with competitive or with individualized learning. In a cooperative classroom, the teacher organizes major parts of the curriculum around tasks, problems, and projects that students can work through in small, mixed-ability groups. Lessons can be designed around active learning teams in a way that helps students combine energies as they reach toward a common goal.

Social skills, like interpersonal communication, group interaction, and conflict resolution, are developed as the collaborative learning process goes along. Students soon get the idea that if someone else does well, you do well. After each lesson, the learning group examines what they did well and what they might be able to do better (social processing). Many curriculum programs are using collaborative learning without labeling or making an issue of it; small-group work is simply viewed as part of a well-planned curriculum.

For decades, research has suggested that collaborative learning has the following positive effects (Baker et al., 2013). A selection of findings:

- *Collaborative learning can motivate students who are having difficulties with various subjects.* Students talk and work together on a project or problem and experience the fun of sharing ideas and information.
- Classroom interaction with others causes students to make significant learning gains compared to students in traditional settings.
- *It may help to encourage active listening for disinterested students.* Students learn more when they are actively engaged in discovery and problem solving. Collaboration sparks an alertness of mind not achieved in passive listening.
- *Collaboration may help students with literacy and language skills.* Group work offers students many opportunities to use and improve speaking skills. This is particularly important for second-language learners.
- *It often provides greater psychological health for frustrated learners.* Collaborative learning gives students a sense of self-esteem, builds self-identity, and aids in their ability to cope with stress and adversity. It links individuals to group success, so that students are supported, encouraged, and held responsible individually and collectively.
- *Collaboration can help prepare students for today's society.* Team approaches to solving problems, combining energies with others, and working to get along are valued skills in the world of work, community, and leisure.

- *Many times collaborative learning increases respect for diversity.* Students who work together in mixed-ability groups are more likely to select mixed racial and ethnic friendships. When students cooperate to reach a common goal, they learn to appreciate and respect each other, from those who are physically handicapped to those who are mentally and physically gifted.
- *It can improve teacher effectiveness with all learners.* Through actively engaging students in the learning process, teachers also make important discoveries about their students' learning. As students take some of the teaching responsibilities, the power of the teacher can be multiplied (Snodgrass & Bevevino, 2000).

SOCIAL NETWORKS AND UNDERAGED USERS

We all know about young adults and their enthusiasm for social networks. But there are a surprising number of children using sites like Facebook and MySpace. In one fourth-grade class we visited, nearly half the children were familiar with Facebook, even though there is little intended for children (On the surface, games and digital socializing were prime attractions).

Social networking sites realize that they have a problem and try to protect youngsters from predators. Still, there is general agreement that verifying age over the Internet is somewhere between difficult and impossible. Social networking sites generally require users to be thirteen years old or older, but age inflation is common (Eighteen is the magic number for some activities).

Students need to realize that unflattering information, images, and comments they post on Google, Facebook, Twitter, LinkedIn, and other social networking sites are hard to erase. Flickr photos and personal item references placed on Wikipedia can be edited and moved around by anyone. So it should be clear that callous oversharing is a threat to privacy and reputation—as well as future personal, school, and job prospects. Of course, it is technically possible to remove unwanted items, but it is difficult, and you can never be completely sure that you have gotten everything.

The fact that the Internet can be a vehicle for damaging someone's life online has serious implications for life offline. Whatever the required age, children and young adults who pretend to be older can bypass safeguards. And there seems to be little anyone can do about it. In one sense, it's a little like other imaginative technologies in that social media can subvert and disrupt traditional arrangements.

The good news is that many of the parents we interviewed said their youngsters are carefully monitored and used social networks responsibly. It is important to note that those parents who were involved in their children's online activities had the most positive views of the results. Whatever the reality, it is especially hard to keep young adults off social media. In fact, one parent told us that she would rather let her child join Facebook in the open than have him go behind her back.

SOME SUGGESTIONS FOR ARRANGING
THE COLLABORATIVE CLASSROOM

In schools across the country, teachers are spending less time in front of the class and more time encouraging students to work together in small groups. Straight rows are giving way to pods of three, four, or five desks. Of course, collaborative learning is more than rearranging desks. It involves changing how students interact with one another and designing lessons so that teamwork is required to complete assigned tasks.

In the collaborative classroom, group learning tasks are based on shared goals and outcomes. Teachers structure lessons so that to complete a project or activity, individuals have to work together to accomplish group goals. At the same time, they help students learn teamwork skills such as staying with the group, encouraging participation, elaborating on ideas, and providing critical analysis.

One of the keys to success is building a sense of cooperation in the classroom. Teachers often start by providing the class with a collaborative activity. The second step is to have groups of three or four students work together on an initial exploration of ideas and information. To encourage group interdependence, teachers can use a small-group version of a strategy like K-W-H-L-S.

What do we *know*?
What do we *want to learn*?
How will I *work with others to learn it*?
What have I *learned*?
How have I *shared* what I learned from others?

We suggest that teachers give time for individual and group reflection in the last phase of any collaborative learning activity. This way, struggling learners can analyze what they have learned and identify strengths and weaknesses in the group learning process. Questions like "what would help us work better next time?" and "how did you contribute to the quality of the group work?" also help in this social processing stage. Teachers might go on to have student groups engage in activities to reshape their knowledge or information by organizing, clarifying, and elaborating on what has been learned. It's often a good idea to ask student groups to present their findings before an interested and critical audience.

Besides encouraging a sense of group purpose, teachers need to help each student feel that he or she can contribute actively and effectively to class activities. The group may sink or swim together, but individuals are still held accountable for understanding the material. In the collaborative classroom, teachers do more than set standards for group work. They use various assessment tools to evaluate group projects, assignments, and teamwork skills. To get at individual accountability, consider randomly quizzing group members after group work is completed. Whether or not you decide on interrupting the group is one thing, but providing for some form of individual assessment is a basic requirement.

COLLABORATIVE LEARNING IN THE INTEGRATED EDUCATION CLASSROOM

Collaborative learning has been cited as an instructional strategy that can connect a wide range of struggling students to the regular classroom routines (Slavin, 1990). It has become popular because of its potential for motivating and academically engaging all students within a social setting.

It is difficult to arrange educational policy around a single policy—especially one that may change with the political winds. We suggest that a variety of approaches and a wide range of educational research are needed to determine what works best in certain situations.

Mounting evidence suggests that integrated applications and collaboration can provide positive outcomes for all students (Gillies et al., 2008). It requires the combined talents of the regular classroom teacher and those of the special educator as well as the related service providers.

THE ADVANTAGES OF COLLABORATIVE LEARNING

Understanding the important role that collaboration plays in the process of integrated education provides a way to look at the benefits of collaboration:

1. Each person brings experiences to the collaborative process that are shared with others.
2. Support is provided for the classroom teacher.
3. Realistic expectations are determined.
4. Classroom teachers are given support for making modifications.
5. Students can be successful when appropriate modifications are made.
6. Teachers become part of a team in dealing with learning and behavior problems.

It is frequently the case that when a student with disabilities is included in the regular classroom, the assumption is made that he or she is there for academic reasons. The reality is that he or she is there to learn. The regular classroom provides a wealth of opportunities for learning.

APPLYING THE POWER OF COLLABORATIVE LEARNING

By engaging students in the process of making sense of what they are studying, children have more power to explore freely and meaningfully connect to the subject. In a collaborative environment, the teacher assists children in the construction of meaning and acts more like a facilitator and less like a transmitter of knowledge. When questions that connect to student experience are raised collectively, ideas and strengths can be shared in a manner that supports the cooperative search for understanding.

A supportive team structure leads to greater productivity for all students. To be successful, each child needs to be held responsible for doing a fair share of the group work. At their best, cooperative groups go beyond individual learning to promote an informal style of question asking, critical thinking, and action plans for all students. Critical analysis and creative problem solving are a natural part of this active learning process.

Some common characteristics of collaborative groups are that the small group of students shares learning tasks and outcomes, and positive group collaboration is developed by setting mutual goals by the teacher and the students. When this is achieved, there is a group task commitment and individual accountability.

Group learning thrives in an atmosphere of mutual helpfulness where students know what's happening—and why. Part of creating the right environment means having *the teacher* define objectives, talk about the benefits of collaborative learning, and explain expectations and behaviors such as brainstorming, peer teaching, and confidence building.

PROMOTING ACTIVE LEARNING

Whether finding out about new concepts, solving problems, or questioning factual information, a collaborative approach has shown that it helps develop academic skills. At the same time, it taps students' self-esteem and builds students' understanding and attitudes about the subject. Working together to accomplish shared goals is the key to collaborative learning. Academic success, future employment, and even everyday life demand the ability to sort through information, educate others, make sound judgments, and work as a team. Learning to work with others, persevering, solving problems, and dealing collectively in a rapidly changing world are all part of the challenges facing today's students.

Struggling learners often face a difficult challenge in trying to keep up with today's classroom activities. The key to assisting students is to identify who is going to have trouble early on and provide a number of ways for students who are at risk to receive support. For example, early intervention programs can provide intensive support at the onset of a child's school career. There is growing evidence that such programs can also prevent problems from occurring in later years.

COLLABORATION AND HUMAN BEHAVIOR

Cooperation is a major factor that differentiates humans from most other species. In addition, small-group human collaboration sets up the infrastructure that allows for all sorts of transformational changes. From complicated language patterns to complex technology, teamwork makes all the difference in the world (Tomasello, 2009). Individuals can't, for example, build a large airplane alone; it takes thousands of people cooperating to get the job done. In most other species, only related individuals help each other. With humans, it is more broadly based, and the larger social network can develop knowledge and innovations more easily. In fact, many assume that a shift in social behavior was a key factor in making humans unique (Chapais, 2008).

TEAMWORK SKILLS

No matter how you view collaborative student teamwork, there are many common principles involved. Instruction is not viewed as something that isolated students should have done to them; learning is something done best in association with others. The social context matters. And the way different communications are authored or coauthored affect the understanding, reception, and production of information and knowledge.

Teamwork skills do not develop automatically. They must be taught. As group members work together to produce joint work projects, teachers need to quietly help students having problems promote each other's success through sharing, explaining, and encouraging. Teachers may not be on center stage all the time, but with collaborative learning, they constantly guide, challenge, and encourage students. They can also help build supportive group environments by explaining collaborative procedures to students, monitoring small-group questions, and helping students assess group effectiveness at the end of an activity.

Crafting group work that supports learning for all students requires content and activities that support cohesive small groups and meet the needs of individuals. Some teachers use some form of collaborative learning in pairs or groups of three or four students about half of the time. Others may set aside less time for cooperative group work. However you set it up, collaborative learning can help your students move beyond competitive and individualistic goal structures.

As individuals within a group come to care about one another, they become more inclined to provide each other with academic assistance and personal support. They are also more likely to make suggestions for what might be done to improve group efforts in the future. As each person adds their unique spirit, the cooperative group takes on enough power to illuminate the consequences of alternative courses of action. It sometimes takes a little time to get cooperative groups up to speed, but it's worth the effort.

MAKING COLLABORATIVE LEARNING WORK

Like anything else, the ability of the teacher is the key to successfully using collaborative learning. By arousing interest and broadening horizons, teachers can amplify the joy and curiosity that are natural parts of the teaching and learning process. For these things to happen, teachers must be masters of content and be equally familiar with the characteristics of effective interactive instruction.

Getting collaborative learning to work for you requires more than giving well-meaning instructions to "work together" and "be a team." Not all groups are collaborative. To structure lessons so that students do work collaboratively with each other requires an understanding of what makes collaboration work.

An important part of collaboration is structuring an environment where group members understand they are connected with each other in a way that one student cannot succeed unless everyone succeeds (*Your success benefits me and my success benefits you*). Group goals and tasks must be designed and carefully communicated so that students believe they share a common fate (*We all sink or swim together in this class*). When the team is solidly structured, it tells students that each member has a unique contribution to make to the joint effort (*We cannot do it without you*). This creates a commitment to the success of the group as well as the individual student. No group member has all the information or all the skills. Even the least able student can recognize this.

TEACHING SUGGESTIONS FOR USING
COLLABORATIVE LEARNING

• Use your existing lessons, content, and curricula and structure them in cooperative groups. Take any lesson in any subject area with a student of any age and structure it collaboratively.
• Tailor collaborative learning lessons to your unique instructional needs. This may mean that you may need to provide additional time for planning.
• Diagnose the problems some students may have in working together and intervene to increase the effectiveness of the group process.
• Teach students the skills they need to work in groups. Social skills do not magically appear when collaborative lessons are employed. Skills such as "use quiet voices," "stay with your group," "take turns," and "use each other's names" are the beginning of collaborative skills.
• It is important to have students discuss how well their group is doing. Groups should describe what worked well and what was harmful in their team efforts. Continuous improvement of the collaborative learning process results from careful analysis of how members are working together.

ARRANGING THE CLASSROOM FOR
COLLABORATIVE LEARNING

Effective teachers know that an important step in changing student interaction is changing the seating arrangement. Architecture and the organization of our public and private spaces strongly influence our lives at every level. The same principle applies to schools and individual classrooms. The way teachers arrange classroom space and furniture has a strong impact on how students learn. When desks are grouped in a small circle or square, or when students sit side by side in pairs, collaborative possibilities occur naturally. Straight rows send a very different message.

A classroom designed for student interaction makes just about anything more interesting. The way you design the interior space of your classroom helps focus visual attention. It also sets up acoustical expectations and can help control noise levels. Natural lighting, carpets, comfortable corners, occasional music, and computers that are arranged for face-to-face interaction can all help set the general feelings of well-being, enjoyment, and morale. Classroom management is actually easier if students know that they can't shout across the classroom but they can speak quietly to one, two, or three others depending on the size of the small group. Even many questions that students are used to asking the teacher can come after asking one or two peers. All students benefit in this kind of group learning situation, even the most reluctant student.

As students engage in collaborative learning, they should sit in a face-to-face learning group that is as close together as possible. The more space you can put between groups, the better. From time to time, it is important to remix the groups so that everybody gets the chance to work with a variety of class members. The physical arrangement should allow you to speak to the whole class without too much student movement. Struggling students benefit from this grouping arrangement. Teachers can give students more of their attention and better differentiate instruction. When the whole class is together, you should be able make eye contact with every student in every group without anyone getting bent out of shape or moving desks (Joiner et al., 2000).

WAYS TEACHERS CAN ORGANIZE FOR COLLABORATIVE LEARNING

1. Formulate objectives.
2. Decide on the size of groups, arrange the room, and distribute the materials students need.
3. Explain the activity and the collaborative group structure.
4. Describe the behaviors you expect to see during the lesson.

   Group behaviors:

   • share ideas
   • respect others
   • ask questions
   • stay in your group
   • encourage your group mates
   • stay on task
   • use quiet voices

5. Assign Roles.
   Classes new to the collaborative approach sometimes assign each member of the group a specific function that will help the group complete the assigned task. For example: the *reader* reads the problem, the *checker* makes sure that it is understood, the *animator* keeps it interesting and on task, and the *recorder* keeps track of the group work and tells the whole class about it. If you have groups of three, then everyone can share the animator's role. Struggling learners need to be included in these roles. No matter how you set up collaborative learning, group achievement

depends on how well the group does *and* how well individuals within the group learn (Spooner, 2015).

6. Monitor or intervene when needed.
   While you conduct the lesson, check on each learning group when needed to improve the task and teamwork. Bring closure to the lesson.
7. Evaluate the quality of student work.
   Ensure students that they themselves will evaluate the effectiveness of their learning groups. Have students construct a plan for improvement. Be sure that all students are on task. Groups may be evaluated based on how well members performed as a *group.* The group can also give individuals specific information about their contribution. Groups can keep track of who explains concepts, encourages participation, checks for understanding, and who helps organize the work (Harvey & Daniels, 2015). Learning with a small circle of friends can help students navigate around the untidy clutter of doubt and strive for things that had previously exceeded their grasp. Working in community with others is the best way for struggling students to gain the confidence and the power to see what can be that isn't yet.

PROBLEM SOLVING IN A SOCIAL SETTING

Problem solving and collaboration are common themes that cut across the content standards and the curriculum. But learning to solve problems in school is often different than the way it happens outside of school. When they get out in the real world, students may feel lost because nobody's telling them what to solve. In real life, we are usually not confronted with a clearly stated problem with a simple solution. Often, we have to work with others to just figure out what the problem is. The same thing is true when it comes to asking and answering questions. When teachers and students can relate to other people, it can bring out the best in themselves and in others.

Knowledge is constructed over time by learners within a meaningful social setting. Students talking and working together on a project or problem experience the fun and the joy of sharing ideas and information. When students construct knowledge together, they have opportunities to compare knowledge, talk it over with peers, ask questions, justify their position, confer, and arrive at a consensus. Even students who usually struggle with a project will feel a sense of belonging to the group.

Collaboration will not occur in a classroom that requires students to always raise their hands to speak. Active listening is not sitting quietly as a teacher or another student drones on. It requires spontaneous and polite interruptions where everyone has an equal chance to speak and interact. Just let others complete a thought and don't break into the conversation in mid-sentence. Try to get everyone to ask a question or make a comment. It may be best not to make students put their hand up first. Encourage the more talkative class members to let everyone make a contribution before they make another point. The inattentive listener may need to assume a leadership role and help monitor the discussion.

Collaborative learning will involve some change in the noise level of the classroom. Sharing and working together even in controlled environments will be louder than an environment where students work silently from textbooks. With experience, teachers learn to keep the noise constructive. Whether you are a parent or a teacher, you know that a little reasoning (regarding rules) won't hurt children. Responsible behavior needs to be developed and encouraged with consistent classroom patterns.

When collaborative problem solving is over, students need to spend time reflecting on the group work. A basic question at the end: "What worked well and how might the process be improved?" Students and teachers need to be involved in evaluating learning products and the collaborative group environment.

Effective interpersonal skills are not just for a collaborative learning activity; they also benefit students in later educational pursuits and when they enter the workforce. Social interactions are fundamental to negotiating meaning and building a personal rendition of knowledge. Mixed-ability learning groups have proven effective across the curriculum. It is important to involve students in establishing rules for active group work.

CLASS RULES FOR COLLABORATIVE LEARNING

Rules should be kept simple and might include the following:

- Everyone is responsible for his or her own work.
- Productive talk is desired.
- Each person is responsible for his or her own behavior.
- Try to learn from others within your small group.
- Everyone must be willing to help anyone who asks.
- Ask the teacher for help if no one in the group can answer the question.

Group roles and individual responsibilities also need to be clearly defined and arranged so that each group member's contribution is unique and essential. If the learning activities require materials, students may be required to take responsibility for assembling and storing them. Avoid getting too many materials too fast. Three or four problems with materials are enough for the struggling learner. All students want to be using materials. Unlike competitive learning situations, the operative pronoun in collaborative learning is *we*, not *me*.

TEACHING THE COLLABORATIVE GROUP LESSON

During the initial introduction of a lesson, you can help your students understand what it is they're supposed to do by establishing guidelines on how the group work needs to be conducted. Present and review the necessary concepts or skills with the whole class, and pose a part of the problem or an example of a problem for the whole class to try. Provide a lot of opportunities for your students to discuss a wide range of issues meaningful to them. Present the actual group problem after you finish the conceptual overview. Then, encourage them to discuss and clarify the problem task.

When they're ready, students start to work collaboratively to solve problems. You'll need to listen to the ideas of the different teams and offer assistance when you detect that some of them are getting stuck. You're also responsible for designing extension activities just in case the faster teams finish early. There are different ways of handling teams that are stuck. One way would be for you to help them discover what they know so far, and then pose a simple example, or, perhaps, point out a misconception or erroneous idea that may be getting in their way. For example, team members may have trouble getting along with each other or focusing on the one very specific task they're supposed to be doing. Pull their energies together by asking them simple questions like, "What are you supposed to be doing now?" "What is your team's task?" "How will you get organized from where you are now?" "What materials do you need?" "Do you think you have enough time to cover everything you set out to do?" "Do you know who will do what?" This is very helpful for disengaged students.

After students complete the problem task and group exploration stages, they will need to meet again as a whole class to summarize and present their findings. Each team needs to present their solutions and tell their classmates how they worked toward their resolution as a group. You or the other students in class could very well ask questions like "How did you organize the task?" "What problems did your team have?" "What method did you use?" "Was your group method effective? Why or why not?" "Did anyone have a different method or strategy for solving the same or similar problem?" "Did your team think that your solution made sense?" Encourage your students to listen and respond to their classmates' comments. You may, in fact, point out to them that they could earn participation points in this exercise by responding precisely to their classmates' remarks and building upon them. Ask the recorder in the group to make notes on the chalkboard and write down students' responses to help summarize class data at the end of the lesson.

HELPING ALL LEARNERS SUCCEED

This section introduces classroom strategies for helping all students succeed in a regular classroom setting. Ten suggestions are offered from a variety of research studies from "Strategies for Helping At-Risk Students" (Snow, Barley, & Bauer, 2015) to "Alternative Approaches in Planning for Academic Content" (Yard & Vatterott, 1995).

A collaborative group structure allows for high levels of flexibility and creativity. One approach that has promise is the use of flexible grouping strategies essential in collaborative learning, which according to a number of studies improves everything from achievement to self-esteem (Johnson & Johnson, 1991; Slavin, 1990). Here, we describe a flexible grouping strategy that can be used with students of all ability levels.

1. *Assign Students to Flexible Groups.* Organize the class into four-student groups. One way to accomplish this is to use partner groups. Rank the class from the most prepared to the least prepared for the subject (e.g., number the students from one to thirty). Next, divide them into subgroups (1 to 10, 11 to 20, 21 to 30) so that the groups are similar to the traditional high-, middle-, and low-ability groups. Finally, achieve mixed grouping by assigning the top student in each of the three groups to one group, the second-highest student in each to another, the third highest to another, and so on. You will, then, have students 1, 11, students 10, 20, and 30. In this way, the mixed groups should comprise students who are sufficiently different in ability that can benefit from each other's help but not so different that they find one another intimidating.

   Inform students of their group assignments, and tell them that they are partners and must help each other as needed, whether by reading each other's work before it is turned in, by answering questions regarding assignments, by showing a partner how to do something, or by discussing a story and sharing their ideas. Let them know that this is only one of many grouping arrangements that you will be using. Grouping procedures may be based on skills, levels, or interests. Collaborative groups can be based on tasks or goal achievement.

2. *Focus on the needs of students.* Students learn best when they satisfy their own motives for learning the material. Some of these motivations include the need to learn something in order to complete a particular task

or activity, the need for new experiences, and the need to be involved and to interact with other people (Yard & Vatterott, 1995).

3. *Make students active participants in learning.* Students learn by doing, making things, writing, designing, creating, and solving problems. The first step is to honor the different ways that students learn.

4. *Help students set achievable goals for themselves.* Often students fail to meet unrealistic goals. Encourage students who are struggling to focus on their continued improvement. Help students evaluate their progress by having them critically look at their work and the work of their peers.

5. *Work from students' strengths and interests.* Teachers may give students interest inventories to help them find areas where they have a special talent or interest, such as sports, art, or car mechanics. Ultimately, each student selects an area of special interest or curiosity and discusses the topic with the teacher and their peers. Then, they begin a search for more information, which may lead to a group project or a team presentation.

6. *Be aware of the problems students are having.* Meet with your students one on one for a brief conference. It's helpful to tape the conversation so that you have an oral explanation of their understandings. Play the tape for your student and ask questions if the student is confused.

7. *Organize a conducive team-meeting environment.* Oftentimes, students are easily distracted by the sights and sounds in the room. Choose an area of the classroom that presents the fewest distractions, and keep visual displays purposeful.

8. *Incorporate more time and practice for students.* Students who are having difficulties remembering skills need small doses of increased practice throughout the day. This increases performance.

9. *Provide clarity.* Clarity is achieved by modeling and using open-ended questions so you can adjust your approach to different students.

10. *Intervene early and often.* The key to intervention strategies are identifying students who need extra help and to provide ways for struggling students to receive support.

COLLABORATIVE LEARNING ACTIVITIES

A carefully balanced combination of integrated education, subject matter knowledge, knowledge of the students, instruction, self monitoring, and active group work help meet diverse needs of all students. The activities suggested here are designed to provide a collaborative vehicle for active learning in math and science.

Activity 1: Build a Square

[This activity can be used with just about any elementary or middle school class. It relates to the geometry standard in math and the communication standard in both math and science.]

Materials: An envelope containing five puzzle pieces. Either the teacher or the students can make the puzzle pieces from three-inch squares of index cards. Cut the index cards into three pieces. Place the puzzle pieces in an envelope.

Procedures: Five people around your table will all make an individual square. Each square has three pieces. Each group leader opens the envelope and passes out the puzzle pieces like a deck of cards so each person has three pieces. *No one is allowed to talk or gesture during this activity.* Group members can pick up a piece and offer it to someone in their group. They can take it or refuse it. *No reaching over and taking pieces!* Raise your hands when all the exchanges have been made and all the five squares are completed. Students work together silently. They are eagerly trying to get their squares done. It is almost impossible for a struggling student to fail when the whole group is focused.

Evaluation: Next, try the activity again, only this time everyone is allowed to talk.

Take time to have a class discussion concerning the problems your group had. Suggest ideas that would make this activity work better.

Activity 2: Back-to-Back Communication

[This can be used from third grade on up through middle school. It relates to the geometry and measurement standards in math and the communication standard in both math and science].

Materials: Cut out shapes that can be easily moved on a desk. Make many geometric shapes, and make each shape a different color. Colored paper is the simplest material, but Attribute Blocks or Pattern Blocks can also be used.

Procedures:

1. Give each group of two people two envelopes with matching sets of shapes. Students at a beginning level should get five or six shapes. More advanced students might use a dozen or more.

2. Have children get into groups of two, seated back to back, with their envelopes in front of them.
3. Tell students that one of them is the teller, and the other listens and tries to follow directions exactly.
4. The teller arranges one shape at a time in a pattern. As the teller does this, he or she gives the listener exact directions—what the shape is and where to place it.
5. When the pattern is finished, have students check how well they have done.
6. Switch roles and do it again.

Evaluation: Have students explain the activity to a partner and describe what was difficult and how they worked through it.

Activity 3: Investigate Your Time Line

[This works from third grade on up through middle school. Among other things, it relates to the measurement standard in mathematics].

Objectives:

1. Working in groups of four or five, each group makes a time line of the ages of the people in their groups and the events in their lives.
2. Students will compare the events in their lives with those of other students. (For example: "The most important event for me when I was five years old was . . . ")
3. Students record and report the results.

Background Information:

• A time line can show different cultural and ethnic patterns.
• Students are able to see how maturity affects decisions.
• A time line exercise is designed to find out how time changes students' math and science perceptions.

Materials: A thirteen-foot-long piece of butcher paper for each group, rulers, fine point markers, and a time line model prepared by the teacher to post on the board for the students to use as a model.

Procedures:

1. The teacher will explain that the students will be working in collaborative groups to make time lines of the ages and lives of the people in their groups.

2. The teacher will divide students into groups of four or five students.
3. The teacher and students will pass out the materials to each group.
4. The teacher will explain his or her model time line and give students directions for making their own time lines:
   • Students will find out the ages of the people in their group: who is the oldest, next oldest, youngest, and so on.
   • Students will start the time line on January first of the year that the oldest person in the group was born.
   • Students will end the time line on the last day of the current year.
   • Each student will use a different color marker to mark off each year.
   • Each year equals one foot, and an inch equals a month.

At the bottom of each year, the students will write the important events in their lives.

A color key with the colors of markers and each student's name will identify the student. Students can put a dot or star by the important events in their lives such as birthdays, birth of siblings, and other important events in their lives.

Evaluation: A volunteer from each group will present their group's time line and post it up on the classroom bulletin board.

Activity 4: Bridge Building

[This is intended for grades three through nine. It supports the measurement, geometry, and communication standards in math and the physical science, investigation, and experiment standards in science]. Bridge Building is an interdisciplinary math and science activity that reinforces skills related to communication, group process, social studies, language arts, technology, and the arts.

Materials: Lots of newspaper, masking tape, one large, heavy rock, and one cardboard box. Have students bring in stacks of newspaper. You will need approximately a one-foot pile of newspapers per small group.

Procedures: For the first part of this activity, divide students into groups of about four. Each group will be responsible for investigating one aspect of bridge building.

Group One: Research
This group is responsible for going to the library and looking up facts about bridges, collecting pictures of all kinds of bridges, and bringing back information to be shared with the class.

Group Two: Aesthetics, Art, Literature
This group must discover songs, books about bridges, paintings, artwork, and more, which deal with bridges.

Group Three: Measurement, Engineering
This group must discover design techniques, blueprints, angles, and measurements of actual bridge designs. If possible, visit a local bridge to look at the structural design and other features.

Have the group representatives get together to present their findings to the class. Allow time for questions and discussion. The second part of this activity involves actual bridge construction with newspapers and masking tape.

1. Assemble the collected stacks of newspaper, tape, the rock and the box at the front of the room. Divide the class into groups. Each group is instructed to take a newspaper pile to their group and several rolls of masking tape. Explain that the group will be responsible for building a stand-alone bridge using only the newspapers and tape. The bridge is to be constructed so that it can support the large rock and so that the box can pass underneath.
2. Planning is crucial. Each group is given ten minutes of planning time in which they are allowed to talk and plan together. During the planning time, they are not allowed to touch the newspapers and tape, but they are encouraged to pick up the rock and make estimates of how high the box is, to make a sketch of the bridge, or to assign group roles of responsibility.
3. At the end of the planning time, students are given about fifteen minutes to build their bridge. During this time, there is no talking among the group members. They may not handle the rock or the box—only the newspapers and tape. (A few more minutes may be necessary to ensure that all groups have a chance of getting their constructions meet at least one of the two "tests" [rock or box]). If a group finishes early, its members can add some artistic flourishes to their bridge or watch the building process in other groups (With children, you may not want to stop the process until each group can pass at least one "test").

Evaluation: Stop all groups after the allotted time. Survey the bridges with the class and allow each group to try to pass the two tests for their bridge. They get to pick which test goes first. Does the bridge support the rock? Does the box fit underneath? Discuss the design of each bridge and how they compare to the bridges researched earlier. Try taking some pictures of the completed work before you break them down and put them in a recycling bin. Awards could be given for the most creative bridge design; the sturdiest, the tallest, and the widest bridge; the best group collaboration; and so on. Remember, each group is proud of their bridge.

PROBLEM SOLVING IN COLLABORATIVE CLASSROOMS

In a classroom that values teamwork, teachers provide time for students to grapple with problems, try out strategies, discuss issues, experiment, explore, and evaluate. A key element in collaborative classrooms is group interdependence. This means that the success of each individual depends on the success of each of the other group members.

Student investigations, team discussions, and group projects go hand in hand with preparing students for the new information, knowledge, and work arrangements that they will come across throughout life. Also, partner teams can work together, as well as teams of three or four—and better than groups of five or six (Bishop & Allen-Malley, 2004).

Data is a valuable resource and information a valuable commodity, but teamwork is the key to making imaginative things happen. Whatever variation of collaborative inquiry a teacher chooses, students can be given opportunities to integrate their learning through interactive discovery experiences and applying their problem-solving skills.

Activity: Form groups of two, three, or four and come up with captions for pictures or political cartoons from the newspaper. An alternative is to come up with the caption and search for a cartoon or picture that works with it. Students can look for something that relates to whatever topic they are studying. Share with the class.

Across all subjects, it is more important to emphasize the *reasoning* involved in working on a problem than it is getting "the answer." Near the end of a group project, the teacher can develop more class unity by pointing out how each small group's research effort contributes to the class goal of understanding and exploring a topic.

Teachers need to model attitudes and present themselves as collaborative problem solvers and models of learning. They do this by letting students know that learning is a lifelong process for teachers and other adults. A suggestion: let them in on some of your more positive professional development experiences.

ATTITUDES CHANGE AS CHILDREN COLLABORATE

Some students may require a shift in values and attitudes if a collaborative learning environment is to succeed. The traditional school experience has taught many students that the teacher is there to validate their thinking and direct learning. Getting over years of learned helplessness may take time.

Attitudes change as students learn to work cooperatively. As they share rather than compete for recognition, struggling students find time for reflection and assessment. Small groups can write collective stories, edit each other's writing, solve problems, correct homework, prepare for tests, investigate questions, examine artifacts, work on a computer simulation, brainstorm an invention, create a sculpture, or arrange music. Working together is also a good way for students to synthesize what they have learned, collaboratively present to a small group, coauthor a written summary, or communicate concepts.

It is important that students understand that simply "telling an answer" or "doing someone's work" is not helping a classmate learn. Helping involves learning to ask the right question to help someone grasp the meaning or explaining with an example. These understandings need to be actively and clearly explained, demonstrated, and developed by the teacher.

A major benefit of collaborative inquiry is that students are provided with group stimulation and support. The small group provides safe opportunities for trial and error as well as a safe environment for asking questions or expressing opinions. More students get chances to respond, raise ideas, or ask questions. As each student brings unique strengths and experiences to the group and contributes to the group process, respect for individual differences is enhanced.

The group also acts as a motivator. We all feel a little nudge when we participate in group activities. Many times, ideas are pushed beyond what an individual would attempt or suggest on their own. Group interaction enhances idea development, and students have many leadership skills when they become teachers as well as learners. In addition, the small-group structure extends children's resources as they are encouraged to pool strategies and share information.

If the group is small enough, it's hard for the more withdrawn students not to participate. Students soon learn that they are capable of validating their own values and ideas. This frees teachers to move about, work with small groups, and interact in a more personal manner with students.

SKILLFUL COLLABORATION AMPLIFIES
LEARNING AND INNOVATION

If one person's achievement in a group is viewed as another's loss, then cooperation, openness, and generosity fade and self-interest and fear move front and center. Collaborative learning is designed to bring out the positive and stimulate the best that everyone has to offer. It has proven itself as an effective way to provide peer support for imaginative behavior in the classroom.

Collaborative group problem solving, reciprocal teaching, and cross-age tutoring are now generally accepted as useful tools for helping students get the most out of any subject. As technology charms us with its quick and easy attractions, brain functions can get lazy and encourage people to take the easy way out. The brain needs substantial face-to-face offline exercise to operate at its collaborative best (Brown & Fenske, 2010).

By collaboratively exploring new concepts in different contexts, students can internalize mental images, perform actions, and discover underlying concepts. To gain and share expertise, team members challenge each other's thinking in a way that doesn't breed conformity or hostility. Work teams can also be used to provide struggling students with a support network that can gradually be withdrawn as children move to higher levels of confidence.

In the collaborative classroom, mutual achievement and caring for one another can result in learning actually becoming more personalized. Students and teachers can come to view each other as a learning community of collaborators who help group members with cognitive, emotional, physical, and social change.

Adapting to today's social and academic realities requires a common framework and conceptual understanding.

When it comes to successful innovation, the prerequisite skills are teamwork, vision, resources, and time. And remember, failure is an inevitable cul-de-sac on the road to success. Just try to figure out what went wrong and try not to make the same mistake twice.

LEARNING IN COMMUNITY WITH OTHERS

Knowledge is rarely constructed in isolation. At just about any age, individuals do better at building understanding when they have the help of others. In a learning community, individuals collaborate in meaning-making activities. Community members are recognized for what they know (as well as what they need to learn). To be successful, each member of the group must learn how to contribute to the overall outcome. When the class is divided into collaborative groups, helping other team members isn't cheating; it is a highly regarded approach to learning subject matter. Such collaborative group work provides the keystone for building broader learning communities.

Increasingly, educational systems set out to develop individuals who can understand the world and are capable of working with others to alter it for the better. Teamwork skills are at (or near) the top of the job skills ladder. As teachers, it is our responsibility to prepare students to enter an increasingly international world with openness, confidence, and intelligence. Much of what we do is more implicit than explicit. So it is as important for the classroom teacher to embody and to exhibit what we value in students.

To reach group goals, each individual must contribute in some way to the outcome. The result is the development of a kind of social cohesion that stems from students learning how to be contributing members of a learning team. Students who are struggling to learn math and science need to go beyond the lower-level basics that are often designed only to improve test scores, to experience the same high-quality education that many in affluent areas take for granted.

In addition to teamwork skills, a collaborative structure can help students by providing group support for self-discovery, problem solving, and higher-level reasoning for all students. One of the side benefits for teachers is that positive instructional changes are most likely to occur when there is a cooperative school climate and a peer support system in place (Newman, 2014).

YESTERDAY, TODAY, AND TOMORROW

In many ways, collaborative team learning becomes a useful instructional partner because it supports the kind of deep learning that shines toward the future. It is little wonder that in one form or another, cooperative group work has become one of the most widely used instructional innovations. In skillful hands, it can build on social interaction to unleash the full potential of our children's minds.

As students learn to accomplish shared goals, they also learn get the most out of learning and life. In addition, as teachers who have experienced or implemented collaborative group learning will tell you, the habits of the mind and the emotions of the heart associated with successful peer collaboration can be like a breeze of fresh air in the classroom (Bellanca & Stirling, 2011).

Yesterday, today, and tomorrow, successful schools have (and will) come in many colors. But there are a few common features that cut across time and space. Culture is important—this includes family, neighborhood, country, and school. One of the educational constants is the need to create a close-knit learning community where all students and their teachers care for each other. Increasingly, new technologies are enabling students to go beyond the classroom to expand their collaboration and knowledge acquisition.

Social networks, like Facebook, can enhance feelings of social connection among self-confident youth. But social media can have the opposite effect on many; more connected does not mean more invested in the lives of others. Also, connecting with friends and exchanging ideas are fine, but popularity contests are a losing proposition for everyone. For example: when you're looking at someone else's status updates, pictures, and "friend" count, it is a little like those family history (impossibly positive) Christmas letters.

When facial expression and body language are missing (online) context takes a vacation. It is clear that face-to-face social interaction and the group transmission of norms are as essential for learning. The same can be said for developing the perception and instinct that are a large part of the student's academic motivation and personal character (Brooks, 2011).

Student learning teams are natural partners of e-learning and distance learning. Like face-to-face collaborative learning, objectives can be structured so that individual goals are influenced by the actions of other group members (social interdependence). Virtual collaboration is increasingly used in the business world, and schools are starting to realize that geographic distance doesn't necessarily get in the way of learning.

By tapping into students' natural curiosity and creating a caring learning community, teachers can help their students learn how to use collaboration to achieve academic goals. Consistent with this is including all students in daily classroom routines and teams where group accomplishment matters.

SUMMARY, CONCLUSION, AND LOOKING AHEAD

Within collaborative groups, all students can build on one another's strengths to develop a sense of group solidarity and accomplishment. As learners work together, they can share alternative viewpoints, support each other's inquiry, develop critical-thinking skills, and improve on their academic performance (De Prete, 2013).

There are many important findings on the benefits of collaborative learning, including motivation, increased academic performance, active listening, improved language and literacy skills, and a sense of self-esteem. Another major benefit of collaborative learning is that individuals are provided with group stimulation and support.

The learning group provides safe opportunities for trial and error—as well as a safe environment for asking questions or expressing opinions. Students also get more chances to respond, raise ideas, or ask questions. Each participant brings unique strengths and experiences to the group process. Along the collaborative way, respect for individual differences is enhanced and it becomes relatively easy to draw everyone into the group work.

When teachers build on the social nature of learning, students usually become more motivated to explore meaningful inquiry and problem solving. As students learn to cooperate and work in small, mixed-ability groups, they can also take on more responsibility for themselves and helping others to learn. The basic idea is that the social nature of learning builds on the continuous interaction between perception and action.

From the content standards to the Common Core, there are suggestions for supporting and understanding the process of teamwork, creativity, and innovation. Clearly, students' interest in their peers is a resource that can stimulate the learning process through group activities.

New technological tools can help with developing effective groups by encouraging online interpersonal communication that connects to offline relationships. Also, tech tools can help collaborative groups evaluate data and cut through today's information clutter (Caine & Caine, 2011).

Imaginative change begins with imaginative ideas. Virtual instruction has its place, but when it comes to helping students generate new ideas, you can't substitute technology for live teachers. In fact, there is no strong research that suggests that online work or courses are as effective as face-to-face learning experiences (U.S. Department of Education, 2009). Cutting corners and costs is one thing, benefiting students quite another.

Whether it is online or off, the dynamism of frequent and in-depth collaboration can serve as one of the engines of educational transformation. The process includes gradually internalizing instructional concepts through interactions with peers and adults—with individual and group reflection encouraged along the way. The basic idea is to build a cooperative learning environment that allows learners to thrive in a knowledge age.

Today's students *can* succeed individually by working in collaboration with their peers. And by building on group energy and idealism, the thinking, learning, and doing processes can be pushed forward in subjects across the curriculum.

The age of cooperation is approaching.
Teachers and administrators are discovering an untapped resource for
accelerating students' achievement: the students themselves.

—Robert Slavin

REFERENCES

Baker, M., Andriessen, J., & Jarvela, S. (Eds.) (2013). *Affective learning together. Social and emotional dimension of collaborative learning.* London, UK: Routledge [Taylor & Francis Group].

Bellanca, J., & Stirling, T. (2011). *Classrooms without borders: Using Internet projects to teach communication and collaboration.* New York: Teachers Collage Press.

Bishop, P., & Allen-Malley, G. (2004). *The power of two: Partner teams in action.* Westerville, OH: National Middle School Association.

Brooks. D. (2011). *The social animal: The hidden sources of love, character, and achievement.* New York: Random House.

Brown, J., & Fenske, M. (2010). *The winner's brain: 8 strategies great minds use to achieve success.* Cambridge MA: Da Capo Press (Perseus Books Group).

Caine, R., & Caine, G. (2011). *Natural learning for a connected world: Education, technology, and the human brain.* New York: Teachers College Press.

Chapais, B. (2008). *Primeval kinship.* Cambridge, MA: Harvard University Press.

Christian, B. (2011). *The most human human: What talking with computers teaches us about what it means to be alive.* New York: Doubleday.

De Prete, T. (2013). *Teacher rounds: A guide to collaborative learning in and from practice.* Thousand Oaks, CA: SAGE.

Dixon-Krauss, L. (1996). *Vygotsky in the classroom: Mediated literacy instruction and assessment, 1st edition.* New York: Longman Inc.

Gillies, R., Ashman, A., & Terwel, J. (Eds.). (2008). *The teacher's role in implementing cooperative learning in the classroom.* New York: Springer.

Gleick, J. (2011). *The information: A history, a theory, a flood.* New York: Pantheon.

Harvey, S., & Daniels, H. S. (2015). *Comprehension and collaboration: Inquiry circles for curiosity, engagement, and understanding, revised edition.* Portsmouth, NH: Heinemann.

Johnson, D., Johnson, R., & Holubec, J. (2008). *Cooperation in the classroom, revised edition.* Edina, MN: Interaction Book Co.

Joiner, R., Miell, D., Faulkner, D., & Littleton, K. (Eds.). (2000). *Rethinking collaborative learning.* London, UK: Free Association Books.

Jolliffe, W. (2007). *Cooperative learning in the classroom: Putting it into practice.* London, UK: Paul Chapman Publishing, a SAGE Publications Company.

Kahn, P. (2011). *Technological nature: Adaptation and the future of human life.* Cambridge, MA: MIT Press.

National Council of Teachers of Mathematics. (2000). *Principles and standards for school mathematics.* Reston, VA: National Council of Teachers of Mathematics.

National Research Council. (1996). *National science education standards.* Washington, DC: National Academy Press.

Newman, T. (Ed.). (2014). *Collaboratively learning about collaborative learning.* Nacogdoches, TX: Stephen F. Austin University Press.

Shih, C. (2011). *The Facebook era: Tapping online social networks to market, sell, and innovate.* Upper Saddle River, NJ: Prentice Hall.

Slavin, R. (1990). *Cooperative learning: Theory, research, and practice.* Second edition. Upper Saddle River, NJ: Prentice Hall.

Snodgrass, D., & Bevevino, M. (2000). *Collaborative learning in middle and secondary schools: Applications and assessments.* Larchmont, NY: Eye on Education.

Snow, D., Barley, Z. A., & Lauer, P. A. (2005). *Classroom strategies for helping at-risk students.* Alexandria, VA: Association for Supervision & Curriculum Development (ASCD).

Spooner, E. (2015). *Interactive student centered learning: A cooperative approach to learning.* Lanham, MD: Rowman & Littlefield.

Tomasello, Michael. (2009). *Why we cooperate.* Cambridge, MA: MIT Press.

U.S. Office of Education. (2009). *Evaluation of evidence-based practices in learning: A meta-analysis and review of online learning studies.* Washington, DC.

Wolfe, B., & Sparkman, C. (2010). *Team-building activities for the digital age: Using technology to develop effective groups.* Champaign, IL: Human Kinetics.

Yard, G., & Vatterott, C. (1995). Accommodating individuals through instructional adaptation. *Middle School Journal* 24: 23–28.

Chapter 4

Communication Technologies

New technologies have been disrupting existing equilibria for centuries, yet balanced solutions have been found before.

—Pamela Samuelson

Available technologies have always been rocking the social and classroom scene back and forth. Sometimes, new educational products or applications change everything; at other times new tech tools don't work out at all.

Each new technology creates a new human environment and often leads to new ways of thinking and acting. But whether it is in or out of the classroom, new ways of communicating and relating to information require a break from habit.

There are times when the latest gadgets are so fascinating that sensible approaches are overwhelmed. But just because something is technically interesting and doable doesn't mean it should be done. And just because children like something doesn't mean it's good for them.

Devices that keep us continually on course and fixed in time and place can destroy the magic of randomness. Also, the stupefying modern obsession with productivity can deny the whimsy that living fully demands. To avoid negative consequences, it is important to be aware of what is taking place in the world around you, become comfortable with thought-provoking ideas, and know how to sort through the glut of information.

With digital technology, questions must always be asked about the relationship between a problem and the dangers associated with how it gets solved. Has the Internet age made us lazy and forgetful, or has it "created a radical new style of human intelligence" (Thompson 2013)?

Emerging electronic information and communications media can conjure up new environments for critical thinking, creativity, and teamwork. When used intelligently, they can help people do all kinds of things better. When done wrong, digital tools can destroy privacy, reputations, and a broad spectrum of basic rights. Self-discipline and a moral compass are needed to navigate around a wired world.

Although it can help, specific technical expertise is not always required for creative and innovative behavior in an increasingly digital century. There are times when all subjects need to be decoupled from technology so that students can master a topic by interacting with others to find openings to new ideas and invention. Given the amount of time young people spend alone in front of a variety of screens, face-to-face human interaction is more important than ever.

Moving in the direction of new opportunities requires more than preparing technicians. Everything from the humanities to whimsical thinking have roles to play as students strive to master subject matter.

Involving all students (equity) doesn't mean teaching to the lowest common denominator; excellence and acquiring deep knowledge of a topic or subject matter even more.

Lessons need to be designed in a way that helps all learners understand and use technology creatively. An important goal is to engage young people in ways that will help them bring more useful tech tools and innovation to whatever they do.

POSSIBILITIES AND PITFALLS IN A WIRED WORLD

We have been warned for decades that the United States is losing ground to international competitors and will lag even further behind unless it provides its citizens with higher-level math, science, literacy, and technology skills.

The world of globalization and automation requires working harder, smarter, and retooling yourself more often. Literacy, math, and computer skills matter. So does problem solving in a technology-rich environment (digital skills). It is clear that America must upgrade the skills of its citizens, or many will find the doors to the twenty-first-century workplace closed to them (OECD, 2013).

The arrival of new technological possibilities has always been exhilarating, frightening, and finally, it's just part of life. A few decades into the twentieth century it was the telephone that began to be taken for granted. By the 1950s, it was television. Now, many children and young adults see digital devices and the Internet as natural ways to extend their information and communication reach.

In a school setting, digital technologies can encourage analytical thinking and help students connect subjects to collaborative inquiry (Caine, 2011). But still, in some ways, the same technologies and their applications encourage uncritical users to know more and more about less and less. In fact, it is now possible for a person to travel through life or around the globe in a wired cocoon.

As educators increasingly take an active role in the development of educational technology, there is more of a reasoned curriculum connection. And the process itself can have something of a liberating effect on the imagination of all involved. Also, new technological possibilities can encourage new habits of the mind and fresh perspectives. To get all of this right requires everyone involved to view teachers' professional development as a necessity (rather than a luxury).

The same Internet that gives us more and more access to various viewpoints can also narrow our universe to well-worn groves of redundant experiences. Unleashing the potential of digital media requires serious thinking, research, and experimentation to make the connection between technology and the characteristics of effective instruction.

It is possible to use technology in a way that makes classroom learning more exciting and effective than ever. But like science, technology and learning can only progress by valuing thought, evidence, and usefulness over magical wonderment.

There is a lot of uncertainty out on the technological horizon. But when it comes to educating the young, teachers, technology, and the school curriculum will play major roles.

Technology is an important thing, but it's not the only thing. It is only helpful when it helps develop students' imagination, inventiveness, self-discipline, and the ability to ask good questions.

POWERFUL TOOLS AND UNEXPECTED POSSIBILITIES

Done wrong, activities and social connections that rely on digital technology can be sad and lonely. Among other things, learning to avoid the dark side of technology requires limiting the time involved and treating people online the way you would want them to treat you.

When done right (within a limited time frame), digital technology can help an active meaning-centered curriculum to flourish in (and beyond) the classroom. But no matter what, the coming together of technologies like computers, video, satellites, and the Internet is both evolutionary and revolutionary.

Social media and other online activities are not inherently asocial—assuming those using it have the discipline to put down the electronics.

Children, for example, need to get by the dazzle and go outside to play. At school, authentic face-to-face communication and collaborative learning require carving out time for the devices to be disconnected (Zuckerberg, 2013).

Where do creative solutions come from, and what sparks chains of creation?

Computers and their associates are potentially powerful tools for communications, academic work, and innovation. Digital technology has the power to move literacy and learning patterns off established roads. By motivating students through the excitement of discovery, a wide assortment of technological tools can assist the imaginative spirit of inquiry and make lessons sparkle. It can even put students right out on the edge of discovery—where truth throws off its various disguises.

As human horizons shift, a sort of flexible drive and intent is required for innovation and progress. Technology can add power to what we do and help us kick against educational boundaries. The vivid images of electronic media can stimulate students as they move quickly through mountains of information, pulling out important concepts and following topics of interest.

The online process changes students' relationship to information by allowing them to personally shift the relationship of knowledge elements across time and space. Learners can follow a topic between subjects, reading something here and viewing a video segment there. All of this changes how information is structured and how it is used. It also encourages students to take more responsibility for their own learning.

The negative side of online learning is the practice of paying partial attention. Students no longer have time to reflect, contemplate, or make thoughtful decisions. Instead, they exist in a state of constant crisis—on alert for a new contact or a bit of exciting news or information at any moment (Rose, 2010).

All media as extensions of ourselves serve to provide
new transforming vision and awareness.

—Marshall McLuhan

Be ready for the unexpected. Things don't always go as planned. Alexander Graham Bell thought, when he invented the telephone, that it would be used to listen to distant symphony concerts. Thomas Edison thought that the phonograph record would be used to send messages. Some of the best thinkers often miss the potential of their inventions. For example, physicist Heinrich Hertz was the first to generate and detect radio waves, yet he dismissed the notion that his findings might ever have any practical value. Human advances often come from what may go unnoticed or seem trivial at the time.

Anything that changes perspective—from travel to technology—can help generate new ideas. The motivation is also there because it's usually more fun to do things where the unexpected may turn up rather than sticking with the easily predictable. Playfulness and experimentation can often open up to creative possibilities, increasing the capacity to fashion ideas or products in a novel fashion. Creatively playing with various ideas, some of which may seem silly at the time, may result in getting lucky with one or two of them.

It is often difficult to detect the subtle happenstance and how we make room in our own lives for positive accidents to happen. Being exposed to different experiences and paying attention to what's going on in the world help, because all kinds of serendipitous possibilities open up. Training the eye to notice things goes a long way toward making unpredictable advances happen. Each new finding can open up fresh questions and possibilities—breaking the habits that get in the way of creative thinking and change. Rx for thinking in the future: following curiosity, leaving doors open, using technological tools, and making room for good luck to happen.

THE TECHNOLOGICAL DIMENSIONS OF LEARNING IN A NEW ERA

At school, the challenge is getting students to apply the same level of intensity to their schoolwork that they apply to social media and video games. Building a dynamic model of learning requires making good use of everything available. But action without vision can be a nightmare . . . and vision without action often leads nowhere. One thing is certain, new technology is bound to generate new ways of thinking, learning, and working.

The playful gleam in the eye is often an engine of progress. There are multiple tools and modes of expression that schools need to build on to promote the multitude of strengths and imaginations found in all students. Many schools are mired in unproductive routines that prevent teachers from making creative breakthroughs.

Educators are not often able to take enough time to go back to the drawing board and use good data and experience to get it right. Reflection and changing approaches takes time, space, support, and time for collegial professional development to make all the changes required.

Powerful forms of face-to-face learning within schools must not be neglected as we sort out the new media possibilities. Intelligent use of electronic forms of learning has proven to be helpful in improving student learning. But when it comes to the professional development of teachers, their value is not as clear. Electronic learning can, however, make a contribution. And it is a useful supplement to the professional development tool kit.

It is difficult to unravel issues of creativity or analyzing without taking into account influential media, like computers and television. They have a tremendous impact on children. We shape them, and they shape us. Some are often written about as Lady Caroline wrote about Lord Byron: "mad, bad and dangerous to know." Others see technology, such as computers and the Internet, as particularly dangerous enemies, creating a culture of electronic peeping Toms without a moral foundation.

To be valuable, educational technology must contribute to the improvement of education. Digital devices and their accessories should be designed to help open doors to reality and provide a setting for reflection. By making important points that might otherwise go unnoticed, these technological tools can help students refine and use knowledge more effectively. For example, computers can use mathematical rules to simulate and synthesize lifelike behavior of cells growing and dividing. It's a very convincing way to bring the schooling process to life.

The yeast of knowledge, openness, and enterprise raises the need for a multiplicity of learning media and technological tools. Schools can teach students to recognize how technology can undermine social values, human goals, and national intention. They can also help students learn to harness these powerful tools so that they might strengthen and support the best in human endeavors. It is our belief that when the pedagogical piece is in place, technology can support and strengthen the best in student learning. This can not only change what teachers teach but also change how they go about doing it.

As new technologies and related products start to fulfill their promise, students will become active participants in knowledge construction across a variety of disciplines. We have had only a glimpse of the technological gateways to learning that will open in the twenty-first century. As state-of-the-art pedagogy is connected with state-of-the-art technological tools, the way knowledge is constructed, stored, and learned will be fundamentally altered.

THE FUTURE OF NARRATIVE IN CYBERSPACE

The idea of print as an immutable canon may or may not be a historical illusion. One thing for sure, the way print is being mixed electronically with other media changes things. Although the American book industry is rushing into the emerging electronic literary market, book pages made of paper won't go away.

One way or another, print is here to stay. Even the doomsayers usually use books to put forward their argument that the medium is a doomed and outdated technology. In the future, will books be confined to dusty museum libraries? No, they will remain an elegant, user-friendly medium. With books, you don't need batteries and don't have to worry about the technological platform becoming obsolete and unusable.

There are at least two fairly new digital approaches to books that are finding a niche in the literacy universe. One is much like an electronic version of printed books. The other approach to electronic books is interactive and visually intensive. It takes the narrative and places it in randomly accessible blocks of text, graphics, and moving video. With some e-book stories, students must learn to go beyond merely following the action of the plot to learn about characters, explore different ideas, and enter other minds.

An interactive e-book story places students in charge of how things develop and how they turn out. Participants are able to change the sequence or make up a new beginning to a multidimensional story. They can slow up to find out additional information, and they can change the ending. Navigating interactive stories with no fixed beginning, middle, or end can be very disconcerting to the uninitiated. It requires different "reading" skills.

To make sense of the anarchy and chaos, a reader has to become a creator. This means following links around so that they can discover different themes, concepts, and outcomes. "Interactive Storytime" is an early example. It tells stories with narration, print, music, sound effects, and graphics. Children can click on any object and connect spelling to the pronunciation.

Literature has traditionally had a linear progression worked out in advance by the author. The reader brought background knowledge and a unique interpretation to what the author had written. But it was the author who provided the basic sequential structure that pushed all readers in the same direction. Computer-based, multidimensional literature is quite different. The reader shapes the story line by choosing the next expository sequence from a number of possibilities.

With early versions of interactive, computer-based literature, readers are connected to a vast web of printed text, sound, graphics, and lifelike video. When key words or images are highlighted on a computer screen, the reader clicks what they want next with a mouse (or finger on a touch screen) and the reader hops into a new place in the story, causing different outcomes. With a virtual reality format, the "reader" uses their whole body to interact with the story. Whatever the configuration, interactive literature causes the user to break down some of the walls that usually separate the reader from what's being read.

The forking paths in this electronic literature pose new problems for readers—like how do you know when you have finished reading when you can just keep going all over the place? Judy Malloy's *It's Name Was Penelope,* for example, shuffles four hundred pages of a fictional woman's memories so that they come together very differently every time you read it. The ambiguity of these programs isn't as bothersome as it used to be.

Today, children are used to television and computer programs that deal with quick movement between short segments of information. In addition, many video games and computer simulations require students to wander in a maze of ideas. As a result, children are usually not as disoriented by the various forms of interactive literature as adults.

Odd varieties of e-stories can be found, free of charge, on the Internet. Some are free, some are comparable to a traditional book in price, and others require a multimedia or virtual reality platform. Many of these efforts at constructing interactive stories were more like interactive comic books than literature. Programs are becoming more sophisticated and are giving us some advance warning of a new literary genre. One thing is for sure—something important is happening to the future of curriculum and instruction.

ONLINE PEER TUTORING

Whether it is *off* or *on* line, peer tutoring involves several methods. In *cross-age tutoring*, older students tutor younger students. In *cross-ability tutoring*, a student who has a good grasp of the subject can tutor a student who is struggling. *Reciprocal tutoring* involves a structure for interaction that is tied to specific academic goals (Grant, 2010).

CONVEYING MEANING WITH POWERFUL VISUAL MODELS

One way to enhance the power and permanency of what we learn is to use visually based mental models in conjunction with the printed word. Inferences drawn from visually intensive media can lead to more profound thinking. In fact, children often rely on their perceptual (visual) learning even if their conceptual knowledge contradicts it. In other words, even when what's being presented runs contrary to verbal explanations, potent visual experiences can push viewers to accept what is presented.

Children can become adept at extracting meaning from the conventions of video, film, or animation—zooms, pans, tilts, fadeouts, and flashbacks. But distinguishing fact from fiction is more difficult.

The ability to understand what's being presented visually is becoming ever more central to learning and to our society. Most of the time, children construct meaning for television, film, computer, or Internet content without even thinking about it. They may not be critical consumers, but they attend to stimuli and extract meaning from subtle messages.

The underlying message children often get from the mass media is that viewers should consume as much as possible while changing as little as possible. How well content is understood varies according to similarities between the viewers and the content. Viewers' needs, interests, and age are other important factors. Sorting through the themes of mental conservatism and material addition requires carefully developed thinking skills.

Each participant constructs meaning in any medium at several levels. For better or for worse, broadcast television used to provide us with a common culture. When viewers share a common visual culture, they must also share a similar set of tools and processes for interpreting these signals (construction of meaning, information processing, interpretation, and evaluation).

The greater the experiential background in the culture being represented, the greater the understanding. The ability to make subtle judgments about what is going on in any medium is a developmental outcome that proceeds from stage to stage with an accumulation of experience.

Equity doesn't mean designing lessons for the lowest common denominator. Equity and excellence are not mutually exclusive goals.

Relying upon a host of cognitive inputs, individuals select and interpret the raw data of experience to produce a personal understanding of reality. What is understood while viewing depends on the interplay of images and social conditions.

Physical stimuli, human psychology, and information-processing schemes taught by the culture help each person make sense of the world. In this respect, reacting to the content of an electronic medium is no different from any other experience in life. It is just as possible to internalize ideas from electronic visual imagery as it is from conversation, print, or personal experience. It's just that comprehension occurs differently.

Reflective thought and imaginative action play important parts in the growth process of a child. Even with a "lean back" passive medium like television, children must do active work as they watch, make sense of its contents, and use its messages. With a "lean forward" medium like the Internet, this work is fairly evident. Evaluative activities include judging and assigning worth, assessing what is admired, and deciding what positive and negative impressions should be assigned to the content. In this sense, children are active participants in determining meaning in any medium.

ADULTS INFLUENCE HOW CHILDREN
LEARN TO ASSESS MEDIA MESSAGES

Although children learn best if they take an active role in their own learning, parents, teachers, and other adults are major influences. They can significantly affect what information children will gather from television, film, or the Internet. Whatever the age, critical users of media should be able to:

- understand the grammar and syntax of a medium as expressed in different program forms
- analyze the pervasive appeals of advertising
- compare similar presentations or those with similar purposes in different media
- identify values in language, characterization, conflict resolution, and sound/visual images
- utilize strategies for the management of the duration of viewing and program choices
- identify elements in dramatic presentations associated with the concepts of plot, storyline, theme, characterizations, motivation, program formats, and production values

Parents and teachers can affect children's interest in media messages and help them learn how to process information. Good modeling behavior, explaining content, and showing how the content relates to student interests are just a few examples of how adults can provide positive viewing motivation. Adults can also exhibit an informed response by pointing out misleading messages—without building curiosity for undesirable programs.

The viewing, computer, and Internet-using habits of families play a large role in determining how children approach a medium. The length of time parents spend watching television, the kinds of programs viewed, and the reactions of parents and siblings toward programming messages all have a large influence on the child. If adults read and there are books, magazines, and newspapers around the house, children will pay more attention to print. Influencing what children view on television or the Internet may be done with rules about what may or may not be watched, interactions with children during viewing, and the modeling of certain content choices. A tip for parents: it's usually a good idea to keep the computer in the family room.

Whether coviewing or not, the viewing choices of adults in a child's life (parents, teachers, etc.) set an example for children. If, for example, parents are heavy watchers of public television or news programming, then children are more likely to respond favorably to this content. If parents make informed, intelligent use of the Internet, then children are likely to build on that model. Influencing the settings in which children watch TV or use the computer is also a factor.

Turning the TV set off during meals sets a family priority. Parents can also seek a more open and equal approach to choosing television shows—interacting before, during, and after the program. When it comes to the Internet, keep the computer in the family room rather than in a private, isolated space. Time limits must be placed on today's electronic gadgets. Parents can organize formal or informal group activities outside the house that provide alternatives to Internet use or TV viewing.

It is increasingly clear that the education of children is a shared responsibility. Parents obviously play a central role, and they need connections with what's going on in the schools. Working together, parents and teachers can use the television, computers, and the Internet to encourage students to become more intelligent media consumers. When it comes to schooling, it is teachers who will be the ones called upon to make the educational connections entwining varieties of print and visual media with the basic curriculum.

COMMUNICATIONS TECHNOLOGY AND PUBLIC CONVERSATIONS

A democratic community is defined by the quality of its educational institutions and its public conversations. Democracy often becomes what it pays attention to. American national values, supported by our constitution, require an educated citizenry that can think, respond to leaders, and are willing to actively go beyond the obvious. Patriotism isn't just the flag and stern rhetoric; it's a thinking, decent, and literate society. Exercising citizenship in a world of accelerated change requires the preservation of our human values.

Ignoring the societal implications of technology means ignoring looming changes. Whether it's technologically induced passivity or the seductive charms of believing in simplistic technological solutions, it is only through the educational process that people can gain a heightened awareness of bright human and technological possibilities. The question that we need to answer is: How might the technology be used to spark a renaissance in human learning and communication?

The long-term implications of recent changes in information and communications technologies are important, if not frightening. The convergence of technologies is causing a major change in societal behaviors, lifestyles, and thinking patterns. With few people monitoring digital technology or theorizing its health, the human race is being forced to swim in an electronic sea of information and ideas. In today's world, there is little question that reality is being shaped by electronic information and electronic illusions.

ACTIVITIES FOR MAKING SENSE OF VISUAL MEDIA

1. *Help students critically view what they see.* Decoding visual stimuli and learning from visual images require practice. Seeing an image does not automatically ensure learning from it. Students must be guided in

decoding and looking critically at what they view. One technique is to have students "read" the image on various levels. Students identify individual elements and classify them into various categories, then relate the whole to their own experiences, drawing inferences and creating new conceptualizations from what they have learned. Encourage students to look at the plot and story line. Identify the message of the program. What symbols (camera techniques, motion sequences, setting, lighting, etc.) does the program use to make its message? How is a visual ad used to excite interest? Packaging, color, and images on pictures of the product have a lot to do with it—the basic idea is to influence consumers. How might reality be distorted in the process?

Analyze and discuss commercials in different media. How many minutes of ads appear in an hour? How many ads do you have to sort through before you can watch a program or use a search engine to get to some websites? What should be done about the ad glut?

2. *Create a scrapbook of media clippings.* Have students keep a scrapbook of newspaper and magazine clippings on computers, the Internet, Facebook, Google, television, and some of the other inhabitants of cyberspace. Newspapers and magazines are good sources of articles—for instance, the *New York Times* science section is a good example for upper-grade students. Ask students to paraphrase, draw a picture, or map out a personal interpretation of an interesting technology article. Share these with other students.

3. *Create new images from the old.* Have students take rather mundane photographs and multiply the image, or combine it with others, in a way that makes them interesting. Through the act of observing, it is possible to build a common body of experiences, humor, feeling, and originality. And through collaborative efforts, students can expand on ideas and make the group process come alive.

4. *Role-play communicating with extraterrestrial life.* Directions for students: If extraterrestrial life has already contacted us, think about how to respond. Think creatively and scientifically about how you would explain this planet to some inquisitive aliens. Explain human life and media devices; try to view our planet as a whole.

5. *Use debate for critical thought.* Debating is a communications model that can serve as a lively facilitator for concept building. Take a current and relevant topic and formally debate it online or face to face. This can serve as an important speech and language extension. For example, the class can discuss how mass media can support everything from commercialism to public conformity and the technological control of society. The discussion can serve as a blend of technology, social studies, science, and the humanities.

Electronic media and social patterns are constantly shifting through various stages of acceptance and use. Communications now come in many forms and from many locations, served up on a variety of digital devices. So it is little wonder that an important instructional goal is giving young people the skills needed to swim through today's technological crosscurrents.

DIFFERENT MEDIA SYMBOL SYSTEMS

Print and visually intensive media take different approaches to communicating meaning. Print relies upon the reader's ability to interpret abstract symbols. A video or computer screen is more direct. Whatever the medium, thinking and learning are based on internal symbolic representations and the mental interpretation of those symbols. When they are used in combination, one medium can amplify another.

We live in a complex society dependent on rapid communication and information access. Lifelike visual symbol systems are comprised in part of story structure, pace, soundtrack, color, and conceptual difficulty. Computers, the Internet, television, and digital devices are rapidly becoming our dominant cultural tools for selecting, gathering, storing, and conveying knowledge in representational forms (Levy, 2011).

Various electronic symbol systems play a central role in modern communications. It is important that students begin to develop the skills necessary for interpreting and processing the full range of media messages. Symbolically different presentations of media vary as to the mental skills of processing they require. Each individual learns to use a media's symbolic forms for purposes of internal representation.

To even begin to read, for example, a child needs to know something about thought-symbol relationships. To move beneath the surface of electronic imagery requires some of the same understandings. It takes skill to break free from a wash of images and electronically induced visual quicksand. These skills don't just develop naturally; training is required to develop critical media consumers who are literate in interpreting and processing print or visual images.

Unlike direct experience, print or visual representation is always coded within a symbol system. Learning to understand that system cultivates the mental skills necessary for gathering and assimilating internal representations. Each communications and information medium makes use of its own distinctive technology for gathering, encoding, sorting, and conveying its contents associated with different situations. The technological mode of a medium affects the interaction with its users—just as the method for transmitting content affects the knowledge acquired.

The closer the match between the way information is presented and the way it can be mentally represented, the easier it is to learn. Better communication means easier processing and more transfer. At its best, a medium gets out of your way and lets you get directly at the issues. New educational choices are being laid open by electronic technologies. Understanding and employing these technological forces require interpreting new media possibilities from a unique and critical perspective.

UNDERSTANDING AND CREATING ELECTRONIC MESSAGES

Understanding media conventions helps cultivate mental tools of thought. In any medium, this gives the viewer new ways of handling and exploring the world. The ability to interpret the action and messages requires going beyond the surface to understanding the deep structure of the medium. Understanding the practical and philosophical nuances of a medium moves its consumers in the direction of mastery.

Simply seeing an image does not have much to do with learning from it. The levels of knowledge and skill that children bring with them to the viewing situation determine the areas of knowledge and skill development acquired. Just as with reading print, decoding visually intensive stimuli and learning from visual images require practice.

Students can be guided in decoding and looking critically at what they view. One technique is to have students "read" the image on various levels. Students identify individual elements, classify them into various categories, and, then, relate the whole to their own experiences. They can then draw inferences and create new conceptualizations from what they have learned.

Planning, visualizing, and developing a production allow students to critically sort out and use media techniques to relay meaning. Young producers should be encouraged to open their eyes to the world and visually experience what's out there. By realizing their ideas through media production, students learn to redefine space and time as they use media attributes such as structure, sound, color, pacing, and imaging.

The field of technology and its educational associates are in a period of introspection, self-doubt, and great expectations. In a world awash with different types of educational media, theoretical guidelines are needed as much as specific instructional methods. It is dangerous to function in a theoretical- or research-deprived vacuum because rituals can spring up that are worse than those drained away. As schools are faced with aggressive marketing for electronic devices, we must be sure that a pedagogical plan that incorporates technology is in place.

For technological tools to reach their promise requires close connections among educational research, theory, and classroom practice. Across the curriculum, new standards are emerging that place a high premium on creative and critical thinking. So it is clear that the curriculum and professional development will pay even closer attention to such skills.

Reaching students requires opening students' eyes to things they might not have thought of on their own. This means using technological tools as capable collaborators for tapping into real experience, fantasies, and personal visions. This way, previously obscure concepts can become comprehensible, with greater depth, at an earlier age.

Technology and metacognitive strategies can come together as students search for data, solve problems, and graphically simulate their way through multiple levels of abstraction. The combination of thoughtful strategies and the enabling features of media tools can achieve more lasting cognitive change and improved performance.

SOCIAL EQUITY AND A MODERN PHILOSOPHY OF TEACHING

Historically, Americans hadn't needed a rigorous education. Wealth had made rigor optional.

—Amanda Ripley

Equity doesn't mean teaching to the lowest common denominator. For high-quality educational experiences, equal educational opportunities must go hand in hand with academic excellence.

As we put together the technological components that provide access to a truly individualized set of learning experiences, it is important to develop a modern philosophy of teaching, academic standards, learning, and social equity.

Harmonizing students' present with the future requires more than reinventing the schools. Many children are behind on their first day of school, so efforts to improve schooling must extend before and beyond the classroom door. For all learners to thrive academically, it helps to have the benefits of preschool, high-quality teachers, health care, and engaged family support.

When it comes to helping all students reach their educational potential, it takes a lot more than technology. But tech tools can lend a hand in the effort to devolve the corrosive brew of poverty and neglect that eats away at the fabric of democratic life.

While new information and communications technologies have the potential to help make society more equal, they sometimes have the opposite effect. At home and at school, equal access to new technological worlds is a long way from reality.

Many school districts lack the money to train teachers to use digital technology effectively. Searching for information on the Internet is common practice in many schools. But even in the schools that have plenty of computers, focus is on typing, drills, and workbook-like practices.

Affluent schools are more likely to encourage students to use digital technology for creative exploration—like designing multimedia presentations and collaborating with classmates in problem-solving experimentation (Ripley, 2013).

Everyone deserves access to the tools associated with a provocative and challenging curriculum. To become an equal instrument of educational reform, digital technology must do more than reinforce a two-tier system of education. Otherwise, many children will face a discouraging picture of technological inequality.

There will be serious social consequences if the inequalities surrounding the use of the latest telecommunications and information technologies. Connections with other students, databases, and library resources have the potential to change the way information and knowledge are created, accessed, and transmitted. Those denied informed access may well find their ambitions stifled as they fall further and further behind the more fortunate.

The challenge is to make sure that this information is available for all in a twenty-first-century version of the public library.

Digital technology gives us the ability to change the tone and priorities of gathering information and learning in a democratic society. Taking the right path with this tool requires learning to use what's available today and building a social and educational infrastructure that can travel the knowledge highways of the future.

THINKING: SLOW, ACCELERATING, AND FAST

Electronically connecting the human mind to people and global information resources may shift human consciousness in ways similar to what occurred in moving from an oral to a written culture. The ultimate consequences are unclear. But the development of basic skills, habits of the mind, wisdom, and traits of character will be increasingly affected by the technology (Roblyer, & Doering, 2010).

Computer-based simulations can simulate invisible things like molecular reactions and static electricity. Also, with role-playing interactive activities from around the world, it is possible to foster thinking skills and collaboration.

The instructional activities that are most effective and most popular are those that provide social interaction and problem-solving opportunities. Information can be embedded in visual narratives to create contexts that give meaning to dry facts.

Interactive digital technology can challenge students on many levels and even serve as a training ground for responsibility, persistence, and collaborative inquiry. It's relatively easy to buy the hardware and get children interested. The difficult thing is to connect to deep learning in a manner that advances curriculum goals.

New technology is a double-edged sword. Laptops can be used to record or take notes on the day's activities and presentations. They can also be a distraction as students check email and Facebook; a few even use the technology to cheat during class. Cell phones can also be used to gather educationally useful information and record important parts of a class. But they can also be brazenly used to send instant messages and waste time texting during class.

To stay on a useful curriculum and instruction path at school, it is important to recognize the fact that many students today have been brought up in an age of wiz-bang gadgets. Their approach to media and daily life is one of constant contact and multitasking. Technological expertise and curiosity are one thing; constant distraction is quite another.

On the first day of class, teachers need to set and post specific rules and consequences for off-task activities. Decide if or when cell phones or laptops can be used during class. Remember to tell students if you don't want a lesson to be recorded. Do not leave it open for debate—enforce the posted rules consistently and fairly.

Schools need more adults than ever: teachers' aides, parents, older students, and more. Technological tools can get in the way of learning. But on the positive side, they can be unique and useful supplements that allow teachers to enhance their lessons and try out some new things.

GENERATING QUESTIONS ABOUT
TECHNOLOGICAL SURVEILLANCE

When a new medium emerges, it generates new ways of thinking and the opening of new realities. Asking probing questions about such things as the intrusion of surveillance technology and the collection of communications is part of what it means to be technologically literate today.

Internet users may know that websites they use often work with online advertisers to target products and services that might interest you. What isn't as well known is that these companies can track you as you travel around and move between devices like computers, tablets, and cell phones. Also, they make up profiles without an individual's permission that can be accessed by employers and governmental agencies.

Many countries use surveillance technologies, but the United States has them all beat. The National Security Agency (NSA), for example, has a huge collection of American communications and a record of just about every cross-border interaction. To make things easier for themselves, the NSA secretly inserts "back doors" into high-tech products and international encryption systems. Also, they collaborate with big software companies to have special access routes built into their systems.

Confidential information on cloud storage is wide open to some businesses and governmental agencies. A number of NSA employees, for example, have been caught spying on love interests and the personal lives of celebrities. Others—from foreign spy agencies to individual hackers—can play the same game with both personal and commercial data.

Are we doing enough to prepare for the level of surveillance possible today?

The public is just beginning to learn about computerized tools like the Biometric Optical Surveillance System operated by the Department of Homeland Security. The program instantly connects to everything from live video cameras to stored drivers' license photos, Facebook pages, global positioning system (GPS) signals, and Google searches. The result: individual faces are identified by massaging huge amounts of data used to infer what a person is up to at any given moment.

The NSA says that they can collect whatever they want from "anyone, anytime, anywhere" (Risen & Poitrasnov, November 22, 2013). The goal seems to be to have access to virtually everything available in the digital world. Encryption doesn't seem to slow them down as they track anyone who uses a computer, mobile device, or router.

Beyond the gathering of personal information, the NSA intends to influence and shape the trends in high-tech industries in ways that are not known to users.

The end result of any government gathering and storing every conceivable type of personal pictures, conversations, and messages is bound to have a negative effect on the open exchange of ideas. Especially when new algorithms go beyond facts and concepts to interpretation and the labeling of individuals and groups—the whole thing seems to invite mission creep and abuse (Unger, 2012). * The pros and cons of business/ government surveillance make for a good small-group and full-class discussion.

Legal or illegal, data miners and advertisers have the advantage over consumers.

LEARNING TO EVALUATE ONLINE
ACTIVITIES AND SOFTWARE

Curriculum is a cooperative and interactive venture between students and teachers. On both the individual and social levels, those directly involved with the process must be taken seriously. Working together, they can decide what benefits are gained from particular software programs. After all, the software user is in the best position to decide if the program is taking people out of the process, or whether learners are in control of the computers. Good software programs let students learn together at their own pace—visualizing, talking together, and explaining abstract concepts so that they can relate them to real-life situations.

There are time-consuming evaluation issues surrounding the multitude of software programs to be dealt with. Multimedia, simulation, micro worlds, word processing, interactive literature, spreadsheets, database managers, expert (i.e., artificial intelligence or AI) systems, or getting the computer in contact with the outside world all increase the potential for influencing impressionable minds. That is too large a universe for the teacher to figure out alone. Teachers can help each other. Another thing that helps the task become more approachable is getting the students to take on some of the responsibility.

Children can learn to critique everything from computer software to Internet websites much as they learned to critique the dominant media of yesteryear—books. One of the first tenets of book review criticism is to critique what is usually taken for granted. Also, having at least a little affection for what is being reviewed helps. Students can do book reports, review computer software, and discuss the quality of sites on the Internet. It helps if they sift through some of the software reviews in newspapers, magazines, and journals, online and offline.

When examining online activities and software, students can quickly check to see if the flow of a program makes sense. Next, they can try out the software as they think a successful or unsuccessful student might. How easy is it to learn? What happens when mistakes are made? How are the graphics? Do you think you can learn anything from this? Is it exciting?

Without question, teachers and students are the ones who will experience the consequences of making good or bad choices in software selection. And they are the ones who most quickly learn the consequences of poor choices as well.

CRITERIA FOR EVALUATING E-ACTIVITIES

The teacher can apply the same assessment techniques used on other instructional materials when they evaluate courseware. The following list is an example:

1. Does the activity meet the age and attention demands of your students?
2. Does it hold the student's interest?

3. Do the programs, activities, or simulation games develop, supplement, or enhance curricular skills?
4. Does the work require adult supervision or instruction?
5. Children need to actively control what the program does. To what extent does the program allow this?
6. Can the courseware be modified to meet individual learning requirements?
7. Can it be adjusted to the learning styles of the user?
8. Does the program have animated graphics that enliven the lesson?
9. Does it meet instructional objectives, and is it educationally sound?
10. Does the activity or program involve higher-level thinking and problem solving?

Student Evaluation Checklist

Name of student evaluator(s) _____

Name of software program_____

Publisher _____ Subject_____

1. How long did the activity take?_____ minutes
2. Did you need to ask for help doing the work? _____ Yes _____ No
3. What skills do you think the activity tried to teach?

Please circle the word that best answers the question.

4. Was it fun to use? Yes No Somewhat Not very
5. Were the directions clear? Yes No Somewhat Not very
6. Was it easy to use? Yes No Somewhat Not very
7. Were the graphics (pictures) good? Yes No Somewhat Not very
8. Did the activity get you really involved? Yes No Somewhat Not very
9. Were you able to make choices in the? Yes No Somewhat Not very
10. What mistakes did you make?_____
11. What happened when you made a mistake? _____
12. What was the most interesting part of the activity? _____
    _____
13. What did you like least? _____
14. What's a good tip to give a friend who's getting started with this activity?
    _____

Extended work: Make up a quiz about the particular computer program or online activity and give the questions to other students in the class who have used it.

- Create your own soundtrack for part of the activity.
- Make up a student guide for the activity. Use your own directions and illustrations.
- Write or dramatize an interview with one of the characters in a television program or in a movie.
- Interview other students who have used the activity and write their responses.
- Write a review of the activity and post it online.

Remember, there are many *top ten* or *best of* lists out there for consideration.

SERVING PEDAGOGY

The curriculum should drive the technology rather than the other way around. The most effective use of such tools occurs when desired learning outcomes are figured out first. Once standards have been set, you can decide what technological applications will help you reach your goals. Technology can help when it serves clear educational goals. But there is much work to be done to put an *e* and a dash in front of education. However, by working together, teachers can learn from each other, push on to other innovations, and build a medium worthy of our students (Willard, 2002).

Converging communication technologies can serve as a great public resource. Commercial profit alone should not determine how these new technologies will be exploited. The public owns the airwaves and the information highways. Emerging public utilities must show a concern for learning and responsible social action. Any new media system is a public trust that should enable students to become intelligent and informed citizens.

In today's world, children grow up interacting with electronic media as much as they do interacting with print or with people. Unfortunately, much of the programming is not only violent, repetitive, and mindless, but also distracts students from more important literacy and physical exercise activities.

New technologies, software, and interactive media amplify everything. To deal with these new digital realities requires a new approach to curriculum and instruction. It also requires a heightened sense of social responsibility on the part of those in control of programming.

Not only has the media changed, but we also now live in a society that is ruled by profits. It is time to go back to considering the public interest and to devise rules to ensure that the mass media take responsibility for the fact that they influence the foundation on which formal learning takes place.

TIPS ON USING DIGITAL TECHNOLOGY

- Technology is an important thing, but not the only thing.
- Put the learning piece in place first.
- Don't panic or be intimidated by technology.
- Make mistakes and learn from your failures.
- Don't be afraid to learn from your students.
- Bring everybody along; leave no one behind.
- Collaborate with other teachers; invest in teacher training.
- Two-way is the only way. Foster active conversation.
- Have fun. Be sure that there is some joy in it.

Remember, both real and imaginary factors can stir people to action. The human imagination can be enhanced by technology-based instruction in a way that makes actual experiences more meaningful. With computer control, you can speed it up, slow it down, go into an atom, or go back into the past. On occasion, the experience can even transcend print or actual experience as an analytical tool.

LOOKING IN THE DIRECTION OF TOMORROW

Amid all the commercial maneuvering, new media technologies have at least the potential for empowering students to take some control over their learning.

Digital technology can extend a student's reach for new knowledge and assist them in the search for new ways of learning. It can also make information more visually intriguing and provide for two-way communication with live or artificially intelligent experts. Tutoring, for example, is often done with live, recorded, or computer-composed experts.

Digital interactive storytelling techniques will allow plot lines to evolve in almost infinite directions. Characters can even be programmed to surprise us in ways that have never been programmed or written. Lessons can play to our cognitive strengths. There are at least three ways to think of spelling a word, for example. One is to picture it. This may be thought of as an experiential kinesthetic approach. Another way is to sound a word out, an audio approach. A third approach is visual. You see the word in your mind and spell it.

It is important to recognize the fact that digital textuality is quite different from what's found in print culture. It has a different logic and takes a different approach to the construction of knowledge. Although digital literacy is still in its infancy, it has already shown real promise and serious limitations. The result is movement toward a new, hybrid cultural landscape (Doueihi, 2011).

Computer-generated technology has already proved that it can give the user a sense of being in another reality. From airline pilots to surgeons, computer simulations have been used to hone skills for years. As the technology has improved and the cost has come down, real possibilities for learning open up.

Within the multisensory world of virtual reality, people can see, hear, and touch objects. Some of the applications being developed involve what has been called "telepresence," which gives the operator the sensation of putting his/her hands and eyes in a remote location. One could, for example, send a robot to "Mars" or the bottom of the ocean, control the action, see what it sees, and feel what it feels.

Can we predict where all of this wiz-bang technology will take us? The best advice is to pursue multiple paths and not be afraid to change direction. In this way, we can push back the horizon of predictability. The more unsettled things become, the more important it is to have a range of possibilities. Even luck is the residue of design. If the implications of multiple versions of the future are thought through, it is bound to be good preparation for whatever happens.

Learning to separate noise from knowledge is increasingly important in this age of too much information. Making better use of "knowledge machines" (digital technology) means going well beyond electronic workbooks or surfing the Internet to collaboratively explore problems and tinker with disparate ideas. The good news is that it's at least *possible* for technological tools to provide a vehicle for building on students' natural curiosity and promoting real learning through active engagement and collaborative inquiry (Gardner & Davis, 2013).

OPPORTUNITIES AND CHALLENGES

When considered collectively, digital technology is the most powerful representational medium ever invented. It should be put to the highest tasks of society. As far as the schools are concerned, this means using technology to motivate students to explore school subjects with passionate curiosity.

Whether it's in or out of the classroom, many school-age youngsters in developed countries spend much of their time engaged with media. It often becomes their main source of information, knowledge, and experience. They may say that what really counts is real-life encounters, but the reality is that many are more strongly influenced by online activity.

Digital devices will continue to evolve in ways that extend human capabilities and compensate for the limits of the human mind. Clearly, dealing with emerging digital technologies is one of the many challenges that teachers face today. We often lament the fact that new teachers have not been provided the training to use the new technologies available to them.

Unfortunately, enthusiasm is sometimes lacking when it comes to math, science, and technology. Still, to be successful, teachers need to have at least a reasonable level of *comfort* with any subject that they are responsible for teaching. And at the primary level, that means everything.

Some teachers are still coming through teacher education programs that did not prepare them adequately to integrate digital technology with instructional tasks. In addition, some school districts pay little attention to the in-service needs of their teachers. This is not a question of remediation. Rather, it is the fact that any profession requires its members to keep up to date with new findings and cutting-edge technologies.

College classes and outside experts can help with professional development. But schools need to acquire their own in-house capacity for helping teachers with professional development.

Increasingly, today's teachers and students have to navigate a world that is networked and global. Being able to work with others online and offline matters. Collaborators can be sitting next to you—or they can be halfway around the world. In the future, understanding and creating with digital tools will be as important as basic reading, writing, and math skills (Ferriter & Garry, 2010).

The future of education and technology is bound to be invaded by the present. From social networks to search engines, digital tools will continue to redefine literacy and reshape the architecture of learning. A wide range of new technological tools are already helping students learn in different ways— while permitting them to explore a much broader world of knowledge and learning. There is much more to come.

Perhaps artificial intelligence can be used to help enhance and develop the human variety. But since we still don't have a clear understanding of human *or* machine consciousness, it will take a while to really make a big difference. Than again, it might not take too long. After all, we have already become tone deaf to the difference between a human and an AI-assisted computer voice (Christian, 2011).

When it comes to change, it always helps if you are prepared enough to see around some of the corners. Also, everyone involved needs to realize failure is an inevitable cul-de-sac on the road to success. Still, the road to success requires learning from what goes wrong and not making the same mistake twice.

Today, mobile gadgets and social media are redefining how the Web and its technological associates are used. As far as tomorrow is concerned, we can only begin to imagine how new technologies and approaches will change the future of learning and life.

To successfully sail through the crosscurrents of such a transitional age requires the development of stronger intellectual habits and a willingness to learn about what's going on in a technologically intensive world.

SUMMARY AND LOOKING AHEAD

To move technological possibilities in a positive direction requires learning from the past, living in the present, and building for the future. It also requires asking questions about life in a wired age. For example: Do modern social networks make relationships more shallow—or do they lead to placing greater importance on face-to-face interactions offline?

Clearly, today's youth need to learn how to "navigate identity, intimacy, and imagination in a digital world" (Gardner & Davis, 2013). But no matter how the promises and pitfalls surrounding computers and the Web work out, the undeniable fact is that the digital future is now irretrievably the present.

The human mind can create beyond either what it intends or what it can foresee. Combinations of electronic media will be with us no matter how far the electronic environment expands. The problem is being sure that it works to human advantage. The informing power of technological tools can help change the schools. It can also make learning come alive and breathe wisdom into instructional activities.

Technological application goes a long way toward explaining the shape of everyone's world today. Along the path to the future, many people have grown used to having technology between them and reality. We shape digital technologies, and at the same time, they shape us. Along the way, many strands of possibilities shape the future of people's lives. Clearly, the focus of education must be shifted in a way that helps prepare students for a future that is vastly different from what their teachers have known.

We know that technologies like the Internet are fragmenting the thought processes of young people. Also, there is less and less time for reflection and quiet thought. Still, it is possible that creative minds may, sometimes, be strengthened by the ability to interact with the Web and Wikipedia (Thompson, 2013). But no matter where all the changes and apps take us, reasoning, communication, and teamwork skills are bound to go hand in hand with taking an active part in shaping the future.

We live in a digital, global, and fast-changing world where educators have to explore and invent new ways to engage students and reimagine their approach to instruction. There are times when the integration of digital innovations into classroom routines can improve our teaching. Examples of pathways to learning through technology include active learning, multimedia materials, and tapping the Internet.

Without broad assistance, the schools will not be able provide a good education for all students. New technologies are filled with possibility. But just because we come up with more and more ingenious ways of communicating, this doesn't ensure that we fully understand what's being communicated.

Is access to an infinite amount of information infinitely valuable, or does it simply lead to the collapse of clear and well-thought-out meaning? Whatever your answer, new media has to have a human face, and uncontrolled technological change gets in the way of educational progress.

Although the technology-intensive educational path to the future may be bumpy, it doesn't have to be gloomy. Clearly, dedicated teachers who understand and know how to use their high-tech tools can make a real difference.

We may live in an information age, but a clear understanding of the nature of information remains elusive. With or without an understanding of the concept, increasing the information flow presents at least as many problems as it does opportunities (Gleick, 2011). The same thing might be said about technology in general.

No matter how fascinating the latest digital tools are, it is important to remember that the goal is to develop future citizens who have the skills, values, and tools to understand and question what's going on around them.

What's needed now is a controlling vision that can help explain concepts related to information, technological innovation, and implications for education. But with or without a grand plan, educators can strive to educate the whole person to be productive in a rapidly changing, technology-intensive, democratic society.

We have trod the face of the Moon, touched the nethermost pit of the sea, and can link minds across vast distances . . . But for all that, it's not so much our technology, but what we believe, that will determine our fate.

—Tim Flannery

QUESTIONS FOR READERS TO DISCUSS

- How have your digital gadgets changed how you think, live, and work?
- Is it possible to have a free flow of information when you feel that you are being watched and recorded?
- Is social thought control a serious danger in a wired world?
- Can computer algorithms predict personal or criminal intentions?
- Is there an algorithmic way to predict who will click, buy, lie, or die?
- Should the government (NSA) be allowed to piggyback on the online tools that advertisers use to track consumers?
- How can there be meaningful oversight, transparency, and accountability when it comes to the collection of personal data?

REFERENCES

Brockman, J. (Ed.). (2011). *Is the Internet changing the way you think?: The net's impact on our minds and future.* New York: HarperCollins.

Brown, J., & Duguid, P. (2000). *The social life of information.* Boston, MA: Harvard Business School Press.

Christian, B. (2011). *The most human human: What artificial intelligences teach us about being alive.* New York: Doubleday.

Caine, R., & Caine G. (2011). *Natural learning for a connected world: Education, technology, and the human brain.* New York: Teachers College Press.

Doueihi, M. (2011). *Digital cultures.* Cambridge, MA: Harvard University Press.

Ferriter, W., & Garry, A. (2010). *Teaching the igeneration: 5 easy ways to introduce essential skills with web 2.0 tools.* Bloomington, IN: Solution Tree Press.

Flannery, T. (2011). *Here on earth: A natural history of the planet.* New York: Atlantic Monthly Press.

Gardner, H., & Davis, K. (2013). *The app generation: How today's youth navigate identity, intimacy, and imagination in a digital world.* New Haven, CT: Yale University Press.

Gleick, J. (2011). *The information: A history, a theory, a flood.* New York: Pantheon Books.

Grant, G. (2010). *Hope and despair in the American city: Why there are no bad schools in Raleigh.* Cambridge, MA: Harvard University Press.

Grosswiler, P. (Ed.). (2010). *Transforming McLuhan: Cultural, critical, and postmodern perspectives.* New York: Peter Lang.

Lehrer, J. (2009). *How we decide.* New York: Houghton Mifflin Harcourt.

Levy, S. (2011). *In the plex: How Google thinks, works, and shapes our lives.* New York: Simon & Schuster.

National Educational Technology Standards for Students. (2000). *Connecting curriculum and technology.* Eugene, OR: International Society for Technology in Education.

Organization for Economic Cooperation and Development (OECD). (2013). *Innovation in education.* Paris, France. Accessed April 10, 2015. http://www.oecd.org/education/innovation-education/.

Ripley, A. (2013). *The smartest kids in the world and how they got that way.* New York: Simon & Schuster.

Risen, J., & Poitrasnov, L. (2013, November 22). N.S.A. Report Outlined Goals for More Power. *The New York Times.*

Roblyer, M., & Doering, A. (2010). *Integrating educational technology into teaching.* Boston, MA: Allyn & Bacon.

Rose, E. (2010). Continuous partial attention: Reconsidering the role of online learning in the age of interruption. *Educational Technology* 50, no. 4 (July/August 2010).

Thompson, C. (2013). *Smarter than you think: How technology is changing our minds for the better.* New York: Penguin Press.

Turkle, S. (2011). *Why we expect more from technology and less from each other.* New York: Basic Books.

Unger, D. (2012). *The emergency state: America's pursuit of absolute security at all costs.* New York: Penguin.

Willard, N. (2002). *Computer ethics, etiquette, and safety for the 21st-century student.* Eugene, OR: International Society for Technology in Education.

Zuckerberg, R. (2013). *Dot complicated: Untangling our wired lives.* New York: Harper One/Harper Collins Publishers.

Zuckerberg, R., illustrated by J. Berger. (2013). *Dot.* Harper/Harper Collins Publishers.

Chapter 5

Science and Mathematics

The Power of Inquiry and Problem Solving

The innovation that radiates from the STEM subjects is driven by intellectual curiosity and the ability to act on our beliefs.

To succeed in a world that is changing at a dizzying speed, we need the intellectual and reasoning tools that science and mathematics can give us. The power of the scientific method and mathematical problem solving are processes that matter. They can help anyone approach the wide range of possibilities that occur in today's world—as well as the world of tomorrow (Froschauer & Bigelow, 2012).

There are as many ways to think about "twenty-first-century skills" as there are ways to think about science and mathematics instruction. Here, we limit ourselves to basic content areas, emerging topics, thinking skills, and life skills like adaptability, teamwork, and social responsibility. Attention is also given to the negative consequences that stem from walling science and math off from the liberal arts and the humanities.

At all levels, the offshoots of science and mathematics—like information and communications technology—are moving closer to the center of the instructional stage. It is important that students understand at least some of the ideas and applications of experts. It also helps if learners are encouraged to do creative things with their own informed opinions, insights, and conclusions (Bellos, 2014).

Creating fresh ideas and products requires individuals and groups who can go beyond conventional wisdom, take risks, and learn from mistakes. So it should come as no surprise when we hear that tomorrow's schools and workplaces will highly value those who continually search for fresh ideas and attempt to do new things.

Pushing the sphere of what's known is the essence of creativity and inno-vation. Innovative change is not always immediate and total. It is possible, for example, to work on incremental improvements right now while simul-taneously thinking far ahead. Still, there are times when everything changes all at once.

Innovation takes many forms. It ranges from Facebook's "move fast and break things" to Bell Labs' historical approach of "moving deliberately and building things." Fast or slow, short- or long-term scientific reasoning and mathematical problem solving are the foundations of technological and engineering success.

In an age of instant gratification, it takes more effort than ever to focus on long-term problems like the environment and climate change (Roberts, 2014).

Even in the primary grades, it is important for students to realize that scientific, technological, and mathematical ideas have a thought-provoking role to play in everything from current affairs to literature, music, and sports. A good question: Just how fulfilled and evolved are we if we just use our new tools for distraction, entertainment, and physical disengagement from each other?

TOO IMPORTANT TO BE LEFT TO EXPERTS

Two good questions:

- What are the six most important innovations in human history?
- Is our age of dizzying innovation actually an era of intellectual stagnation? [See the BBC and PBS series *How We Got to Now*.]

Whether they are done individually or in groups, formally or informally, science/math/technology ideas and activities are simply too important to be left to the experts (Johnson, 2015).

Many teachers of science and mathematics at the elementary school level have to teach dozens of topics and subjects. So it should not come as a surprise to find out that many have not received specialist training in every subject (By the middle grades, specialists are more common). Still, when it comes to teaching science, technology, and math, it is important for all teachers to have the intellectual tools needed to help children learn and apply age-appropriate concepts.

Students at any age can learn to ask big questions and think about grand concepts. In fact, those who work deeply with science and math at an early age are more likely to be creative in these subjects later on (Neagoy, 2012).

Technologies like the Internet have made it possible for anyone to learn throughout their lives.

Chose a metaphor: Is the Internet like a glass-bottom boat or a giant experiment where we are all lab rats? (Rudder, 2014). A little skeptical inquiry and questioning are good for everyone. Whether it is done individually or in groups, formally or informally, science, math, and their technological associates are simply too important to routinely accept "expert" opinion.

Only a small percentage of children may become scientists or mathematicians, but everyone must know enough to apply the intellectual tools that are part of these subjects.

Major goals of science, technology, and math education in the twenty-first century include helping students develop more self-understanding and move in the direction of responsible citizenship. Along the way, it is important to recognize that new technologies are altering the way knowledge is conveyed (Barnes, 2013).

When it comes to using the imagination to solve problems in new ways, mastering traditional science and math matters. But so does interacting imaginatively with others and communicating individual values.

Alan Kay had a good point when he said that the best way to predict the future is to invent it. The future is uncertain and unmade. But for things to turn out well, we all need the intellectual tools provided by science and math to be productively involved in creating it.

CORE CURRICULUM STANDARDS FOR SCIENCE AND MATHEMATICS

The National Research Council (NRC) has published *A Framework for K–12 Science Education: Practices Crosscutting Concepts and Core Ideas* (2011). This publication takes one of the most important steps forward in science and math education since the National Science Standards (1995) and the National Mathematics Standards (2001). The NRC constructed the science framework and is working on the next generation of science standards.

The standards bring an imaginative perspective to learning science and math. They emphasize the importance of having students actually *do* science and mathematics.

The science framework, for example, identifies key scientific ideas and practices that all students should learn. Among other things, it is designed to help students gradually develop their knowledge of core ideas in four interdisciplinary areas over multiple years, rather than the shallow knowledge of focusing on many topics.

The standards suggest that students should be encouraged to ask questions, carry out investigations, and solve problems based on evidence (National Academy Press, 2011). Along the way, it is important that all students have an appreciation of the beauty and wonder of what they are studying.

It is the teacher's role to help students develop the capacity to discuss and think critically about science, engineering, and math-related issues. Who knows, some may even decide to pursue careers in these fields.

Over the last few decades, both teaching methods and subject matter content have changed. So have the textbooks. Increasingly, students have e-textbooks, e-books, and e-zines that can be accessed on all kinds of mobile devices. Still, hard-copy books have a role to play in any pedagogical version of the future. It is up to educators to decide the technological mix that works best in different situations.

Although lobbyists for high-tech companies may dazzle legislators, there is no proof that technology alone improves learning. Basic technology is fine, but when it comes to using the digital technology at the K–3 level, the supporting evidence is thin. Also, at all grade levels, there are times that in order to benefit from new technologies, we need to use them less.

SCIENCE, MATH, TECHNOLOGY, AND THE SCHOOL CURRICULUM

The rapidly evolving nature of science, mathematics, and technology is one of the reasons that there is so much debate about its classroom utility within the educational community and in the general public. But whether or not learning involves basic or digital technology, students must learn how to collaboratively put the skills they learn into practice.

In science education, for example, the science interdisciplinary areas include: life science, physical science, earth/space science, engineering, technology, and the application of science. Some core ideas that cut across these fields include matter and interactions and energy. Students understand the same is relevant in many fields. These concepts should become familiar as students progress from kindergarten through grade twelve.

Both the science and the math standards emphasize key practices that students should learn: asking questions, defining problems, and analyzing and interpreting data. Other important practices include explaining ideas and designing solutions. These practices need to be linked with the study of interdisciplinary core ideas and be applied throughout students' education.

The Math Framework merges the Common Core standards for grades K–12. The 2011 math framework connects the standards to classroom practice. They describe math-proficient students, present a coherent progression, and provide a strong foundation that prepares students for future math activities.

GUIDING PRINCIPLES FOR MATHEMATICS

1. Learning: Math ideas should be explored in ways that stimulate curiosity, create enjoyment of math, and develop a depth of understanding. Students should be actively engaged in doing meaningful mathematics and discussing ideas and applying math in interesting, thought-provoking situations.
2. Math tasks should be designed to challenge students. For example, some short- and long-term investigations connect procedures and skills with conceptual understandings. Tasks should generate active classroom talk, promote conjectures, and lead to the understanding of the necessity of math reasoning.

STANDARDS FOR MATH PRACTICE

1. Make sense of problems and be persistent in solving them.
2. Reason and draw conclusions.
3. Create reasonable arguments.
4. Model with math and science situations.
5. Use appropriate tools.
6. Be precise.
7. Clearly express your reasoning.
8. Interpret results.
9. Report on the conclusions and the reasoning behind them.

MATHEMATICS: A TOOL OF SCIENCE

Although it is usually best for children to construct knowledge for themselves, we should recognize that students frequently have false understandings about math-related concepts. Some of the misconceptions that students have are natural; some are picked up from the media and the home environment. Just have your students draw a picture of a mathematician or a scientist and you will have some graphic evidence of stereotypes. You might also have them keep track of representations in film and on television.

Children have a natural curiosity when it comes to using science and math to examine the natural world. They learn by experiencing things for themselves, building on what they have already learned, and talking with other students about what they are doing. Observing, classifying, measuring, and collecting are just a few examples of the processes that children of all ages can learn and apply (Leinwand, 2012).

UNDERSTANDING SCIENCE AND MATHEMATICS

1. *Science and math are methods of thinking and asking questions.* How students make plans, organize their thoughts, analyze data, and solve problems is *doing* science and mathematics. People comfortable with science and math are often comfortable with thinking. *The question* is the cornerstone of all investigation. It guides the learner to a variety of sources revealing previously undetected patterns. These undiscovered openings can become sources of new questions that can deepen and enhance learning and inquiry. Questions such as "How can birds fly?" "Why is the sky blue?" or "What leads to lightning and thunder?" have been asked by children throughout history. Obviously, some of their answers were wrong. But the important thing is that the children never stopped asking—they saw and wondered, and sought an answer.

2. *Science and math require a knowledge of patterns and relationships.* Children need to recognize the repetition of science and math concepts and make connections with ideas they know. These relationships help unify the science and math curriculum as each new concept is interwoven with former ideas. Students quickly see how a new concept is similar or different from others already learned. For example, young students soon learn how the basic facts of addition and subtraction are interrelated (4 + 2 = 6 and 6 – 2 = 4). They use their science observation skills to describe, classify, compare, measure, and solve problems.

3. *Science and math are tools.* Mathematics is the tool scientists and mathematicians use in their work. It is also used by all of us every day. Students come to understand why they are learning the basic science and math principles and ideas that the school curriculum involves. Like mathematicians and scientists, they also will use science and mathematics tools to solve problems. They will learn that many careers and occupations are involved with the tools of science and mathematics.

4. *Science and math are fun (a puzzle).* Anyone that has ever worked on a puzzle or stimulating problem knows what we're talking about when we say science and mathematics are fun. The stimulating quest for an answer prods one toward finding a solution.

5. *Science and math are art forms.* Defined by harmony and internal order, science and mathematics need to be appreciated as art forms where everything is related and interconnected. Art is often thought to be

subjective, and by contrast, objective science and mathematics are often associated with memorized facts and skills. Yet the two are closely related. Students need to be taught how to appreciate the scientific and mathematical beauty all around them; for example, exploring fractal instances of science and math in nature. A fractal is a wispy, tangled curve that seems complicated no matter how closely one examines it. The object contains more, but similar, complexity the closer one looks. A head of broccoli is one example. If you tear off a tiny piece of the broccoli and look at how it is similar to the larger head, you will soon notice that they are the same. Each piece of broccoli could be considered an individual fractal or a whole. The piece of broccoli fits the definition of fractal appearing complicated; one can see consistent, repetitive, artistic patterns.

6. *Science and math are languages—both are means of communicating.* Science and mathematics require being able to use special terms and symbols to represent information. This unique language enhances our ability to communicate across the disciplines of technology, statistics, and other subjects. For example, a young child encountering $3 + 2 = 5$ needs to have the language translated to terms he or she can understand. Language is a window into students' thinking and understanding.

   Our job as teachers is to make sure students have carefully defined terms and meaningful symbols. Statisticians may use mathematical symbols that seem foreign to some of us, but after taking a statistics class, we, too, can decipher the mathematical language. It's no different for children. Symbolism, along with visual aids such as charts and graphs, are an effective way of expressing science and math ideas to others. Students learn not only to interpret the language of math and science but also to *use* that knowledge as well.

7. *Science and math are interdisciplinary.* Students work with big ideas that connect subjects. Science and mathematics relate to many subjects. Science and technology also are obvious choices. Literature, music, art, social studies, physical education, and just about everything else make use of science and mathematics in some way. If you want to understand what you are reading in the newspaper, for example, you need to be able to read the charts and the graphs taught in science and math classes.

ACTIVITIES THAT HELP STUDENTS UNDERSTAND SCIENCE AND MATHEMATICS

1. *Science and math are methods of thinking*: List all the situations outside of school in which you used science and math during the past week.

2. *Science and math require knowledge of patterns and relationships*: Show all the ways fifteen objects can be sorted into four piles so that each pile has a different number of objects in it.
3. *Science and math are tools*: Solve these problems using the tools of math and science:
   • Will an orange sink or float in water?
   • What happens when the orange is peeled? Have groups do the experiment and explain their reasoning.
4. *Having fun, solving a puzzle with science and mathematics*: With a partner, play a game of cribbage (a card game in which the object is to form combinations for points). Dominoes is another challenging game to play in groups.
5. *Using science and math as an art*: Have a small group of students design a fractal art picture.
6. *Applying the language of science and math*: Divide the class into small groups of four or five. Have the group members brainstorm about what they would like to find out from other class members (favorite hobbies, TV programs, kinds of pets, and so forth). Once a topic is agreed on, have them organize and take a survey of all class members. When the data are gathered and compiled, have groups make a clear, descriptive graph that can be posted in the classroom.
7. *Designing interdisciplinary activities with science and math*: With a group, design a song using rhythmic format that can be sung, chanted, or rapped. The lyrics can be written and musical notation added.

LOOKING AT SCIENCE, TECHNOLOGY, AND MATH: THE TWENTY-FIRST CENTURY

Science, technology, and mathematics in the twenty-first century emphasize the processes of good practice, problem solving, reasoning, proof, communications, making connections, and forming scientific and mathematical relationships. Also, digital technologies have a major role to play (Marshall, 2013).

Websites, search engines, data mining, social networks, and other Internet technologies are all part of today's media mix (Andrews, 2012). A good point for discussion: What can be done about the fact that our digital tracks are collected by for-profit companies? Have central privacy rights been violated in cyberspace? Can Internet users demand respect from companies and governments?

Teachers can help students develop important twenty-first-century coping skills—like making better online choices and gaining more control over their personal data. When it comes to basic subject matter, the challenge for today's teachers is how to motivate students for lifelong learning—while awakening curiosity and encouraging creativity.

In the last century, teachers emphasized the memorization of facts and answering questions correctly. Now, more attention is paid to helping students learn how science and mathematics relate to social problems, technology, creative innovation, and their personal lives (Peters & Stout, 2011).

A new pattern for teaching science, technology, and mathematics is emerging. It's called STEM (science, technology, engineering, and mathematics). As pointed out by Vasquez and others, the real power in taking a STEM approach lies in the integration of the subject areas so students begin to see how the concepts and skills from the different disciplines can work together to help them answer intriguing questions and solve meaningful problems.

STEM attends to content and the characteristics of effective instruction by engaging students in active and interactive learning and thus deepening their involvement in their academic work and their understanding of the subjects we teach. The basic idea is to provide students with many opportunities to interpret science, technology, and math ideas and to construct understandings for themselves.

Whether or not you follow one of the STEM approaches, it is important to make science and math teaching purposeful by providing meaningful activities with real applications that touch one's daily life. The process involves collaborative inquiry, building on curiosity, and valuing students' ideas in ways that make science and math subjects more accessible and interesting.

A COLLABORATIVE MODEL FOR TEACHING SCIENCE AND MATH

Views of learning emphasize thinking processes within the learner and point toward changes that need to be made in the way that educators have traditionally thought about teaching, learning, and organizing the school classroom. Central to creating such a learning environment is the desire to help individuals acquire or construct knowledge.

Knowledge is to be shared or developed—rather than held by the authority. It holds teachers to a high standard, for they must have both subject matter knowledge and pedagogical knowledge based on an understanding of learning and child development.

The collaborative learning model for inquiry in science and math emphasizes the intrinsic benefits of learning rather than external rewards for academic performance. Lessons are introduced with statements concerning reasons for engaging in the learning task. Students are encouraged to assume responsibility for learning and evaluating their own work and the work of others. Interaction may include a discussion of the validity of explanations, the search for more information, the testing of various explanations, or a consideration of the pros and cons of specific decisions.

The characteristics that distinguish new collaborative science and mathematics learning revolve around group goals and the accompanying benefits of active group work. Instead of being told they need information, students learn to recognize when additional data is needed. Student success is measured by performance, work samples, projects, and applications.

Scientific reasoning and mathematical problem solving involve testing ideas through experimentation as learners creatively search for new ideas and applications.

Learning science and math in today's schools has a lot to do with exploring a problem, thinking, and proposing a solution. This involves peers helping each other, self-evaluation, and group support for risk taking. This also means accepting individual differences and having positive expectations for everyone in the group.

Students should understand the purpose of their tasks as contributing to their own learning and self-development as well as that of the group. If the teacher can help children push these elements together, the result will be greater persistence and more self-directed learning.

Allowing plenty of time for active collaborative learning enables students to jointly address common topics at many of levels of sophistication. This instructional method commonly involves having all students work on the same topic during a given unit. The work is divided into a number of investigatory or practical activities in which the students move from working alone to working in small groups.

Differentiated activities are organized to include basic required work and optional enrichment work. This way, the groups that move more slowly should accomplish the basic requirements and still be able to choose some of the options. The more able groups should move on to more challenging assignments after completing the basic tasks. Because topics are not sequenced linearly, each new topic may be addressed and differentiated instruction provided for.

IMPROVING TEACHING AND LEARNING

You can't fire your way to fantastic teachers for all students. As things are today, we are already losing a high percentage of new teachers every year. These losses include teachers at every level of job performance. Still, some school districts insist on using test scores, along with other factors, to rank teachers—and then, make the results public.

Whatever your line of work, how would you feel if a narrow range of evaluation procedures were used to put a questionable job performance rating of you out there for all to see? In any field, individuals are more likely to improve when they feel valued and appreciated. If the goal is improving the quality of teachers' work, the best approach is to harness their talent rather than publically shaming "low performers."

A constructive, active set of methods reflects the way science and math should be taught today. The implication here is that classroom learning experiences should stimulate learners, build on past understandings, and encourage an exploration of students' own ideas. The comprehension process is helped along when students are given multiple chances to interpret concepts and construct understandings for themselves.

The human brain has the ability to scan a vast warehouse of information, knowledge, and past experience to come up with unique solutions to problems. For many problems on the horizon, it is important to remember that solutions often take longer than you thought they would—and then, change happens faster than you thought it could (Catmull, 2014).

Thinking and reasoning in science and math today have a lot to do with how things turn out in the future. Energizing students in a way that helps them grow into participants in tomorrow's social and technological changes requires engaging them in problem-solving investigations and engaging projects today (Lannin et al., 2011).

One of the good approaches to teaching math and science involve working with a partner for feedback on written work that relates to how problems were solved. To encourage peer review and joint authorship, we suggest that students keep daily logs or journals. As students talk together, they can better understand what they have been working on (before presenting their understandings in a group situation).

With the renewed emphasis on thinking, communicating, and making connections between topics, students are more in control of their learning. With collaborative inquiry, students have many experiences with manipulatives, calculators, and computers, and working on real-world applications.

There are more opportunities to make connections and work with peers on interesting problems. The ability to express basic math and science understandings, estimate confidently, and check the reasonableness of their estimates are part of what it means to be literate, numerate, and employable.

OVERVIEW OF THE INTEGRATED SCIENCE AND MATH STANDARDS

All students should:

• Understand numbers and operations and estimate and use computational tools effectively.

- Understand science and math subject matter including physical, life, and earth/space science, algebra, and geometry.
- Understand and use various patterns and relationships.
- Use observation and special reasoning to solve problems.
- Understand the themes and processes of science and mathematics.
- Understand and use systems of measurement.
- Become familiar with inquiry skills (pose questions and organize and represent data).
- Focus on problem solving.
- Recognize reasoning and proof as essential and powerful parts of science and mathematics.
- Communicate ideas clearly to others by organizing and using thinking skills.
- Understand the relationships among science, math, and technology, and make connections among them.
- Identify with the history, culture, and nature of science and mathematics.
- Understand and practice science and mathematics from a personal and social perspective.

These selected integrated standards are derived from the National Science Education Standards (National Academy Press, 2011) and the Curriculum and Evaluation Standards for School Mathematics (National Council of Teachers of Mathematics, 2010).

SAMPLE ACTIVITIES

In an effort to link the integrated standards to classroom practice, a few sample activities are presented. The intent is not to prescribe an activity for a unique grade level, but to present activities that could be modified and used in many grades.

Activity 1: Compare and Estimate

Objectives: In grades K–4, the curriculum should include estimation so students can:

- explore estimation strategies
- recognize when an estimate is appropriate
- determine the reasonableness of results
- apply estimation in working with quantities, when using measurement, computation, and problem solving

Science and math instruction in the primary grades tries to make classifying and using numerals essential parts of the classroom experience. Students need to go beyond counting and writing numerals to identifying quantities and seeing relationships between objects.

When developing fundamental concepts, learners need to manipulate concrete materials and relate numbers to problem situations. They benefit by talking, writing, and hearing what others think. In the following activity, students are actively involved in estimating, manipulating objects, counting, verbalizing, writing, and comparing.

Directions:

1. Divide students into small groups of two or three students. Place a similar group of objects in color-coded containers, one for each group. Pass out recording sheets divided into partitions with the color of the container in each box.
2. Have young students examine the container on their desks, estimate how many objects are present, discuss it with their group, and write their guess next to the color on the sheet.
3. Next, have the group count the objects and write the number they counted next to the first number. Instruct the students to circle the greater number.
4. Switch cans or move to the next station and repeat the process. A variety of objects (small plastic animals, marbles, paper clips, colored shells, etc.) add interest and are real motivators.

Activity 2: Adding and Subtracting in Real-Life Situations

Objectives: In the early grades, the science and mathematics curriculum should include concepts of addition and subtraction of whole numbers so that students can

- develop meaning for the operations by modeling and discussing a rich variety of problem situations
- relate the mathematical language and symbolism of operations to problem situations and informal language

When children are learning about the operations of addition and subtraction, it's helpful for them to make connections between these processes and the world around them. Story problems using ideas from science help them see the actions of joining and separating. Using manipulatives and sample word problems gives them experiences in joining sets and figuring the differences between them. By pretending and using concrete materials, learning becomes more meaningful.

Directions:

1. Divide students into small groups (two or three students in each group).
2. Tell stories in which the children can pretend to be animals, plants, other children, or even space creatures.
3. Telling stories is enhanced by having children use unifix cubes or other manipulatives to represent the people, objects, or animals in the oral problems.
4. Have children work on construction paper or prepare counting boards on which trees, oceans, trails, houses, space stations, and other things have been drawn.

Activity 3: Solving Problems

Problem solving should be the starting place for developing understanding. Teachers should present word problems for children to discuss and solve, working together, without the distraction of symbols. The following activities attempt to link word problems to meaningful situations:

Objectives:
Students will:

- solve problems
- work in a group
- discuss and present their solutions

Directions:

1. Divide students into small groups (two or three students in each group).
2. Find a creative way to share 50¢ among four children. Explain your solution. Is it fair? How could you do it differently?
3. The children in your class counted and found there were 163 sheets of construction paper. They were given the problem of figuring out how many sheets each child would receive if they were divided equally among them.
4. Encourage students to explain their reasoning to the class.
5. After discussing each problem, show the children the standard notation for representing division. Soon you will find students will begin to use the standard symbols in their own writing.

Activity 4: Using Statistics: Supermarket Shopping

Statistics is the science or study of data. Statistical problems require collecting, sorting, representing, analyzing, and interpreting information.

Objectives:
Students will:

- collect, organize, and describe data
- construct, read, and interpret displays of data
- formulate and solve problems that involve collecting and analyzing data

Problem:

1. Your group has $2 to spend at the market. What will you purchase?
2. Have groups explain and write down their choices.
3. Next, have groups collect data from all the groups in the class.
4. Graph the class results.

Activity 5: Promoting Mathematical Modeling in STEM Activities

Modeling requires that students develop procedures to work on problem situations. The purpose of models is to explain or predict results, draw conclusions, and answer questions about real situations as they encounter.

Fifth graders explored a modeling experience by finding out the relationship among weight, distance, and balance using a lever. Students were divided into groups. They were to make sense of the problem by identifying, observing, and manipulating a mysterious lever. The mysterious problem included four steps:

1. *Introduction.* The teacher showed students a lever to examine without telling how it worked. A lever and some weights were provided for each group. Students were to share ideas, take notes, and describe how the tool would work.
2. *Exploration.* Some students tried to manipulate the lever using one of its holes. After trying several holes, they recognized that when they used the hole in the middle, they attained balance. They hung weights on both sides of the bar to see how the lever worked. After several tries, they realized that the weights they hung changed the balance.

   When they hung only one weight at a time from the middle hole, they observed that balance was achieved. Students recorded their observations on a recording sheet.

3. *Evidence.* Students had to organize their observations and provide a model based on the weights and distance on the lever to achieve balance. Students worked collaboratively together and wrote their findings.
4. *Scientific Model Testing.* Science, technology, engineering, and mathematics use a predictive process using models. The lever project is just one example. Students need to convert their experiences to other balance tasks and show it mathematically. One student revealed her thinking: "$2 \times 4 = 4 \times 2$." The numbers showed the weights on the lever.

MAKING INTERDISCIPLINARY CONNECTIONS

Mathematics and technology have always served as important tools for work in the sciences. All three have major roles to play across the curriculum.

Science and math inform everything from history to the evening news. They enrich the visual and performing arts—as well as sports and physical education. As an extension of our natural language, they provide a context for language learning.

As science and mathematics continue to become more integrated into society, their interconnectedness with other school subjects becomes an important goal (Burns, 2007).

INTERDISCIPLINARY MATH AND SCIENCE ACTIVITIES

It is best to get away from the idea of splitting up the curriculum; instead, the new focus is looking at fusing various disciplines together. The next few activities try to accomplish this goal.

Activity 5: Using the Sun to Teach Geometry

Objectives:
Students will:

- describe, model, draw, and classify shapes
- investigate and predict the results of combining, subdividing, and changing shapes
- develop spatial sense
- relate geometric ideas to number and measurement ideas
- recognize and appreciate geometry in their world

Directions:

1. Have students investigate figures and their properties through shadow geometry, exploring what happens to shapes held in front of a point of

light. They can also explore what happens to shapes held in the sunlight when the sun's rays are nearly parallel.

2. Have children discover which characteristics of the shapes are maintained under varying conditions. For this activity, provide pairs of children with square objects such as wooden or plastic squares.

3. Take students to an area of the playground that has a flat surface. Have the children hold the square regions so that shadows are cast on the ground. Encourage the children to move the square regions so that the shadow changes.

4. Have students talk about the shadows they found. Discuss how they were able to make the shapes larger and smaller. See what other observations they have made.

5. To make a permanent record of shapes, have a student draw a shape on a piece of paper and put the piece of paper on the ground. Let the shadow fall on the paper. Have that student draw around the outline of the shadow.

6. When each student has had a chance to draw a favorite shape, there will be a collection of interesting drawings that can serve as a source for discussion, sorting, and display.

7. For a challenge activity: Students may also wish to discover if they can make a triangle or a pentagon shadow using the square region. Using outlines, children drew the shadows cast by square shapes to see if students can find things that are alike and different in the drawings.

8. Have students count the number of corners and sides of each shape and compare those numbers. Encourage them to discuss and record their conclusions.

Precaution: Be sure you direct students not to look at the sun directly.

Activity 6: Creating Maps

Objectives:
Students will:

- recognize, describe, extend, and create a wide variety of patterns
- represent and describe math and science relationships
- explore the use of variables and open sentences to express relationships

As students measure many geometric figures, they uncover patterns and see relationships. After students have explored different shapes, the next part of the activity looks at patterns. The topic is called map making. A map is a pattern that we follow. It tells us where to go and how we go about getting there. The following activity has students follow a map, recording as they go.

Directions for the Map Exercise:

1. Have children use graph paper and a pencil to draw a path. Each unit on the grid will represent one city block.
2. Write the labels for north, east, south, and west. Begin your map in the middle of the graph paper. Then follow this route.
    A. Walk two blocks south.
    B. Turn east and walk three blocks.
    C. Turn south and walk one block.
    D. Turn east and walk three blocks.
    E. Turn south and walk four blocks.
    F. Turn east and walk one block.
    G. Turn south and walk three blocks.
    H. Turn west and walk half a block.
3. Compare your map to those of other students. How are they the same? How are they different? How would the map change if step B were a ninety-degree turn west?
4. As a challenge problem: With your group, make a scale model of the local area. Include a "key" identifying symbols and directions.

Activity 7: Estimate and Weigh Different Materials

Objectives:
Students will:

• estimate the weight of different objects
• relate everyday experiences to the math/science measuring activity
• check their estimates

Children establish a link between their concrete everyday experience and their understanding of math and science abstractions through many different experiences in representing quantities and shapes. Representation helps children remember an experience and make sense by communicating it to others.

Directions: Measuring Activity

1. Fill several milk cartons with different materials such as rice, beans, clay, plaster of Paris, and wooden objects.
2. Seal the cartons and label them by color or letter. Tell the children what the materials are but do not identify the contents of a particular carton.
3. Have the children guess how to order the cartons by weight according to what they contain. Then, let the children order the cartons by weight,

holding them in their hands and using the pan balance to check their estimates.

Activity 8: Which Will Melt Quicker?

Objectives:
Students will:

* explore reasoning in science and mathematics
* measure and compare quantities
* write about their findings in their science and math journals

Problem: Suppose you have a glass of water. It has the same temperature as the air. Would an ice cube melt faster in the water or air? Invite students to find out.

Materials: thermometer, water, ice cubes, two glasses (same size), small plastic bag, salt, spoon

Directions:

1. Fill one container with warm water and leave the other container empty.
2. Let the children see and feel the cups and the water. Explain: "We are going to put an ice cube in each container. Our problem: Which ice cube do you think will melt first?" Write the guesses on the board.
3. Have students measure the temperature inside the empty glass. Also, measure the temperature inside a glass of water. It should be about the same as the air temperature. If not, let the water stand a while.
4. Find two ice cubes of the same size.
5. Put one cube into the empty glass. Put the other in the glass of water.
6. Compare how fast the ice cubes melt.

Questions for Further Investigation:

1. How can you make an ice cube melt faster in water? Will stirring the water make a difference? Will it melt faster in warmer water? Does crushing the ice make a difference? Does changing the volume of the water matter?
2. How will ice cubes melt when other things are added to the water?
3. Will an ice cube melt faster in salt water? Does the amount of salt make a difference?
4. Students will measure and compare temperatures, hypothesize, experiment, and arrive at conclusions.

Evaluation: Have students explain their reasoning through writing about their experiment in their journals. Direct their discussion by asking them to explain what mathematics they used. What science skills were involved? What is the best way to show their data?

Activity 9: Science and Math Metric Challenge

Objectives:
Students will:

• solve problems working as a team
• explain directions

Directions:

1. Divide the class into teams of three or four students.
2. Give each team a list of challenges.

Team Challenges:

1. Find how many square meters of floor space each person in your classroom has.
2. If there are one hundred students in the gym, how many cubic meters does each student have?
3. How many square meters does the school playground have?
4. Find the number of meters you must walk from our classroom to the principal's office and back.
5. Create a game with your group involving meters. Establish rules. Is luck involved? Write out the rules. Explain to the class how to play the game.

Activity 10: Design an Escher-Type Art Drawing

Students become aware of the properties of shapes through many experiences; they manipulate, visualize, draw, construct, and represent shapes in a variety of interesting and creative ways.

Objectives:
Students will:

• create patterns
• explain their designs

Directions:

1. Introduce the idea of making a repeated pattern (tessellation). Teachers may wish to talk about artists who use the concept of tessellation in their artwork.
2. Have students represent a three-dimensional object on paper.
3. Ask students what shapes can be seen in different objects.
4. Have them try to make a symmetrical design. What shapes will tile a floor (or tessellation)?
5. Begin by having students make a tessellated design. Encourage students to explain their pattern and the relationships between the figures they've chosen. Students who are adept at tessellating (drawing repeated patterns) may wish to extend that skill in artwork designs.

Through direct experiences with three-dimensional objects and then transferring those objects into a two-dimensional world, students become aware of the relationships and properties of geometric shapes. They are also able to notice symmetry in the designs they create. They investigate how patterns look if they're moved or rotated. They draw, build, and describe many shapes from a variety of perspectives.

Activity 11: How Long Are You?

Objectives:
Students will (see figure 5.1):

- collect, organize, and describe data
- measure and compare theirs and their partner's body parts
- explain the measurements

Activity 12: Finding Your Heart Rate

Objectives:
Students will:

- understand the heart and its system
- learn how to calculate their heart rate
- understand that heart rate changes depending on physical activity
- chart heart rate data

Materials: classroom with room to move around, calculate-your-heart-rate worksheet, pencils, timer or clock

---

1. With a partner, measure and compare the following body parts

	You		Partner	
	Inches	Feet	Inches	Feet
a. Head to toe:				
b. Arm span: fingertip to fingertip:				
c. Forearm:				
d. Foot:				
e. Circumference around head:				
f. Hand (pinky to thumb)				

2. Explain your measuring technique and state your measurements.

3. Artwork: Draw yourself and your partner's measurements and color.

4. Comparison Sentences: What did you learn? _____

_____

_____

5. Share with the rest of the class.

Figure 5.1   How Long Are You Worksheet.

Background Information: The heart is a pump. The heart pumps blood to parts of our body. The number of times the heart pumps per minute is called *heart rate*. Heart rate changes when we do different activities.

Procedures: Introduce heart rate, and have students guess how many beats per minute their heart is beating. Ask students to name activities they believe would change heart rate. Then, ask if they think these activities would make the heart beat faster or slower than normal. Explain to students that there are two main areas on the body where it is easiest to find your heart rate (neck and wrist). Have students find their pulse. Make sure each student has found it. Practice counting while being timed for ten seconds.

Directions:

1. Pass out the heart rate worksheet. Have students count their heart rate while sitting.

2. Have students enter their number on the chart. Explain to students that this is the number of times their heart beats in ten seconds.
3. Explain that heart rate will be taken in one-minute intervals. Help students multiply their number by six in order to have the number of times their heart beats in one minute. Enter the number on the worksheet.
4. Do the same for the activities of standing and running in place for thirty seconds.
5. After the worksheet chart is filled in, ask students to write a sentence about a time when they felt their heart rate change.

Evaluation: Students' performances will be evaluated according to how much of the chart they are able to fill in and how well they participated in the activity.

Heart Rate Worksheet

Your heart rate is how many times your heart beats per minute.
Your heart rate changes.
Your heart rate is your pulse.
Your pulse is found in your neck and wrist.

Record your heart rate below:
Sitting   *Standing*   *Running in place* 10 seconds
_____
_____
60 seconds

A useful instructional procedure: determine the purpose and scope of the lesson. Next, build on student interests as you provide space for thinking, reflection, and discussion. Be prepared to push student thinking forward with purposeful activities. Finally, share some of your lessons with other teachers and get suggestions for improvement.

Whether it is individual or group work, it also makes sense for inquiry, scientific reasoning, and mathematical problem-solving skills to be integrated and used across the curriculum.

A SAMPLE OF ONLINE RESOURCES FOR STEM

Connected science, technology, engineering, and math activities and projects are part of today's science and mathematics curriculum. The learning process associated with STEM views science and math as underlying all engineering problems. Technology is viewed as an essential tool in the search for answers.

Organizations like the National Science Teachers Association (www.nsta. org) and the National Council of Teachers of Mathematics (www.nctm.org) can help. So can the following websites:

- *AAAS Science NetLinks* (http://sciencenetlinks.com)
  The American Association for the Advancement of Science has made available a wide range of lesson plans for just about every grade level.
- *Discovery Education* (www.discoveryeducation.com/teachers)
  Here the content fits in nicely with state standards, and there are links to a large number of teacher-friendly math websites.
- *National Science Digital Library's K–6 Science Refreshers* (http://nsdl.org/ refreshers/science)
  This site gives teachers a quick review of science concepts before they have to teach them. Also, there is a wide range of short lessons—covering everything from symbiosis and simple machines to weather forecasting.
- *PBS Teachers STEM Education Resource Center* (www.pbs.org/teachers/ stem)
  Here, teachers and students can choose from thousands of resources— including lesson plans, videos, and interactive activities.
- *NASA's Planet Quest Exoplanet Exploration* (http://planetquest.jpl. nasa.gov)
  If students or teachers want to connect to experts, this is a good place to do it. Possibilities range from NASA's Jet Propulsion Laboratory (JPL) and images from space to the "Ask an Astronomer" podcast. Other possibilities: online games, activities, and submitting questions to experts.

All of the sites referred to here invite curiosity in a way that stretches students' minds. Some of the visuals instill a sense of wonder, while many of the activities engage learners in a way that helps them ask insightful questions.

TEAMWORK AND INDIVIDUAL INQUIRY

The ability to work in small groups is an important twenty-first-century skill that reaches across the curriculum. Being able to function as part of a team is something that is important at any age. This is as true in math and science as anywhere else. In the world outside of school, projects that rely on science and math often build on different points of view within the group to produce a coherent whole (Eichinger, 2004).

What about personal temperament and cultural imperatives? The cultural milieu we find ourselves in offers us templates while leaving plenty of room for a variety of choices. Culture and psyche make each other up. In other words, we shape our templates, and they shape us.

In and out of school, having groups functioning as a team sometimes results in more persistence when it comes to working through a problem in today's diverse classrooms. As a consequence of group work, individuals can often be more motivated. The end result is often more enthusiasm and success for everyone.

Most tasks can be made more interesting by making at least some space for a team approach. Small, cooperative groups can handle more sophisticated problems than individuals working alone. Organizing students in a way that leaves space for both individual and group work allows teachers to channel energy into productive communication and problem solving. Such an arrangement also gives students an opportunity to take more responsibility for their own learning. Of course, there is no freedom in a vacuum.

Even when students are working in small groups, the teacher guides, mentors, and advises. It is, after all, the teacher who sets up groups and encourages everyone to take responsibility for themselves and for other team members. An example from mathematics instruction: a good approach is to set up situations in which student groups can develop math arguments that are based on representations and go on to describe consistencies across problems (Russell et al., 2012).

When students focus on their own investigations, discussions, and group projects, the teacher's role shifts to that of an expert manager. The whole-class setting can be used for initial brainstorming, giving directions, summarizing data, reviewing different strategies, and coming to common understandings about the questions that come up. From time to time, the whole class can come together for a brief explanation of group work.

To prepare for an uncertain future, it is important for teachers to raise provocative questions. At the same time, it also makes sense to encourage students to use what they have learned to illuminate a new phenomenon.

A good teacher knows how to ask the right question in different situations. Some of these questions can be worked on alone, then discussed in small groups, and finally brought up with the entire class. Teachers may also want to use the larger class setting to summarize and highlight important ideas that come from the work of the small groups (Witzel, 2012).

At some point, it is important for both individuals and learning teams to move from freewheeling idea creation to sorting the good ideas out from the bad. Working with one, two, or three peers can help diminish some of the fear surrounding science and math and amplify student understanding. Small, collaborative groups can also help generate an appreciation of the power and beauty of science and mathematics.

Call it collaborative, cooperative, or team learning, the essential point is that strategies for teaching science and mathematics that involve social interaction result in children gaining more control of the math and science curriculum. This in no way diminishes the need for individual students learning to ask hard questions as they take risks in a supportive community (Wedekind, 2011).

CHALLENGING SCIENCE AND MATH ACTIVITIES

The next section brings together the science and math standards to elementary and middle school classrooms. Meaningful activities that employ the core ideas and practices of observing, comparing, measuring, recording data, and making good conclusions are emphasized. These activities are based on the 2010 National Framework for K–12 Science Education Standards. Whenever possible, the Mathematics Standards (2011) are included.

Activity 1: Mysterious Stories

Stories are a means of communication. Even before written language, people drew pictures on walls of their caves to show a successful hunt or the animals they met. Stories are told of accomplishments whether found in dance, pictures, art, or words. It is important to view stories as a desire for people to communicate their thoughts, dreams, and mysteries across generations.

Looking at stories as mysteries is exciting, providing students with characters they can identify with and thus allowing them to be included and be part of the adventure.

Activity 2: Invent a Mystery Story

Create your mystery story. Choose a topic of interest to you.

Activity 3: The Mystery of Gravity and Yo-Yos

Grade level: Elementary and junior high

Content Standards:

- applying the core ideas of physical science
- comparing movement and gravity

Objectives/Importance: Students observe objects concerning force, acceleration, friction, and gravity. Students apply physics to real-world situations.

Background information: Students should review the basic physics principles of gravity and inertia.

- gravity: a natural force of attraction that tends to draw objects together
- inertia: a property of matter whereby it remains at rest or continues in uniform motion unless attracted by some outside force
- velocity: rate of change of an object's position

Questions:

How do yo-yos reflect physics?
What is an example of inertia?
How does your yo-yo show force?
Can you make your yo-yo accelerate?
What causes friction when using a yo-yo?
Can you explain why a yo-yo shows gravity?

Other Student Activities: Students work in pairs with their yo-yos.

1. Estimate the direction your yo-yo moved in one minute.
2. Record the velocity of your yo-yos. What speed do you think they traveled?
3. Write a mystery story of your yo-yos and how they demonstrate gravity.
4. Why does a yo-yo act as it does?
5. There are some professional yo-yo groups. Find out more about them. Record your findings.

Accelerated Student Activities:

1. Slow down your yo-yo, then try to speed it up.
2. What happens when the yo-yo is thrown in a different direction?
3. What makes the yo-yo slow down?
4. When does the yo-yo move fast?
5. Describe the physics involved in these activities.
6. Record your yo-yo movements. Compare your observations with those of other students.
7. With other students, describe the force, speed, gravity, and friction of your yo-yos. Record your findings.
8. Make a class chart so other classes can see your physical science achievements.

Activity 4: Flowing Mysteries

Grade level: Elementary, junior high

Content Standards:

- applying the physical science standards
- using basic ideas and procedures in science
- putting personal views to practical use
- practicing oral and written communication skills
- employing science and technology skills

Procedures:

Students are experimenting with household chemicals.
Student tools for each work station:

    six small plastic bottles
    six flowing substances (vinegar, soap, alcohol, cooking oil, vanilla, water)
    six short, glass tubes with rubber bulb
    one wide-mouthed drinking cup
    one small drinking cup
    one flat-bottomed container for holding articles
    one piece of plastic wrap
    one sheet of aluminum foil
    one sheet of waxed paper
    one sheet of white paper

Directions:

1. Prepare the containers with food coloring added.
2. Have students discuss how scientists perform experiments.
3. Prepare the trays and tools for each group.
4. On the chalkboard, list the experiments that students might try:
    - substance races
    - floating ability
    - density
    - combining liquids
    - other suggestions

Student Task

Discover what the six chemicals are using the following rules:

- Use your sense of sight to find out what the flowing mysteries are.
- You are not to smell, touch, or taste the chemicals.
- Each dropper can be used to pick up only one substance.

Students rotate among the workstations, experimenting as they try to discover what the flowing mysteries are. They conduct several tests during the process.

Work Station 1 Substance Race
Lesson steps:

1. Choose a substance and a sheet of paper to cover your tray (waxed, white, aluminum foil, plastic wrap).
2. Place a drop of each substance on the paper.
3. Tip the tray so the substance moves.
4. Record the movement of the chemicals.
5. Try the experiment with all of the flowing chemicals.

Work Station 2 Floating Ability
Lesson steps:

1. Select a small plastic container.
2. Add drops of each colored substance.
3. See which substances will float.
4. Encourage students to experiment.
5. Jerk, shake, and maneuver the container to detect which chemicals move to the top.
6. Record the movement of the chemicals.

Work Station 3 Density

1. Select a small plastic container.
2. Add drops of each colored substance.
3. See which substances will sink.
4. Encourage students to experiment.
5. Jerk, shake, and maneuver the container to detect which chemicals sink.
6. Record the movement of the chemicals.

Work Station 4 Mixing Chemicals

1. Guess what each substance is and test your guesses by observing which substances blend together.
2. Record your guesses.

blue chemical
green chemical
red chemical
yellow chemical
purple chemical
clear chemical

Which will mix? Write your reasoning:

oil
soap
water
vanilla
vinegar
alcohol

Connecting the Math Standards to the Core Content Standards

Standard 1: Understand Number and Operations
Students need to understand counting (represent one-to-one correspondence with concrete materials, match a set to a numeral).

Standard 2: Ability to Use Patterns, Algebra, Functions, and Variables
Students will understand and use functions (plus +, minus −, times x, divide /).

Standard 3: Geometry
Apply geometry, understand shapes, and use size, symmetry, congruence, and similarity.

Standard 4: Measurement
Use measurements to measure and compare lengths and widths; tell and write time in hours, half-hours; use analog and digital clocks.

Standard 5: Data Analysis, Probability
Organize data; use charts, tables, graphs, and statistics.

Standard 6: Problem Solving
Find solutions, use strategies, take risks, make decisions, and get results.

Standard 7: Reasoning
Reasoning is connected to students' language development. Thinking and reasoning are important to math learning. Students should have experiences with deductive reasoning (moving from guesses to conclusions). Learners

should also be aware of inductive reasoning (informal reasoning using specific examples) and use evidence to make assumptions and form conclusions.

Standard 8: Communicating
This includes working in groups talking, listening, and expressing ideas. Students share information, explain ideas, and help each other.

Standard 9: Forming Conclusions
Many relationships are learned everyday by students making connections through their own experiences and applying math content to real-life situations.

Standard 10: Representing Math Relationships
Representing "0" (zero) shows connections among math concepts and improves understanding. When students are able to use different blocks, colored math squares, and fraction pieces while performing math skills, learning becomes more enjoyable.

CAPTURING STUDENT INTEREST/ENGAGED LEARNING

It makes sense to emphasize cognitively challenging and developmentally appropriate activities. In the primary grades, it is especially important that children begin to have science/math experiences involving the exploratory use of materials, open-ended discussions, dramatic play, music, and art.

Making connections with other disciplines and real-world concerns energizes both students and their teachers. It also helps make science and math more meaningful—a key to making sense of these subjects and capturing student interest (Hand, 2014).

Student learning teams are a powerful way to approach mathematics and science instruction. To help students achieve a deeper understanding, more attention is being given to application and social interaction. Collaborative inquiry and problem-solving activities are important routes to deeper understandings of science and mathematics.

The best academic mix of individual and group work has a lot to do with a person's preferred social style (Cain, 2012). So for some students, it may sometimes be best to begin a lesson by encouraging them to individually embrace the power of reflective thinking. The first step might be working alone for a while. Next, discuss their thoughts with a partner; then, move to a group of three or four.

Small groups work well in the classroom. Being socially connected can turn into a wasteful distraction from real experiences. But *on* or *off* line, nonstop socializing can be a distraction. It almost seems as though some people just can't stop talking or texting. *Individual* experience, playfulness, spontaneity, and intellectual curiosity still matter. And leaving a little space and quiet time for personal reflection may help encourage independent thinking.

TEAMWORK, REFLECTION, AND MOVING THE FURNITURE

In tomorrow's classrooms, interactive learning by small groups of students will be the norm. This makes sense because peer support helps learners feel more confident and willing to make mistakes and engage in scientific inquiry and problem solving in mathematics. Collaboration, in concert with a little human friction, has a lot to do with how scientists and mathematicians advance their fields.

Criticism and debate do not necessarily inhibit imaginative thinking or innovation. In fact, informed criticism can actually encourage people to dig deeper and come up with more useful and less predictable ideas. After all, every new idea is not useful nor equally worthy of praise. In fact, false praise actually has a negative effect on the quality of a student's imaginative work.

With any subject or topic, a brainstorming or freewheeling approach is fine—just leave a little space for collaborative evaluation. For example, when it comes to the technological products of science and mathematics, it is important to question the significance of things like the Internet, social networks, and collaborative computer games.

Try asking students to explain the ideas that drive their work, the hypothesis they generate from those ideas, and why their conclusions make sense. This kind of circular thought/discussion process is likely to result in a deeper understanding of what is being studied.

Whatever approach you take incorporating creativity into your lessons, it is important to remember that failure is widely recognized as part of the creative process (It certainly helps if you know how to learn from false starts and mistakes). Although many ideas initially generated may not be good, the more new ideas that are produced in the process, the more likely something unique and useful will turn up.

Whether what they come up with is good, bad, or in between, at some point, students must learn to pool their creative thoughts and figure out what's useful and how to put what they have learned into practice. Keep in mind that with some topics, there is very little that is completely new. So sometimes, the most imaginative thing to do is to figure out new ways of illuminating what is familiar.

The road to the future should be paved by the deepest wells of information. Exposure to other ways of thinking—and testing convictions against competing ways of viewing the world—has a lot to do with what education is all about.

It is always wise to encourage children and young adults to become familiar with a wide range of perspectives. The next step is moving on to draw imaginative conclusions that are based on what they have studied and what they believe.

Individual idea creation, critical thinking, teamwork, and debate are all sure to be part of any future science/math package. So in the classroom, get used to the furniture, the quiet spaces, the ideas, and the discussion getting moved around.

A good question: What is something about the future that you think is true, but most people disagree with you on? (Thiel & Masters, 2014). One potential point of disagreement: *the future needs to be radically different from the present.*

Is it true? A. Yes B. No C. I doubt it.

SUMMARY, CONCLUSIONS, AND LOOKING FORWARD

Many of the insights of modern science have come about with the help of mathematics and technology. Combining these tools with the processes of scientific reasoning opens up possibilities for discoveries that lead to a better understanding of the world (Ackerman, 2014).

The imaginative implications of science, math, and their technological associates reach well beyond the schools. Mastering these subjects may not result in innovation, but they certainly increase the odds of it happening.

As far as mathematics instruction is concerned, teachers have to go beyond teaching students basic arithmetic, how to balance a checkbook, or estimate how long it will take to get from one town to another. Students should learn to ask the big questions as they consider how math might be applied to broader human problems.

When specific classroom content is concerned, it is not enough to teach computation and procedures in isolation from the situations that require those skills. Teachers also have a responsibility to appreciate the problems and the promises of science, math, and technology.

To thrive in a creative way in the classroom, it helps if students can see the unique work of others. And they need to be in an environment where imaginative work is valued. Cognitive capacity and subject matter knowledge matter, but creative individuals tend to have a risk-taking personality and temperament. Still, like the idea of multiple intelligences, there are many different kinds of creativity—and there are multiple paths to imaginative ideas (Sinclair, 2006).

Being naive or afraid of science or mathematics can be a real problem in school, in the workplace, and for citizens in a democracy. The key to academic success in these subjects is fostering habits of the mind such critical thinking, problem solving, agility, adaptability, curiosity, and imagination. Also, in a world filled with the technological products of science and math understanding, these subjects are more important than ever.

The need for analytical skills and social intelligence goes with any version of the future. Curiosity, along with the tools of math and science, has always driven innovation. But in spite of certain agreed-upon principles, uncertainty and change goes with the territory.

Essential twenty-first-century skills include knowing how to use a wide range of scientific and mathematical tools to solve problems in an imaginative way. It is also important to have some idea how science and math impact life on a daily basis. At any grade level, academic competency in science and math includes understanding some of the roles these subjects serve in society.

Twenty-first-century skills include having some idea about how to use the intellectual tools of science and its associated tools (like math and technology) in thoughtful, purposeful, and meaningful ways. Also, sometimes being creative and innovative in the present requires pushing preconceptions about the past and the future out of the way.

In any discussion of what is going to crop up just over the horizon, it is important to keep in mind the caution that history is more likely to rhyme than to repeat itself. A good way to get ready for the situations and big ideas of tomorrow is to look around today. Get prepared. Along the way, notice how the future often gets mashed up with the past.

The future is already here. It's just not evenly distributed yet.

—William Gibson

REFERENCES

Ackerman, D. (2014). *The human age: The world shaped by us.* New York: W. W. Norton & Company.

Andrews, L. (2012). *I know who you are and I saw what you did.* New York: Free Press.

Barnes, M. (2013). *Role reversal: Achieving uncommonly excellent results in the student-centered classroom.* Baltimore, MD: ASCD.

Bellos, A. (2014). *The grapes of math: How life reflects numbers and numbers reflect life.* New York: Simon & Schuster.

Burns, M. (2007). *About teaching mathematics: A K–8 resource.* Sausalito, CA: Math Solutions.

Cain, S. (2012). *Quiet: The power of introverts in a world that can't stop talking.* New York: Crown.

Catmull, E. (2014). *Creativity, Inc.: Overcoming the unseen forces that stand in the way of true inspiration.* New York: Random House.

Eichinger, J. (2004). *40 strategies for integrating science and mathematics instruction: K–8.* Upper Saddle River, NJ: Prentice Hall.

Esler, W., & Esler, M. (2001). *Teaching elementary science.* Belmont, CA: Wadsworth.

Etheredge, S., & Rudnitsky, A. (2003). *Introducing students to scientific inquiry: How do we know what we know?* Boston, MA: Allyn & Bacon.

Froschauer, L., & Bigelow, M. (2012). *Rise and shine: A practical guide for the beginning science teacher.* Arlington, VA: NSTA (National Science Teachers Association).

Gibson, W. (2012). *Distrust that particular flavor.* New York: G. P. Putnam's & Sons.

Hand, D. (2014). *The improbability principle: Why coincidences, miracles and rare events happen every day.* New York: Scientific American/ Farrarr, Straus & Giroux.

Johnson, S. (2015). *How we got to now.* New York: Riverhead Books.

Krauss, L. (2012). *A universe from nothing: Why there is something rather than nothing.* New York: Free Press (Simon & Schuster).

Lannin, J., Ellis, A., Elliot, R., & Zbiek, R. (2011). *Developing essential understanding of mathematical reasoning for teaching mathematics in grades preK–8.* Reston, VA: NCTM.

Leinwand, S. (2012). *Sensible mathematics: A guide for school leaders in the era of common core standards.* Second edition. Portsmouth, NH: Heinemann.

Lowrey, L. F. (1997). *NSTA Pathways to the science standards—elementary school edition.* Arlington, VA: National Science Teachers Association.

Marshall, J. C. (2013). *Succeeding with inquiry in science and math classrooms.* Arlington, VA: National Science Teachers Association.

National Academy Press. (2011). *National science education standards.* Washington, DC: National Academy Press.

National Council of Teachers of Mathematics (NCTM). (2000). *Principles and standards for school mathematics.* Reston, VA: National Council of Teachers of Mathematics.

National Council of Teachers of Mathematics (NCTM). (2001). *Principles and Standards March 2001.* Accessed on April 15, 2015. http://www.nctm.org/Publications/teaching-children-mathematics/2001/Vol7/Issue7/Principles-and-Standards-%282001%29---March-2001/.

National Research Council. (2012). *A Framework for K–12 Science Education: Practices, Crosscutting Concepts and Core Ideas.* Washington, DC: The National Academies Press.

National Research Council. (2015). *Next Generation Science Standards: Framework for K–12 Science Education (2015).* Accessed on April 15, 2015. http://www.nextgenscience.org/framework-k%E2%80%9312-science-education.

Neagoy, M. (2012). *Planting the seeds of Algebra, PreK–2: Explorations for the early grades.* Thousand Oaks, CA: Corwin.

Peters, J., & Stout, D. (2011). *Science in elementary education: Methods, concepts, and inquiries.* Eleventh Edition. Boston, MA: Allyn & Bacon.

Roberts, P. (2014). *The impulse society: America in the age of instant gratification.* New York: Bloomsburg Publishing.

Rudder, C. (2014). *Dataclysm: Who are we (when we think no one's looking).* New York: Crown Publishing Group.

Russell, S., Schifter, D., & Bastable, V. (2012). *Connecting arithmetic to algebra: strategies for building algebraic thinking in the elementary grades.* Portsmouth, NH: Heinemann.

Sinclair, N. (2006). *Mathematics and beauty: Aesthetic approaches to teaching children.* New York: Teachers College Press.

Thiel, P., & Masters, B. (2014). *Zero to one: Notes on startups, or how to build the future.* New York: Crown Publishing Group.

Vasquez, J., Sneider, C., & Comer, M. (2014). STEM Lesson Essentials. Portsmouth, NH: Heinemann.

Wedekind, K. (2011). *Math exchanges: Guiding young mathematicians in small group meetings.* Portland, ME: Stenhouse Publishers.

Witzel, D. (2012). *Teaching science and math: Resources and strategies for K–12 science and math teachers.* Arlington, VA: National Science Teachers Association.

Whitin, P., & Whitin, D. (2000). *Math is language too: Talking and writing in the mathematics classroom.* Reston, VA: National Council of Teachers of Mathematics and Urbana, IL: National Council of Teachers of English.

Chapter 6

Language and Literacy

Communication Skills in a Digital Age

> *Language and creation are so interconnected that you cannot have one without the other . . . We manipulate language so we can manipulate the world. Innovation is whatever remains when all of our failures are removed.*

> —Kevin Ashton

Language arts provide many of the intellectual tools needed to create something new and different. When cognitive, creative, and collaborative skills are allowed to flourish in language and literacy classes, every student has a chance to develop the skills needed to create and innovate.

Invention and discovery are amplified in language-rich classrooms as learners are encouraged to express themselves in unique ways. It doesn't take long for young people to realize that reading and writing skills help them discover and create something new. Most would agree that it's more about hard work than lightning bolts full of insights coming out of nowhere.

It is important to recognize the fact that language and literacy development depend on the quality of what students read—or have read to them. Reading strongly influences writing—and both can be integrated with the other language arts to reach across the curriculum. It should also be noted that whether it is at home or at school, the quality of the words adults use are as important as the quantity.

By the time children reach the upper elementary grades, teachers often use digital technology to enhance the development of communication skills. Screens and machines can help and/or hinder the development of reading, writing, speaking, and imaginative skills. Yes, new media may be able to help with old problems, but it can also create some new ones. Texting and multitasking during class, for example, will destroy even the best lesson.

137

Today's cloud-based information technology structures are bound to help us refine the information and language that we use. Along the literacy glide path, our tech tools are bound to strongly influence the way we discover and create things.

Smart machines and artificial intelligence are increasingly shaping how information is collected and used. Not only that, but we now have robo-writers that can go beyond reprocessing data to creating human-sounding printed pages. So it's hard to avoid the fact that new media will increasingly influence how children and young adults construct meaning with language and literacy.

As far as innovation itself is concerned, the process is less about solo inventors than about collaboration. In the right environment, the ability to work in teams can make individuals even more creative and empowered (Catmull, 2014). Add the right mix of supportive social and cultural factors to the mix and you can create something very human and very special.

It is often in the space between individual differences and imaginative group activities that discoveries are made and new insights created. Examples of collaborative work: parallel computation technologies, better algorithms, and big data collection. Taken together, these developments mean that we had all better get used to a higher level of predictive strength.

A note of concern: the technology may be helpful in predicting what we want online and even foresee a few over-the-horizon events, but we better move quickly to fine-tune the technology before it fine-tunes us.

Uncertainty rules in today's ambiguous and quickly changing world. But whatever happens, you can be sure that change favors enthusiasm, energy, teamwork, and *the prepared mind.*

ADVANCING LITERACY IN A NEW AGE

How might the Web and its digital associates have a detrimental or positive effect on language and literacy development?

Whatever your answer, becoming too dependent on digital technology isn't a good idea.

No one knows for sure what will crop up just around the corner, but when it comes to education, diminishing the face-to-face human factor can undermine both the individual and the society. Good literature and collaborative small-group work are and will continue to be two of the keys to advancing literacy (Taylor & Duke, 2014).

As learners move through the stages of language learning, discussions about what's being read and written helps everyone move toward fluency. The thoughtful use of all available tools can help accomplish shared language, literacy, and creative-thinking goals. What about new ideas? Coming up with them has a lot to do with remixing the metaphors, concepts, and scientific understandings of our time.

Certain simple truths about learning are sometimes lost in the smoky quarrelsomeness of the debate over the best approach to teaching. One of these simple truths is that language learning is social and instruction is most effective when it is taught holistically and within a meaningful context. Another reality is that integrating language arts is a powerful way to connect students to the full range of real communication possibilities.

As language and literacy instruction increasingly expand to include electronic media, it is important to realize that each communications medium relates directly or indirectly to every other. It's much more than learning subskills. Language learning, at its best, involves becoming active, critical, and creative users of print, spoken language, and the visual language of electronic media.

Technological resources can do many things—including linking the classroom to the outside world in ways that extend the boundaries of learning. Still, digital technology has a mixed track record when it comes to improving reading and writing skills at the elementary school level (Johnson, 2014).

Wiz-bang technology, collaborative learning, and a standards-based curriculum all help. But the key to high-quality instruction is a cooperative, language-rich classroom where the teacher knows the characteristics of effective instruction. Meaningful group activities and settings can help students learn how to use language to communicate, solve problems, and meet the diverse literacy demands that they will encounter throughout their lives.

As teachers look for new ways to make the language arts more active, dynamic, purposeful, and fun, it is important to recognize the importance of personal adaptability and creativity. Just as there is no unified educational theory that explains everything, there is no instructional method that will meet the needs of all students all the time (Moline, 2012).

Rigid scripts designed by others have always been a poor substitute for well-educated teachers who can combine professional flexibility with a thorough knowledge of effective instruction. Permanent competency in any field is illusive. The best advice for both teachers and students: do the best you can with what you know today—and work hard to do better tomorrow.

MAKING CONNECTIONS IN GROUPS

Language learners must invent and try out the rules of language for themselves through social interaction as they move toward control of language-for-meaning.

—Pace

Whether its old or new media, the whole range of language skills can be helped by communicating with peers who provide immediate feedback during the reading, writing, and revision processes. It should come as no surprise to learn that the most competent readers tend to be the most competent talkers, listeners, writers, viewers, and thinkers.

Let's look at how younger children can share *big books*:

Steps in sharing a big book:

• The teacher introduces the book and makes the children predict what it is about.
• The teacher reads the book to the students, holding the book up high so children can see the words.
• The teacher sometimes pauses so students can think about what will happen next.
• The teacher rereads the book; students can read along (out loud) with him/her.
• Students may pair up for a rereading, taking turns reading small parts.

Beginning readers may have to be repeatedly exposed to a book by hearing the story read well several times before they develop oral fluency themselves. The old-fashioned round-robin style doesn't work well. Just about anything else will get the job done. If you want to do a lot of oral reading, simply do paired reading in groups of two. Get close, point the chairs in opposite directions, and take turns reading.

Don't assume that student—or even an adult—can make a book sound exciting when reading out loud. Many new teachers have to practice and get suggestions from their peers to do the job well. So you know that young readers will have to go over the text several times with a friend or two.

Just about any activity that you can think of can be used. For example: children can work in small groups to act out a story or practice reading the lines in a reader's theatre activity. They can also work in small groups to discuss the theme, plot, characterization, or difficulty to be overcome in the story. Felt pens and large paper can be used for semantic maps or webs of their answers. These can be put up and shared with the whole class. The most important thing is to get children thinking, discussing, and interacting with literature.

Reading is thinking with the mind of a stranger.

—Jorge Luis Borges

SOCIAL PROCESSING AND THINKING
ABOUT WRITTEN EXPRESSION

The development of a writing community is a very powerful way for students to collaborate in developing their writing voice (Hipsky, 2011). Whether writing is self, peer, or teacher evaluated, it is important not to lose sight of the connection between what is valued and what is valuable. Jointly developed folders (portfolios) have a major role to play in student writing assessment. By selecting samples, these folders can provide a running record of students' interests and what they can and can't do.

To work toward less control, teachers need to help students take more responsibility for their own learning. The ability to evaluate does not come easily at first, and peer writing groups will need teacher-developed strategies to help them process what they have learned. The ability to reflect on being a member of a peer-writing team is a form of metacognition—learning to think about thinking. The skills of productive group work may have to be made explicit. This requires processing in a circular or U-shaped group where all students can see each other. Questions for evaluative social processing might include:

- How did group leadership evolve?
- Was it easy to get started?
- How did you feel if one of your ideas was left out?
- What did you do if most members of your group thought that you should write something differently?
- How did you rewrite?
- Did your paper say what you wanted it to?
- What kind of a setting do you like for writing?
- How can you arrange yourself in the classroom to make the writing process better?
- What writing tools did you use?
- How do you feel when you write?
- What was the reasoning behind what you did?

Remember, it's just as important for students to write down their reasoning as it is to explain their feelings and preferences.

The recognition of developmental stages in social skills must be taken into account as teachers incorporate literature-based writing concerns into their classroom routines. For the younger students, the writing process can take the form of jointly produced language experience stories. These can be placed on large charts with the teacher or an upper-grade student doing the writing. As soon as they can write on their own, the children can keep a private journal where they label drawings, experiences, and writing samples.

As students learn to expand their perspectives, they can begin to carry a story from one page (or day) to the next. Time may be set aside each day for a personal journal entry. Although it's important that the language be in a student's own words, the teacher can make comments without formal grading (Dierking & Jones, 2014).

There are times when teachers have to intervene to assess students' writing or do some final editing before something is widely shared. Remember to stamp "draft" or "creative writing—work in progress" on anything that might go home before it reaches its final form. A "work in progress" stamp would save you from a little embarrassment when a misspelled word or some bad grammar reaches parents.

STRUCTURED AND UNSTRUCTURED POETRY EXPERIENCES

Some twenty-first-century Americans, for example, might disagree with Wordsworth, a nineteenth-century Englishman, who explained poetry as "emotion recollected in tranquility." People often reach for poetry today because in its own peculiar way, poetry tells truths that other communication techniques often miss.

Teachers must have some basic knowledge of the vocabulary of poetry in order to help children enjoy and mature in their understanding and appreciation of it. One thing they can do is to share some of their efforts at poetry with their students—as well as reading published poetry to their class. Reading or writing poetry involves awareness of certain elements that make it unique. Some poetry characteristics that students should know about:

1. Poetry uses condensed language so *every* word becomes important.
2. Poetry uses figurative language (e.g., metaphor, simile, personification, irony). The language of poetry is often rhythmical (regular, irregular, metered).
3. The language of poetry is often rhythmical (regular, irregular, metered).
4. Some words may be rhymed (internal, end of line, runover) or nonrhyming.
5. Poetry uses the language of sounds (alliteration, assonance, repetition).
6. The units of organization are line arrangements in stanzas or idea arrangements in a story (balance, contrast, build-up, or surprise).
7. Poetry uses the language of imagery (sense perceptions reproduced in the mind).

Different Kinds of Poetry

1. *Fixed Forms*
   a. Narrative or storytelling

b. Literary forms with prescribed structures (e.g., limerick, ballad, sonnet, haiku, others)

c. Lyric

2. *Free Verse*

a. Tone: humorous, serious, nonsensical, sentimental, dramatic, didactic

b. Content: humor, nonsense, everyday things, animals, seasons, family, fantasy, people, feelings, adventure, moods

c. Time of writing: contemporary, traditional

3. *An Example of Collaborative Poetry*

Students work in small, collaborative groups. Each team or partnership is given a short time (one or two minutes) to compose the first line of a poem. On a signal from the teacher, each team passes their paper to the next group and receives one from another. The group reads the line that the preceding team has written and adds a second line. The signal is given and the papers rotate again—each time the group reads and adds another line.

Teams are encouraged to write what comes to mind, even if it's only their name. They must write something in the time allotted. After eight or ten lines, the papers are returned to their original teams. Groups can add a line if they choose, revise, and edit the poem they started. The poems can then be read orally with team members, alternating reading the lines. Later, some of them can be turned into an optic poem (creating a picture with computer graphics using the words of the poem) or acted out using ribbons or penlights (while someone else reads the poem).

Writing Poetry in Small, Collaborative Groups

The collaborative writing of poetry intertwines process with content and students with learning. The cooperative linking of poetry concepts will often turn mundane work into poems rich in detail, sentiment, and humor. The importance of an audience for poetry will help at every stage of the writing.

Working in cooperative groups helps students become more responsible in communicating their understanding to other group members and an audience. The sharing of ideas helps each child develop a better understanding of the writing process and stimulates student conversations around literary pursuits.

When poetry is fused with collaborative dreams, emotions, and comedy, it can foster personal and intellectual growth. If poetry is viewed as a solitary and dour undertaking, then little space is left for the role of humor in explaining life's goofy splendors.

A group's interactions encourage building and changing ideas to foster the development of collaborative poetry. Interactions between peers can amplify the process. It's good to stir things up, but sometimes, a few rules will help the group to be more productive:

1. One person should not do all the talking.
2. Accept everyone's ideas.
3. Stick to the topic.
4. Remind each other of the rules or appoint a group leader to help.

Poetry is more than just printed words on a page. Poetry comes alive when the reader and the words connect in a way that provides meaning and builds upon the reader's experiences. External stimuli, like some of the methods presented here, can build on sights, sounds, thoughts, and tensions to create poems. Unsaid inner meanings can be revealed in the "music" or rhythm of a poem. Poetry often happens between sensibility, control of language, and rhythm.

A good place to begin is with a subject that offers a sense of metaphysical possibility. How do real writers write? Beethoven, for example, would write fragments in notebooks that he kept beside him; later, he would develop these themes. He got ideas from every conceivable direction—including other composers, folk music, and myths. Like other writers, he needed a thorough knowledge of the language (music) and a broad range of experience to build upon. Children can do the same thing by keeping a notebook of ideas about experiences, books, and how their thinking changes in regard to different subjects.

Beyond having some mastery of language, being able to think in images is certainly useful (Bogard & Donovan, 2013). So is the ability to concentrate. Poetry, like any kind of writing, requires many revisions along the way. It's important to get something—almost anything—down and go from there. Sketching out an idea and developing it into a clear vision can foster language growth and help illuminate the reading and writing process (Ganske, 2014).

Since what students read influences how they write, there is a natural connection between students' written poetry and the richness of the literature program they are exposed to. By leading students to appreciate literature and poetry across time and cultures, teachers can enhance a child's ability to write.

A variety of children's literature and poetry can become a source of vocabulary, metaphor, and conceptual material. Experiencing the language and rhythm of good poetry gives students the building blocks for creating their own poetic patterns. By exposing students to various kinds of poetry patterns, teachers enable them to do a better job of creating poetry on their own.

EXPERIENCES WITH POETRY

1. Poetry with Movement and Music
   Poems can be put to music and movement. One student can read the poem, and the rest of the group can use streamers and penlights in a

darkened room to move down to the pen. Students can also illustrate picture books to go with poems that they can later share with younger children.

2. Daily Oral Reading of Poetry
   Students sign up and read aloud at the end of each day. Other students "point," commenting on parts of the poem that catch their attention. A classroom anthology of poetry can be illustrated and laminated.

3. Responding During Free Writing Period
   Thirty minutes to an hour and one half is set aside each day for students to write on any topic, in whatever form they choose. A share time follows so that other students may respond to each other's writing by pointing and asking questions.

4. Literature Share Time
   Students gather in small groups once a week to share books they have been reading. The groups are structured so that each student
   a. reads the author and title of each book
   b. tells about the book
   c. reads one or two pages aloud
   d. receives responses from members of the group, specifically pointing out parts they liked and asking questions.

5. Wish Poems
   Each student writes a wish on a strip of paper. The wishes are read together as a whole for the group. Students then write individual wish poems, which are shared.

6. Group Metaphor Comparisons
   Poems containing metaphors are read aloud. Group comparison poems are written on the board. Students write individual comparison poems and share them with the class.

7. Sample Poetry Lesson
   A lesson developed from *Dinosaurs*, a poetry anthology for children edited by Lee Bennett Hopkins.
   a. Teacher reads poems aloud.
   b. Students brainstorm reasons why the dinosaurs died and words that relate to how the dinosaurs moved.
   c. Models of dinosaurs and pictures are displayed and talked about.
   d. Students write poems and share them.

8. Cinquain poetry: five lines long
   • Find a picture (that shows action) that you would like to write about.
   • Discuss what you would like to write about it with a partner.
   • Think of a story that you would like to tell.
   • Count syllables as you write your words or phrases to tell a story.

a. Two syllables in the first line. Title
b. Four syllables in the second line. Description
c. Six syllables in the third line. Action
d. Eight syllables in the fourth line. Feeling
e. Just two syllables in the last line. Conclusion
Write, revise, and share.

9. Shape Poems
   Words should be written to show the shape of the thing being expressed.
       Try to make a picture out of the poem and add some color to outline it.
   Examples: *slippery slithering snake, sliding sensitive.*

10. The Fame to the Name
    This activity can be adapted to suit class and curriculum needs, integrating whole language, cooperative learning, and poetry. It is a simple lesson with lots of flexibility that integrates social studies, history, and mathematics. The form of the poem is in the name. The name chosen is written vertically on a chart pad or on the board.

    Beginning with each letter in the name, the class brainstorms a sentence or phrase that tells something about the name. Here is an example using the state of Alaska:

A lot of fresh air
L and of the froze
Athabaskans, Eskimos, Aleuts
Seals, bears, moose, and more
Kaleidoscope in the night sky
A state to be proud of.

Model the alternate line reading of a poem with the class: you read one line, one of your students reads the second line, and so on to the end of a poem. This will give the children an idea of how it is to be done. Pair students up for poetry, create one or two poems, and practice one poem that each pair presents to the whole class.

Let students know about using alliteration to add excitement. Another idea is to make a list of nouns or adjectives that pertain to the theme. Incorporate cooperative learning by breaking the students into small groups. One method is to have each group work on one letter of the thematic poem or invent its own topic. Be sure to allow time for group presentations.

As a parental involvement activity, have each student with his or her family write a poem using their last name. Families with several names can be encouraged to use both, or individuals can write a poem using their own name.

Motivating poetry activities can be used throughout the whole year. Life experiences can broaden the world knowledge base of these poems.

To incorporate writing across the curriculum, pull names or subjects from the children's life experiences, science and social studies or history and math.

You might encourage the students to write about animals, their habitats, the weather, or other scientific facts about the state or city. Suggested social studies topics might include the people, their culture, and the history of the place.

Children may wish to include personal school or family history in their poem. Math could be incorporated by using population or the area size of a state. Another idea is to have students figure out how many students are in each grade within a school and how many students there are in total.

CREATING POEMS FROM WORDS IN THE ENVIRONMENT

This activity is designed to increase students' observation of words in their environment and create poetry from printed words they observe around them. This can be in the classroom, at school, on field trips, at the bus stop, or walking down the street.

Pair children up or have them grouped in threes. Set the physical boundaries, limiting them to the classroom, hallway, playground, and other areas. Set expectations based on the needs of the class.

SUMMARIZE WITH BIOPOEMS

Biopoems encourage students to make inferences and synthesize by selecting the precise language to fit the form and character. Biopoems are an effective way to write and think about people in the past and present. They are also effective in introducing students to each other.

Creating a collaborative biopoem:

1. Divide the class into groups of two or three.
2. Each partnership produces a biopoem on an author of a book, a historical figure, or someone in the news (Students may have to look up some of the information).
3. Give each pair of students a large sheet of paper and some colorful markers. Instruct the groups to make a poster large enough for the whole class to see.
4. After the group has finished one biopoem, encourage individuals to do a biopoem about themselves.
5. At each stage, group members should be talking to each other and making comparisons. Select one of the poems, and be sure it is big enough to present to the entire class.

The biopoem form is:

Line 1 First Name _____

Line 2 Four traits that describe the character _____

Line 3 Relative (brother, sister, friend, parent, etc.) of _____

Line 4 Lover of _____ (three things or people)

Line 5 Who feels_____(three items)

Line 6 Who needs _____

Line 7 Who fears _____

Line 8 Who gives _____

Line 9 Who would like to see_____

Line 10 Resident of_____

Line 11 Last name _____

Biopoem uses:

– to review a character in a book.

– to understand an historical or well known figure.

– to introduce people.

– as an activator to develop a character before writing a story.

Figure 6.1 Biopoem Worksheet.

COMBINING OLD AND NEW MEDIA

Some upper-grade teachers have had success combining traditional forms of writing with new forms of expression. Social networks and blogging are but two examples. Along the way, students can use the Internet to get their ideas out across the Web.

Newspapers and World Knowledge Are Important

Newspapers can be an excellent supplement to literature, original documents, and oral histories. With upper grades, middle school and high school students' newspaper articles can spark ideas for group discussion and provide writing models for analysis.

Students can see how a composition is organized as they read rather than watch television. They can also compare the evening news, which is often based on items in national newspapers with written stories. The *New York Times*, the *Washington Post*, the *Los Angeles Times*, or the local newspaper can be more stimulating than textbooks. With younger children, simple pieces (with pictures) and publications like the *My Weekly Reader* (Scholastic) can replace more difficult newspapers.

The daily newspaper, particularly if it's in a second language, can be an intimidating document for students to tackle. It is imposing in format and vocabulary for early readers who are accustomed to materials geared toward their competency levels. By preparing imaginative exercises using a newspaper or a clip from a national newscast, a teacher can provide an introduction and demystify those pages filled with newsprint and connect to a second-language video segment.

It is important that the newspaper and video segment cover some of the same ground. The TV news items or conversations should be shown first so that what the students have listened to (and seen) is then applied to print. This means using print and video material from the same stories.

The following example called The Newspaper Scavenger Hunt is an exercise that can be applied to a variety of reading levels. A list is drawn up with columns of words and phrases extracted from a sample paper. This list of cartoons, pictures, words, concepts, and short phrases (to be found in the newspaper) is handed out to pairs of students along with the paper. They are then asked to begin the hunt. Students put the page number on which the item is located on the answer sheet and then circle the item in the newspaper. A time limit is set for the search to take place. When time is up, the students can compare their "success" rates. This exercise can be modified for a range of ability levels.

The teacher can go over the newspaper with them as the class collaboratively searches for connections with nightly news program the students are asked to watch as homework. Small groups can also make up a creative story composed almost entirely of headlines, subheadings, and a few connections of their own. Political cartoons, with their words removed, can also be presented, and groups can come up with their own caption.

INTEGRATING THE LANGUAGE ARTS
WITH READERS THEATRE

Readers' theater is the oral presentation of prose or poetry by two or more readers. Complete scripts can be provided, or students can write them after reading a story or a poem. The actual story or chapter may be ten or twenty pages long—the finished readers theatre script may only be two or three pages. We recommend trying some prepared scripts first (so that children get the basic idea) and then have the students work as a small group to transform a story or poem into a script.

The typical readers theatre lesson involves script writing, rehearsal, performance, and follow-up commentary for revision. Before the class presentation, children need a chance to practice and refine their interpretation. Everybody eventually gets their own copy so that they can read their role from a hand-held script (A few mistakes in reading are good for a laugh).

When reading, they stand up (from a chair) or turn to face the audience; when their turn is over they sit down or turn their back to the audience. If there are four roles and five children, then two read the same thing at the same time; if there are four students and six roles then two members of the group read two roles.

Lines, gesture, intonation, and movement are worked out in advance. Individual interpretations are negotiated between group members. The performance in front of an audience can intensify the experience and connect the reader to the audience. After going over a prepared script or two, children can take a story that they are reading and create their own scripts.

Readers theatre can be a good, informal, cooperative learning activity where students not only respond to each other as character to character but also in spontaneous responses that tie the group together with the situation of the text. The idea is to use a highly motivating technique to engage children in a whole range of language activities and literate behaviors.

A sample script:
No chairs or turning around for this one. Students jump *up* when their reading turn comes and *down* when they are not reading. If it says "EVERYONE," then the whole group jumps up to read and down at the same time until it's over. "Put some real energy into it or you get to do it twice" (Time for practice first could help).

"Song of the Popcorn"

EVERYONE: Pop, Pop, Pop!
1st child: Says the popcorn in the pan!
EVERYONE: Pop, Pop, Pop!
2nd child: You can catch me if you can!
EVERYONE: Pop, Pop, Pop!
3rd child: Says each kernel hard and yellow!
EVERYONE: Pop, Pop, Pop!
4th child: I'm a dancing little fellow!
EVERYONE: Pop, Pop, Pop!

5th child: How I scamper through the heat!
EVERYONE: Pop, Pop, Pop!
6th child: You will find me good to eat!
EVERYONE: Pop, Pop, Pop!
7th child: I can whirl, and skip, and hop!
EVERYONE: Pop, Pop, Pop, Pop! Pop, Pop, Pop!
EVERYONE should be sure to quickly go up and down with each "Pop, Pop, Pop!" If there aren't enough children for a script, someone can read two roles. If there are too many students, two can read the same role at the same time.

You can connect the readers theatre popcorn activity directly to the STEM subjects by actually popping popcorn and measuring the distance it goes when the top is off (You might want to put something on the floor first). Students can go online to find the science behind the popping. Hint: it has something to do with a tiny drop of moisture inside the kernel turning into steam.

COMBINING POETRY AND READERS THEATRE

Poetry is an art form that allows us to think deeply about ourselves and others. It doesn't have to be solitary, in the schools, and off the streets. Wordsworth may have been wrong when he explained poetry as "emotion recollected in tranquility." Teachers can always be looking for ways to make poetry interactive and stretch the possibilities. Readers theatre is one way to make poetry inclusive and fun.

Students can divide up a poem in several ways, read each version out loud in their small group, and discuss which division lent dramatic effect to the piece. Other questions: Which script has the best logical breaks or shifts? What are the dramatic or thematic advantages to the different arrangements? How would different interpretations of what the poem is saying affect the division? If there are four students and three roles, two students can read in unison.

Script #1

Reader 1: "Abandoned Farmhouse" by Ted Kooser

He was a big man,
says the size of his shoes on a pile of broken dishes by the house;
a tall man too, says the length of the bed in an upstairs room;
and a good, God-fearing man, says the Bible with a broken back—
on the floor below the window, dusty with sun;
but not a man for farming
say the fields cluttered with boulders and the leaky barn.

Reader 2: A woman lived with him, says the bedroom wall papered with lilacs and the kitchen shelves covered with oilcloth,

Reader 3: and they had a child says the sandbox made from a tractor tire

Reader 2: Money was scarce, say the jars of plum preserves and canned tomatoes sealed in the cellar-hole, and the winters cold, say the rags in the window frames. It was lonely here, says the narrow gravel road.

Reader 1: Something went wrong, says the empty house in the weed-choked yard. Stones in the fields say he was not a farmer;

Reader 2: the still-sealed jars in the cellar say she left in a nervous haste

Reader 3: And the child? Its toys strewn in the yard like branches after a storm, a rubber cow, a rusty tractor with a broken plow, a doll in overalls. Something went wrong, they say.

"After Reading" Questions:

Why do you think the characters left? Does this reader's theatre version of the poem help you get to know more about the characters? Does each reader have an equal share? What are the dramatic or thematic advantages to this division?

Script #2

Reader 1: "Abandoned Farmhouse" Ted Kooser

Reader 2: He was a big man,

Reader 4: (echoes) a big man

Reader 1: says the size of his shoes on a pile of broken dishes by the house;

Reader 2: a tall man too,

Reader 4: (echoes) a tall man

Reader 1: says the length of the bed in an upstairs room;

Reader 2: and a good, God-fearing man,

Reader 3: (echoes) good and God-fearing

Reader 1: says the Bible with a broken back on the floor below the window, dusty with sun;

Reader 2: but not a man for farming,

Reader 1: say the fields cluttered with boulders and the leaky barn.

Reader 3: a woman lived with him,

Reader 1: says the bedroom wall papered with lilacs and the kitchen shelves covered with oil cloth,

Reader 4: and they had a child

Reader 1: says the sandbox made from a tractor tire,

Reader 3: Money was scarce,

Reader 1: say the jars of plum preserves and canned tomatoes sealed in the cellar-hole,

Reader 2: and the winters cold,

Readers 3 and 4: "Oh, so cold"
Reader 1: say the rags in the window frames,
Reader 3: It was lonely here,
Readers 3 and 4: "so lonely"
Reader 1: says the narrow gravel road.
Everyone: Something went wrong,
Reader 1: says the empty house in the weed-choked yard.
Reader 2: Stones in the fields say he was not a farmer;
Reader 3: the still-sealed jars in the cellar say she left in a nervous haste,
Reader 4: And the child? Its toys are strewn in the yard like branches after a storm—a rubber cow, a rusty tractor with a broken plow, a doll in overalls.
Everyone: Something went wrong, they say,
Reader 4: (echoes) Something went wrong.

Questions: Are there any dramatic or thematic advantages to this division? Explain the thinking behind your preferences. How would what your conception of what happened to the characters influence how you would divide the poem up?

CREATIVE DRAMA IN THE LANGUAGE ARTS CLASSROOM

Creative drama can serve as a tool for integrating language learning experiences. It also offers teachers a medium that can make important contributions to children's literacy development (Jensen & Nickelsen, 2014). Engaging in literacy-related creative drama should be part of every language arts program. These activities can be done in small groups with few props, no memorization of lines, and no chance for failure.

Dramatic play can be used to bridge the gap between written and visual forms of communication. For example, students can work in small groups to script, act, and even videotape a one-minute commercial. They pick a topic, develop a skit, practice, and perform it for the class. They can, then, critically examine the reasoning behind each group's presentation to the class. The original commercials developed by the students can also be compared to those done on the Internet or on television.

Creative drama can help students reconstruct their own meanings as they respond to literature, writing, and ideas. The way students are asked to go about this process influences their development as readers, writers, and thinkers.

Creative drama:

• Doesn't emphasize performance.
• Adapts to many types of books, lessons, and subjects.

- Encourages the clarification of ideas and values.
- Evokes contributions and responses from students who rarely participate in "standard" discussions.
- Can be used to assess how well students understand what they are reading—characterization, setting, plot, conflicts, etc.
- Provides a stimulating prewriting exercise.

Teaching Story Dramatization and Teamwork

1. Select a good story—and then tell it to the group.
2. With the class, break the plot down into sequences, or scenes, that can be acted out.
3. Have groups select a scene they wish to dramatize.
4. Instruct the groups to break the scene or scenes into further sequence, and discuss the setting, motivation, characterizations, roles, props, and more. Encourage students to get involved in the developmental images of the characters—what they did, how they did it, why they did it. Have groups make notes on their discussions.
5. Meet with groups to review and discuss their perceptions. Let them go into a conference and plan in more detail for their dramatization.
6. Have the whole class meet back together and watch the productions of each group. Instruct students to write down five things they liked and five things that could be improved in the next playing.
7. Let the players return to their groups at the end of all group performances and evaluate the dramas using the criteria in number 6.
8. Allow groups to bring back their group evaluations to the whole class. Discuss findings, suggestions, and positive group efforts.

Creative Drama with Active Learning Teams

1. Personification (This can also be used as a prewriting activity)
   Each student draws the name of an inanimate object (pencil sharpener, doorknob, waste basket, alarm clock, etc.). Students pick a partner and develop an improvisation.
2. Using Drama to Extend a Story
   Creative drama can extend a story. Try "blocking" a play as you read it aloud in class. Giving such a visual perspective increases concentration.
3. Increasing Research and Journalism Skills
   Using techniques of role-playing and creative drama, have student groups show *how* to interview (give good and bad examples). Short excerpts from TV news or radio information programs provide good models for discussion and creative drama activities.

Creative drama has long been used to help students learn speaking, listening, thinking, and social skills. After they reflect the theme and action of drama, children can compare character development in plays and written literature. By drawing on prior knowledge and tapping so many modes of expression, creative dramatics ties in nicely with Howard Gardner's ideas about multiple pathways to learning.

Creative dramatics can be a motivating foundation linking all of the language arts by engaging students in the full range of language expression. Reading, writing, and the other language arts often occur in less of a social context. As students experience puppetry, pantomime, improvisation, and other dramatic activities, they develop teamwork skills that can be applied to a wide range of comprehension strategies.

Are innovative leaps in language and the arts different from those in science and engineering?

Try making a Venn diagram of overlapping circles with these subjects. Similarities are where they overlap and differences are where the subjects have their own part of the circle. It's a little difficult with four circles, so using two subjects at a time is an alternative.

CONNECTING LANGUAGE, THINKING SKILLS, AND LITERATURE

Reading is seeing the world through the mind of a stranger.

—Jorge Borges

Reading and writing have traditionally been at the core of the elementary curriculum. Now, we have integrated language arts instruction; a special place is reserved for critical and creative thinking. Although the language arts curriculum is not changing at the same speed as technology, new developments and approaches are evolving in reading, writing, speaking, listening, and integrated instruction.

How might the different parts of language arts influence each other and contribute to work in other subjects?

Literature is one of the keys to language and literacy. However, to reach its full power, it must be integrated with the other language arts. Students can, for example, use oral language to talk about what they are reading, listen to others, write in response journals, and dramatize stories (Fredricksen et al., 2012).

Connecting a story to creative drama and writing are good ways for students to share imaginative ideas with their peers. This can create an atmosphere in which unconscious thought can flow freely.

Activity: You might use creative drama and have students act out a dream or a daydream. Put four students in each group, have them each share a dream, and choose one to act out. Everyone in the group has to play a role, even if they're just a tree or rock. Each group practices for a sixty-second skit and then presents it to the entire class. Have the whole class guess whose dream it was and have that person explain the dream.

Students can be asked to record how they think and make inferences about what they see, hear, or read. They might even use pictures to tell the tale. Any combination of these techniques can also be used to help learners realize that creativity and innovation have a lot to do with many small steps and a bit of luck.

Spoken History: Exploring the lives of elders in the community can be more than informative; it can make use of the full range of communication skills to connect generations. We like to ask five or six elders in for an oral history project. Each group gets one person to interview. Each elder gets assigned to a small group and is interviewed by students who take notes and later write up the "history." After the interviews, a student from each group stands and briefly explains the questions and answers.

To do this spoken history activity, students need to do a little homework on the time period in question and prepare some questions. The local newspaper may even be willing to come in and cover the event. In a small town, the local newspaper might even carry the final version of what the students write about each visitor.

The integrated language arts approach encourages long periods of self-selected reading, teachers reading out loud to students, the use of technology, and the sharing of books and response projects. Response projects emphasize reflection and interpretation, not summarizing the plot of a story. These methods for analyzing literature can also help the teacher find special student interests in an author, illustrator, or theme.

Students and teacher can occasionally plan a unit together—choosing books around a topic or person of interest and planning reading and response activities. Students can also keep response journals and focus on a few favorite books through writing, art, drama, or a particular line of research (Stock et al., 2014).

Some teachers like to use what they call a "think-aloud." They choose one or two strategies to teach, such as prediction, visualization, confirming, elaborating, or summarizing. Next, they talk about how they use these strategies to activate prior knowledge as they read. The next step is to have the students practice the meaning-construction strategy—working with a partner as they read, think out loud, and jot down a few notes. This helps students develop their own critical reading and writing skills as they experience a variety of viewpoints.

LITERACY AT HOME SUPPORTS LITERACY AT SCHOOL

Innovation is often the result of a series of mental steps involving problem, solution, and revision. Directing personal energy onto a path of positive action requires knowledge of the subject, the purpose, and the means needed to make something new happen. At every stage, it is difficult to isolate creative achievements from the environmental contexts that individuals and groups happen to be in.

When children learn language and literacy skills in active ways, they can construct their own meaning with the full range of communication tools. This means interacting with peers, electronic media, and literature to accomplish genuine goals. All of the adults in a child's life can help create a rich learning environment while providing information that students need to know when they need to know it. Parents, as much as teachers, need to create a literate environment, mediate the learning, and be good literacy models.

Whatever adults want to make important to children, they must make important to themselves as well. For example, it's hard for a teacher to teach reading if they don't read newspapers and books. Likewise, it's hard for a parent to instill a love of literature if there are no reading materials (books, magazines, and newspapers) around the house. If parents read and have a highly developed vocabulary, children follow suit. Reading in the home environment precedes reading in the world.

Parents need to know what's going on so that they can help out at home. In the twenty-first century, many parents are employed. A few can't read well in any language; others can't read English. Parents with the most highly developed language skills are most likely to be working outside the home. With some parents caught between fifty-hour workweeks and functional illiteracy, it is little wonder that teachers have more trouble than ever with home-school connections.

When teachers change their methods and classroom organizational structures, they need the understanding of parents and administrators. When professional colleagues help each other, things usually work out for the better. Some teachers meet with parents before school starts to set cooperative goals and ask parents about the student's strong and weak points—what works for their child and what doesn't.

We need to leave no stone unturned when it comes to helping parents realize how they can make a big contribution to their child's success in language and literacy. They can do this by helping their children use reading, writing, listening, speaking, and communication technology for real purposes (Dole et al., 2014).

ALGORITHMS AND NATURAL LANGUAGE GENERATORS

[See if you can tell which paragraph within this subtitle was written by a robot-writer].

It has been said that language is what makes us human. Well, if that was ever true, it's less true now. Algorithms and natural language generators are getting faster and a lot better.

Revision is the key to good writing—and right now robot writers don't seem as good at that as humans.

Automated Insight's Wordsmith Platform is the robot-writer program that the Associated Press uses, cutting a lot of newspaper jobs in the process. Two examples of robot-writer programs that we like are Narrative Science and Wordsmith. Tell these software programs your intended audience and what writing style you prefer. You can even choose the style of a particular author if you wish. Then, your robot-writer will mine a tremendous amount of data, sort out what's useful, and quickly provide you with an original report—or an entire book.

Big data may provide too much information for humans to sort through, analyze, and quickly write about. But would turning the sorting and *composition process* over to computer algorithms cause us to miss out on some of the things that the curious and inventive human mind might come up with?

E-BOOKS AND E-READERS

Critics like Nicholas Carr have looked at the Internet and argue that the Web has had a detrimental effect on language, literacy, and thinking (Carr, 2014). Might digital technology dictate human literacy acquisition and thought processes in detrimental ways?

Amazon's Kindle readers have helped make e-books ubiquitous. There are differences between reading on your computer (slower) and reading on one of the Kindle devices (faster).

In spite of a little early criticism, the technology now allows for the constant upgrade of nonfiction works. Also, it is sometimes a possibility of customizing the information you want and upgrading articles. Special features let you adjust the size of the print, the sound, or the background lighting. And unlike paper books, e-books can be read in the dark.

Electronic books are able to search for strings of ideas or words within the text and quickly find information, interesting passages, and references. A menu lets readers jump quickly to a particular chapter or a favorite scene.

Some e-book software can be read out loud to you in ways that reinforce the speaking and listening dimensions of language and literacy. As you might imagine, children are very attracted to these digital reading tools. A common question when they see one: "When can I read my books on one of these?"

In spite of its many possibilities, many students and teachers still prefer the elegance of the printed work on paper. Some believe that print will be diminished in importance in a sea change from paper to electronic books. Don't count on it. Paper books will *not* "go the way of the quill pen."

At school and at home, both old and new electronic media are increasingly reshaping the way language and literacy acquisition takes place. Although much of language arts instruction will continue along traditional paths, the schools cannot avoid the most powerful information and communication technologies of our time. Caution at the primary level is one thing, but complete avoidance in the upper grades is quite another (Spectrum, 2014).

The more powerful our digital gadgets become, the more important it is to connect the technology to language and literacy learning—as well as higher-level thinking. Artificial intelligence will not replace original human thought. But digital technology will work together with people to extend their reach. So it is more important than ever to design applications and devices that work well with users.

OLD AND NEW MEDIA FOR LANGUAGE LEARNING

When it comes to using digital technology at the elementary level, the evidence of usefulness is thin. Teachers should not assume the new thing is always better than the old thing. E-books and online reading devices may have found a comfortable niche, but there is something elegant and sensual about print and illustrations on paper.

In spite of inevitable changes, the wood pulp business has little to fear. Paper documents have proved more resistant than expected. In fact, print on paper is doing much more than hanging on. So many new avenues for paper documents continue to develop that we are using more paper than ever.

Books in the traditional mode will be with us throughout the twenty-first century. They are, after all, a user-friendly medium that will not become unreadable when the technology changes. Best of all, you can share a real book or article with a friend (Recent laws like the Digital Millennium Copyright Act make online sharing of materials difficult legally).

People who use specially designated software to read an e-book are identified every time they read something. If you aren't authorized to read a specific e-book, you are committing a "crime." Fortunately, we still have the freedom to read and share paper books. And it is still possible to go to the library.

Since e-books and reading online are part of our future, we had better consider them in a social and educational context. There are some advantages to carrying fifty pounds of books on an e-book reader. Although they are not superior to printed books, the e-book opens a range of possibilities for helping readers master words, passages, and concepts in a new way. Stumble over a word that you can't pronounce or a concept that you don't understand and the e-book will give you the correct pronunciation and an explanation.

It is unlikely that any electronic media will become the main container of content. E-books are simply one of the new waves from the literary future. They will become part of the many ways we will use digital tools to read, watch, and investigate.

Being able to use digital devices to leverage "big data" may have some advantages. Yes, new media may offer the possibility of providing new experiences and new approaches to language and literacy learning. And just as importantly, it can enhance existing learning environments.

An array of digital products will continue to evolve as they spread across the landscape. An exotic collection of literary hybrids will change how we read, write, and communicate. Books and magazines can be reduced to digital pieces where readers only have to pay for the pages or chapters that they want to use. Already, many books have become part of distant databases, allowing readers to extract and combine what they want from pools of digital information.

Some upper-grade teachers have had success combining traditional forms of writing with new forms of expression. Social networks and blogging are but two examples. Along the way, students can use the Internet to get their ideas out across the Web.

CHANGING THE WAY WE COMMUNICATE AND THINK

A few large tech companies are accelerating the harvesting and centralization of data in a way that redefines how we relate to just about everything in the world. Algorithms are changing the way we read. Also, it is now possible to chop different books up into interchangeable parts and provide a highly targeted text.

Facebook, Twitter, and Google News are three examples of search engines and social media that customize what you read with mathematical formulas (algorithms). Whether it is book passages, newspapers, or magazines, predictions about what you might want to read (based on prior choices) are constantly being placed in front of you.

It's a vague new world of information fragments arranged by code and delivered online. Although the Internet can expand the range of things to read, social networks like Twitter and Facebook tend to connect you with people who share your point of view. Automation may help or hinder our work across the curriculum. The trick is to avoid the dull, the surveillance, and the manipulation.

Using personalized algorithms and artificial intelligence, it is possible to sort out some of the things that you want to see. It is a feeble data set when compared to a knowledgeable human. So in the classroom, it is never a good idea to allocate control over what is going on to the latest software or digital gadgets.

Both old and new media are important things. But they are far from being the only things. Many new ideas have been found at the intersection of art and science. But as far as the classroom is concerned, nothing beats a teacher who understands the characteristics of effective instruction.

Digital texts have transformed what and how many of us read, write, and communicate. Still, it is a mistake to assume that the new media is automatically better than the old. In fact, polls have shown that even digital natives strongly prefer the printed page for pleasure and learning (See Barron's *Words on Screen: The Fate of Reading in a Digital World*, 2015).

Whether it is a book printed on paper or an e-book, the key to quality language and literacy instruction is a language-rich classroom with a caring and capable teacher. If you want to use the latest technology, be sure to put the pedagogical and curriculum piece in place first. The next step is figuring out how the digital tools can help you achieve instructional goals.

In and out of school, completely avoiding the most powerful information and communication technologies of our time is not an option. But buyer beware. There are plenty of entrepreneurs out there who would like to sell all kinds of tech things. If you let them, they would be happy to impose their version of the future on you. A better arrangement is for educators, policymakers, and the public to exert some control over the vested interests and the rough edges that surround new technologies.

The world is an uncertain place, and being able to get some sense of the probabilities certainly helps. The future is, after all, not just some place that we are going to but one that all of us should be involved in creating. Being aware of what's going on can help you be proactive as you go about constructing tomorrow's instructional environment.

Information and communication technologies are part of the fabric of contemporary life—and they are an increasingly important part of classroom instruction. And there may be times when tech tools can provide a powerful lever for opening doors to learning. But when the teacher doesn't know how to make good use of them, these technologies can be just another annoying distraction.

The more powerful technology becomes, the more indispensable good teachers are.

SUMMARY, CONCLUSION, AND LOOKING AHEAD

Language and literacy learning is, at its best, a shared and expanding set of experiences. With parents with younger children this means stories at bedtime, a discussion of the news, adults who read, museum excursions, and library visits. At school, it means encouraging a cooperative environment so that students can actively construct knowledge together. As Vygotsky put it: What children can do together today, they can do alone tomorrow.

Clearly, there is a direct relationship among language, literacy, teamwork, and innovation in the STEM subjects and beyond. Also, being able to discover and create helps young people develop the skills needed to innovate and solve many of the problems that come up today, tomorrow, and in the years ahead.

A common element in successful classes and successful schools is a socially integrating a sense of purpose and a shared sense of community. By building on the social nature of learning, teachers can encourage students to believe that they have the ability to learn. Along the way, learners will (hopefully) realize that by making a real effort, they can maximize their potential (Johnson, 2014).

Active team learning provides students with opportunities to jointly interpret and negotiate meaning, and make connections between prior knowledge and new ideas. Starting with the child's own experiences and background knowledge, the collaborative process can lead to both a shared group idea and a more elegant individual expression.

When students have regular opportunities to talk, read, write, go online, and solve problems together, language learning really comes alive. Remember, small collaborative groups need time to share, clarify, suggest, and expand concepts.

The interpersonal and integrated nature of literacy development gives students new tools for using and reflecting on a wide range of communication possibilities. By sharing knowledge among peers, the seeds of literacy can grow—allowing students to adjust the language medium that they are using so that they can communicate effectively with a variety of audiences (Bainbridge & Heydon, 2012).

Programs with connected language and literature components provide a solid foundation for approaching language instruction in a natural and holistic manner. It is up to the teacher to make sure that young people learn to apply a wide range of strategies for comprehending, critiquing, and appreciating written, spoken, and visual language.

Powerful approaches to language and literacy instruction require intrinsically motivating activities that help students draw on cultural and personal resources to develop productive habits of the mind.

As children develop the different language skills needed to communicate about problems, they also gain the intellectual tools they need to create with others. Engaging youngsters in an active group exploration of ideas is an exciting and powerful way for children to take an active role in their learning community. The ultimate goal is to understand and influence the direction of change in their world.

A major goal of language and literacy instruction is to enable young people to make sense of the world around them. The specific methods that a teacher chooses to teach reading, writing, and other language skills will probably reflect a unique combination of professional knowledge, policy requirements, personal choice, and a passion for the subject being taught.

Like many things in the classroom, the quality of language and literacy instruction depends on the positive energy of the teacher. When teachers are truly enthusiastic and energized, their students are more likely to read, write, invent, and communicate with others.

As you navigate the shoals of doing too little and daring too much, it is important to remember that good teachers take surprisingly different paths. Still, *informed enthusiasm* is a trait that all successful teachers have in common. To paraphrase William Blake, "Energy is an external delight."

REFERENCES

Ashton, K. (2015). *How to fly a horse: The secret history of creation, invention, and discovery.* New York: Doubleday.

Bainbridge, J., & Heydon, R. (2012). *Constructing meaning: Teaching the language arts.* 5th edition. Toronto, ON, Canada: Nelson Education Ltd.

Bogard, J., & Donovan, L. (2013). *Strategies to integrate the arts in language arts.* Huntington Beach, CA: Shell Education.

Borges, J. (1957). *Book of imaginary beings.* New York: Penguin Classics.

Carr, N. (2014). *The glass cage: Automation and us.* New York: W. W. Norton & Company.

Catmull, E. (2014). *Creativity, inc.: Overcoming the unseen forces that stand in the way of inspiration.* New York: Random House.

Dierking, C., & Jones, S. (2014). *Oral mentor texts: A powerful tool for teaching reading, writing, speaking, and listening.* Portmouth, NH: Heinemann.

Dole, J., Donaldson, E., & Donaldson, R. (2014). Reading: Across multiple texts, K–5. [Common Core Standards in literacy.] New York: Teachers College Press.

Fredricksen, J., Wilhelm, J., & Smith, M. (2012). *So, what's the story? Teaching narrative to understand ourselves, others, and the world.* Portsmouth, NH: Heinemann.

Ganske, K. (Ed.). 2014. *Write now! Empowering writers in today's K–6 classroom.* Newark, DE: International Reading Association (IRA).

Hipsky, S. (2011). *Differentiated literacy and language arts strategies.* Upper Saddle River, NJ: Pearson Education.

Jensen, E., & Nickelsen, L. (2014). *Bringing the common core to life in K–8 classrooms: 30 strategies to build literacy skills.* Bloomington, IN: Solution Tree.

Johnson, D. (2014). *Reading, writing, and literacy 2.0: Teaching with online texts, tools, and resources, K–8.* New York: Teachers College Press.

Moline, S. (2012). *I see what you mean: Visual literacy K–8.* Portland, ME: Stenhouse Publishers.

Murray, J. (1997). *Hamlet on the holodeck: The future of narrative in cyberspace.* New York: The Free Press.

National Council of Teachers of English & International Reading Association. (1996). *Standards for the English Language Arts.* Urbana, IL and Newark, DE: International Reading Association (IRA).

Pace, G. (1991). When Teachers Use Literature for Literacy Instruction: Ways That Constrain, Ways That Free. *Language Arts* 68 (1) (January): 12–25.

Smith, M., & Wilhelm, J. (2002). *Reading don't fix no Chevy's.* Portsmouth, NH: Heinemann.

Spectrum (Compiler). (2014). *Common core language arts and math, Grade K.* Greensboro, NC: Carson-Dellosa Publishing Company.

Stock, P., Stock, T., & Schillinger, T. (2014). *Entering the conversation: Practicing literacy in the disciplines.* Urbana, IL: NCTE.

Strickland, D. (2004). *Improving reading achievement through professional development.* Norwood, MA: Christopher-Gordon Publishers, Inc.

Taylor, B., & Duke, N. (Eds.). (2014). *Handbook of effective literacy instruction: Research-based practice K–8.* New York: Guilford Press.

Vygotsky, L. S. (1978). *Mind in society: The development of higher educational processes.* Cambridge, MA: Harvard University Press.

Chapter 7

Arts Education

Connections, Knowledge, and Informed Encounters

Imagination is to break through the limits.

—Thoreau

Many twenty-first-century models of education suggest that the arts can serve as a connection within and across disciplines. Projects involving the arts can also serve as a prism that allows students to connect with multiple subjects, dimensions, and directions of focus (Gardner, 2011). Along the way, art investigation can also help with synthesis, interconnection, and generating a sense of community.

At school, engaging methods of teaching the arts can spark students' imagination and open up inventive possibilities. Related critical thinking, creativity, and collaboration are all related parts of a process cutting across a wide range of subjects and real-world challenges.

The arts provide unique problem-solving possibilities that often trigger unpredictable changes in other areas. Innovation is often a by-product of imaginative efforts to solve a particular problem. The value of education in the arts can also be justified on the basis of its distinctive value in human life as a tool in preparing for unpredictable change.

In some ways the arts, like other subjects, is often part of a composition that is independent of the whole in which it participates. Whether it is the visual arts, music, dance, or drama, the arts have the possibility of providing active entry points to inventive thinking and global skills. The challenge is building on that potential in a way that makes some of the possibilities a reality.

The visual arts, dance, poetry, plays, and music have long been organizers or points of integration for a whole range of human activities. Opening up the classroom to such powerful motivators involves having students think for themselves and explore ways to reinvent their world. The whole process has a lot to do with actually *doing* art—while paying attention to culture, aesthetics, technology, and how the arts relate to other subjects.

New media can sometimes be a powerful amplifier for arts education. A good example is how images of visual art from museums around the world can be studied and analyzed online. Digital technology can also influence music education by making sampling and blending music relatively easy by providing students with the digital tools needed to mix and edit the compositions of others as they add pieces of their own compositions.

In an arts-rich classroom, learners come to appreciate what happens at the intersection of art and technology—a powerful way to engage learners in subjects across the curriculum. You can paint, compose a song, develop a dramatic script, or dance about just about anything. To paraphrase Isadora Duncan, "If I could write about it I wouldn't have to dance it."

Along the path to understanding and creating, instruction in the arts energizes students as they develop the skills to create, adapt, and take risks in the future (Chatterjee, 2013). To paint, sing, dance, or take part in creative dramatics are all good examples of activities that enable young people to learn how to deal with the world of today and fashion the world of tomorrow.

THE ARTS AS AN EYE TO THE FUTURE

The merger of globalization and information technology requires that we all adapt quicker, work smarter, and better understand the world. Along with helping students deal with a connected world, the arts can enhance awareness of the aesthetic qualities of their own surroundings.

National content standards in arts education are playing an important role in quality control and supporting efforts to develop assessment techniques to measure student achievement in the arts. All curriculum frameworks for teaching the arts assume that *all* students—not just the gifted—deserve high-quality experiences in this area. Like science or math, you do not have to be aiming at becoming a scientist or mathematician to profit from developing some understanding of the subject matter.

The arts have a lot to do with enshrining some reproduction of experience, gaining some control over the process, and influencing the future. Encounters with the arts also have a unique capacity to provide openings for imaginative breaks from the expected. They continue the universal human practice of making *special* certain objects, sounds, movement, or representations that have been linked with human survival for countless generations.

The arts are showing more potential than ever for enriching technology, science, the environment, and the world around us. In the classroom, they can challenge students to integrate what they are learning—while widening and deepening their imagination. Clearly, if the arts are missing from daily life, it opens doors to the danger that is inherent in dividing science from humanism. Tired of email, Twitter, and Buzzfeed lists? Matthew Crawford is in your corner. He calls spending too much time distracted by media "a kind of obesity of the mind" (Crawford, 2015). From the sciences to the arts, mental energies can be dissipated by too much screen time. The solution is to become "absorbed in some worthy object that has intrinsic appeal, the kind that elicits our involvement in such a way that our mental energies get gathered to a point. And once that gets under way, I think it feels more like abandon than self control" (Crawford, 2015).

Real artists sometimes focus on their work by picking up hints of cultural and technological challenges well before they result in transforming changes. Using new media to create art is but one example that students could study and emulate. David Hockney, for example, likes to turn digital play with his iPhone and iPad into onscreen images and paintings. He has even called the iPad the "most spontaneous medium" he has ever found.

The *Globe and Mail* newspaper (July 26, 2011) reports that David Hockney likes using his digital gadgets for "luminous subjects like landscapes, plants, sunrises and sunsets." This highly regarded artist has exhibited his digital artwork in museums. He also likes spontaneously drawing informal "iPictures" and sending them to friends.

Hockney has a history of constructing artwork with a wide range of media for a variety of purposes. He has made use of paint, photography, iPads, computers, fax machines, photocopiers, and opera set design. In every case, the medium has always influenced—and often determined— the end result.

You can use some of Hockney's approaches in the classroom.

With the help of two elementary school teachers, we tried one of his techniques with fifth- and sixth-grade students. He calls the method we used a "joiner."

Our approach: students were put into teams of two or three and asked to take pictures of the same thing from different distances and slightly different angles. For example, students used cameras to take seven or eight pictures of each other and/or things in the environment. The next day, the teacher brought in the prints, and students made an arrangement and glued or taped them on construction paper (Some of the students liked laminating the end result). Finally, the results were posted in the room and in the hallway.

Some teachers prefer to have student teams use digital cameras to compose a "joiner" and print the pictures (immediately) right in the room. The same procedure was followed for art construction, but the lesson went from start to finish in one class period (Note: some students started by going online to see how Hockney did it).

Universally acclaimed for his use of paint on canvas, British artist David Hockney has always liked experimenting with old and *new media.* A good digital example is his use of the iPad and the Brushes app. For his iPad drawings, he uses a stylus—you can see the results and the arrangement of pixels from a color inkjet printer.

The reviews of Hockney's digital work have been mixed. Some say that he uses the iPad in the same way that artists used to work with pastels, watercolors, or oil paints. Hockney certainly thinks the medium is here to stay. Questions: Does his new work energetically engage with newness, while creatively juggling digital and analog possibilities? *or* Is there something dull, bland, and contrived about the work?

We live in a time of technological upheaval and fast change. Still, it can take a very long time for the full effect of an innovation to fully sink in (Holmes, 2014). It has long been a responsibility of the arts to address technical and social issues. From the visual arts to music and drama, artists have always used the latest technology to draw on the raw material of life and the environment.

PROVIDING A SENSE OF OPENING

The arts have always provided a space, a sense of opening, a loving of the question, and a unique communal resource. In addition, the work of artists has often refashioned what is around them in a way that provided creative sparks for the cultural conversation. Today's school reform process should not push aside such a basic aspect of social consciousness and interdisciplinary knowing. If there are no arts in a school, there are fewer alternatives to exploring subjects by the spoken and written word.

The arts can open some collective doors of the mind and provide new spaces for the active construction of knowledge. Also, they are powerful tools for countering the tendency toward standardization. Of course, at the classroom level, it will take the skill of teachers to move forward and use the arts to shape the interconnected exuberance of learning—keeping light from the arts at the center of the human spirit.

Extending education in the arts with other subjects must go hand in hand with other new aspects of schooling and daily life. The notion that the arts can encourage wonder, inquiry, speculation, and technological literacy has for too long been lost in a morass of indifference, nostalgia, crafts, didacticism, and an already overcrowded curriculum. To dig it out requires a greater emphasis on professional development to help teachers become more familiar with the arts and discipline-based arts education.

There is an increasing trend for teachers around the world to be asked to encourage students across a number of art forms. The art forms teachers deal with include: painting, photography, music, drama, media, technology, dance, and performance (Sinclair et al., 2008). These and other art forms give students the opportunity to engage meaningfully with cultures from around the world of today and the world of yesterday (history).

Whatever waves of change sweep over the schools, performance, creation, and understanding will continue to be important. However, arts education is becoming a little more focused on analysis, history, and culture. In the field, this is referred to as a "discipline-based approach." It depends more than ever on the intellectual preparation and commitment of the teacher. Specialists can help, but it is the regular classroom teacher who will continue to be the primary source for instruction in the arts.

FROM DREAMWORKS ANIMATION: A TABLET FOR YOUNG CHILDREN

DreamWorks and a technology company, Fuhu, have a product we have used with five-year-olds; it is called DreamTab. The two companies worked together to create a device that has original content and frequent updates. For example: DreamWorks animators have designed interactive drawing lessons for young children. Some of the best animators in the country share their approaches to their art form. Along the way, young children are invited to experiment with related art of their own. A major goal is to change the way children interact with technology.

You can arrange it so that when children turn on the DreamWorks tablet, up pops the penguins from *Madagascar* to get children to do a creative dance. It is about as far as you can get (on a tablet) from the days of solitary confinement in front of a computer screen. Still, it is important to remember that there are frequent times when it is best to turn off the devices and work in small groups—or *go outside to play.*

Although most of the experiences are at a primary level, the DreamTab comes with a stylus that is similar to what professional animation artists use. It is also possible to get on the Web and do things like email and instant messaging. Fortunately, everything is designed to fit within the guidelines set by the Children's Online Privacy Act.

A NATIONAL SECURITY AGENCY (NSA) WEBSITE FOR CHILDREN

Like DreamWorks, the NSA uses animation to put a smiley face on its mission. No, it is not to inform on their parents—at least not yet. Children are encouraged to construct their own secrets by using furry animals and reptiles. Breaking colorful codes and recovering signals from around the world are part of the game.

Decipher Dog and CrypoCat are just two of the cartoon characters that help children learn about spying duties and to think about what they want to do when they grow up. After entering the How I Can Work for the NSA section of the site, a bunny rabbit comes along and says it likes listening to hip-hop and rock. In his free time, he uses cutting-edge technology-derived intelligence from a variety of signals from all over the world.

The NSA animation takes children into games of identifying the purpose, content, and user. Cellphones, emails, Google searches, Facebook records, and other signals are all part of the fun. The CyberTwins (Cy and Cyndi) even have some good tips on stopping and thinking before sharing private information on social network sites. The whole process resembles efforts by many businesses, educators, and other governmental agencies to promote self-serving messages and related interaction with children. *A note to parents and teachers:* you had better keep an eye on what youngsters are doing on the Internet.

Schools, families, and communities need to share responsibility for getting students engaged and motivated to learn about competing societal dilemmas.

The early years has a lot to do with later success. Impulse control, social skills, and tenacity are dispositions that develop early on.

Although they are hard to measure, social and emotional development are key factors at any age. Problems at school are often the result of things going on outside the classroom. Sometimes it takes programs that bring parents on board. At other times it may take counseling and treatment.

The arts can help address a whole range of issues—from early childhood through the teenage years.

THE ARTS—PAST, PRESENT, AND FUTURE

Even at the beginning of human civilization, the arts had a central place in ceremonies that connected cave paintings to ritual, religion, and daily life. In fact, humanity has been shaped by the synthesis of science, math, art, and the imagination (Gurche, 2013).

In the future, will our culture be as filled with the arts as it now is with television and sports? Of course, a lot depends on how you narrow or stretch the definition of what "the arts" mean. But no matter what the definition, the arts and social change will continue to shape each other.

Both the arts and the sciences have many things in common; both are always looking for interesting problems to solve. Making or exploring something that we are unfamiliar with is the essence of creativity across subjects. And we all have a certain amount of creativity in us.

Arts education, at its best, helps students develop an interpretation of the world collectively, to adapt, and to make sense of the world around them. No one works in total isolation to create a masterpiece. There is always a collective influence. But this doesn't mean that individuals should jump on any bandwagon without an interest in its destination.

Many educators and artists suggest that children without knowledge of the arts are as ignorant as children without knowledge of literature or math (Eisner, 2005). Schools are good at transmitting knowledge, but a deep knowledge in the arts requires going beyond factual information to developing practical knowledge. In a paint-by-numbers world, you have to know when to depart from the cookbook. This involves avoiding tunnel vision and building on imitation, imagination, and actual experience to create things that go beyond the textbook or lesson.

De Tocqueville predicted that American democracy would diminish the character of art. It took decades to prove him wrong—at least for a while. Now, some artists have worked hard to break down the disconnection between the nation's establishment (including the arts, academia, and the press) and the people.

Whether it's visual arts, music, or the theater, the arts have the potential to help us be receptive to new thinking and generous toward the production of something fresh. Far from being beaten down, American artistic expressions, especially film and music, have been some of our most successful exports.

Some people think of the arts as elitist, therapeutic, frivolous, impractical, or mindless entertainment. They are not always wrong, but they miss the point. The arts can provide important intellectual tools for understanding many subjects. They also build on qualities that are essential to revitalizing schooling: teamwork, analytical thinking, motivation, and self-discipline (Donahue & Stuart, 2010).

In the twenty-first century, the arts have a lot to offer new approaches to curriculum and instruction; for example, skills and perspectives of art to show what thinking, learning, and life can be. The arts also provide cultural resources that people can draw on for the rest of their lives. But in this era of accountability, attention has to be given to the substance of the disciplines involved. Otherwise, the arts may be dismissed as expendable in an era of curriculum gridlock and financial difficulties.

VISUAL ANALYSIS AND THE CRITICAL FUNCTION OF THE ARTS

Efforts are now being made to deepen and extend education in the arts by connecting them to critical thinking, problem solving, aesthetic analysis, technology, and new ways of working. This increasing influence of discipline-based art education (DBAE) curriculum addresses more than the traditional issues of creative expression and performance. It provides an interdisciplinary framework for connecting arts education to aesthetic criticism within a cultural, historical, and social context.

In a literature-based reading curriculum, for example, students are expected to develop the thinking skills necessary for "literary criticism." Should we expect less when it comes to the arts? A renewed emphasis on artists, criticism, aesthetic discourse, and the importance of discipline-based arts education will accompany education into the next century.

DO MUSIC LESSONS HAVE A COGNITIVE BENEFIT?

Cognitive skills like spatial reasoning may be enhanced, but the research on the subject isn't conclusive. But even if future studies rule out major gains in academic achievement, music education generates joy and cultural knowledge along with the development of musical skills.

Some Selected Examples of Discipline-Based Art Education Activities (Practical Ideas for Teachers)

The following discipline-based art activities are organized around an interdisciplinary unit theme titled "You and Your World." This approach was selected so that critical-thinking skills and interdisciplinary content could be linked and included as an integral part of classroom life.

As part of an integrated approach, it is important that children learn to be more flexible and move freely between different communications media. To accomplish this, children need exposure to many different communication forms.

Unit Introduction Activity

Before beginning this unit, discuss with children the need all people have to communicate ideas and how there are many ways to do this. Encourage children to brainstorm all the ways people use to communicate. List the suggestions on the board or a chart. Young children may wish to find or draw pictures that can be placed on a bulletin board. Such a chart becomes an ongoing resource for students to refer to, and additions can be incorporated throughout the year.

Unit: You and the World

When you think of how you are related to others, the thing that most people say is family. But even if you were alone in the world, you wouldn't be unrelated. The fact that you have read these words makes you a member of English-speaking people. As a student, you have a relationship with those who attend your school and with those who work there. The music you listen to and enjoy is enjoyed by others. Your relationships with your fellow humans are marked by the foods you think are good, the clothes you think are fashionable, the jokes you tell, and more.

In the nineteenth century, Ralph Waldo Emerson viewed the relationship between the arts and your day-to-day work with others as central to imaginative thinking. He felt that people depended on their relationships in order to understand what they read, wrote, painted, or sang. Emerson thought that each person is related to a few others and to all people; each of us has within ourselves the sum of human history.

You may never have thought of yourself as part of an ongoing historical record. But chances are you have watched characters in movies or on television and sensed that they felt as you have felt and acted as you would have acted—that they were, in a sense, related to you. Your relationships with actual or fictional others are the basis of sympathy and one of the keys to imaginative thinking.

Unit Activities

1. Make a map of significant relationships in your life. Put your name in the center of a sheet of paper. Then begin thinking of the important people in your life. As you think of them, write their names on the paper. Organize or group the names that belong together. You may wish to connect the names with lines to show the relationships.
2. Make a list of ten words you chose at random from the dictionary. Next, write or make up something about you that uses all the words you have listed. It could be a paragraph in the form of a news report, a story, a creative drama, or whatever works with the words you have. Just make sure you *use* the words, not just mention them.

   For example, the word *hare*.
   Use: I saw a *hare*, chewing on a carrot in my garden.
   Mention: *Hare* is another word for a rabbit.
   Let the words guide what you write.

3. Suppose there is a lottery in your state. A three-digit number is picked at random. For $1, you can buy a ticket picking any number from 000 to 999. If the number on your ticket matches the number on the ticket drawn you win $500. Is that a good payoff? Why or why not? How much of the money the state takes in does it keep?
4. Try reflecting on and then describing an episode from a television series that you regularly watch. Here are some questions that may help you think

about the program. Jot down your answers. Then, write a paragraph or two about what you've learned.

a. For what sorts of people is the program produced?

b. Are the main characters people like yourself? Are they people you want to be like?

c. Are the main characters unusual in some way? If so, in what way? Are they usually attractive? Do they have special skills?

d. If the program is a comedy, what are the jokes about? Is there a laugh track? Do you laugh as often as you hear people in the audience laughing?

e. What kinds of problems do the characters in the program have? Are they the same sorts of problems you have?

f. Are the characters in the program richer or poorer than you are?

g. Describe the plot. Does it make sense? Do the characters in the program act the way real people act?

h. Does the program use background music? What sort of music? What does the music contribute to the mood of the program?

i. Try looking at the program without listening to the sound. What do you notice? Try listening to the program without watching the picture. What do you notice?

j. Do you know what is going to happen before it happens, or are you surprised? How do you feel when the program ends?

CONNECTING SUBJECT MATTER WITH THE ARTS

The arts can also help get a dialogue going between disciplines that often ignore each other. When knowledge from diverse subject matter areas are brought together, the result can be a new and valuable way of looking at the world. The arts and humanities have proved to be very useful tools for integrating curricular areas and helping students transcend narrow subject matter concerns.

Teachers at many levels have used intellectual tools from the fine arts as a thematic lens for examining diverse subjects. Some schools have even worked out an integrated school day, where interdisciplinary themes based on the fine arts add interest, meaning, and function to collaboration. Whether it's reading, writing, arithmetic, or anything else, the arts can be wrapped around central themes in the arts so that rich connections stimulate the mind and the senses.

The research suggests that using a thematic approach improves students' knowledge of subject matter and aids in the transfer of the skills learned to other domains outside the school. An additional finding is that good units organized around themes can improve the students' abilities to apply their knowledge to new subjects.

In collaborative art projects, language development flourishes when children are encouraged to discuss the materials they are using and reflect on the nature of their artwork through writing. Whatever the combination, an important result of integrating various subjects around a theme results in an enhancement of thinking and learning skills—*the metacurriculum.*

Before we can deal with teaching the thinking process, children need some solid content to think about. After that, teachers need to provide continuity between activities and subjects. The thinking skills engendered in one area can serve as a connection between subjects. In making curriculum connections, it's often helpful for teachers to see model lessons that include cross-disciplinary suggestions and activities.

The relationships established between subjects and the way teachers facilitate these relationships are important. When disciplines are integrated around a central concept, students can practice the skills that they have learned from many subjects. This helps students make sense out of the world.

The goal of an interdisciplinary curriculum is to bring together different perspectives so that diverse intellectual tools can be applied to a common theme, issue, or problem. Thematic approaches can help by providing a group experience that fosters thinking and learning skills that will serve students in the larger world.

By its very definition, "interdisciplinary" implies cooperation among disciplines and people. The notion that students of different abilities and backgrounds can learn from each other is a natural outgrowth of the collaborative tendency inherent in this approach. Everyone's collaborative involvement not only allows input into the planning process but it can also help with self-responsibility and long-term commitment to learning.

Organizing parts of the curriculum around themes means that each subject is mutually reinforcing and connected to lifelong learning. Subjects from the Greek classics to radiation theory need the historical, philosophical, and aesthetic perspectives afforded by interdisciplinary connections.

Curriculum integration provides active linkages between areas of knowledge, consciously applying language and methods from more than one discipline to examine a central theme, issue, topic, or experience. This holistic approach focuses on themes and problems and deals with them more in depth rather than memorizing facts and covering the text from cover to cover.

There is always the danger of watering down content in an attempt to cover all areas. We can, however, teach the work of Newton on one hand while paying attention to the history of the times on the other. The history of ideas, political movements, and changing relationships among people are part of the fabric of our world. We cannot narrowly train people in specialist areas and expect them to be able to deal with the multifaceted nature of twenty-first-century jobs.

THEMATIC STRATEGIES FOR CONNECTING
SUBJECTS AND PEOPLE

Artists have the right—and possibly the obligation—
to reinterpret the history of our time

—Oliver Stone

Like the arts, innovation in science can experience ups and downs and cul-de-sacs. These different ways of knowing, the arts, and the sciences do not need to grow further apart. The unity of all cultural and scientific efforts was the unwritten rule until the eighteenth century. But as art and science have progressed over the last two hundred years, both have become more narrow, specialized, and extensive.

The arts can help connect the mind and the senses—uniting the cognitive and affective dimensions of learning.

Whether the collaboration is in the distant past, a computer chip, or a peer sitting nearby, collaboration in art involves creating, interpreting, and connecting to others. Socially useful art requires *hard* thinking about the location and the intended audience in order to understand how best to engage local modes of expression and needs.

Themes can also direct the design of classroom activities by connecting classroom activities and providing them with a logical sequence and scope of instruction.

One set of steps for developing thematic concepts is to:

1. Determine what students know about a topic before beginning instruction. This is done by careful questioning and discussion.
2. Be sensitive to and capitalize on students' knowledge.
3. Use a variety of instructional techniques to help students achieve conceptual understanding.
4. Include all students in discussions and cooperative learning situations.

Thematic instruction values depth over breadth of coverage. The content should be chosen on how well it represents what is currently known in the field and its potential for dynamically making connections.

THEMATIC UNITS

The design of thematic units brings together a full range of disciplines in the school's curriculum: language arts, science, social studies, math, art, physical education, and music. Using a broad range of discipline-based perspectives can result in units that last an hour, a day, a few weeks, or a semester. They are not intended to replace a discipline-based approach; rather, they are expected to act as supportive structures that foster the comprehensive study of a topic.

Teachers can plan their interdisciplinary work around issues and themes that emerge from their ongoing curriculum. Deliberate steps can be taken to create a meaningful and carefully orchestrated program that is more stimulating and motivating for students and teachers. Of course, shorter, flexible units of study are easier to do than setting up a semester or yearlong thematic unit.

Collaborative thematic curriculum models require a change in how teachers go about their work. It takes planning and energy to create effective integrated lessons, and more time is often needed for subject matter research because teachers frequently find themselves exploring and teaching new material. Thematic teaching also means planning lessons that use nontraditional approaches and arranging for field trips, guest speakers, and special events.

Contacting parents, staff members, and community resources that can help expand the learning environment is another factor in a teacher's time and planning efforts. Long-range planning and professional development for teachers are other important elements of the process.

The arts have a power beyond aesthetics for making us "see." They can also enhance the ability (flexibility) to change your mind in the light of new information.

The arts can help us view ourselves, the environment, and the future differently—even challenging our certainties about the arts themselves. In connecting the basic concerns of history, civilization, thought, and culture, the arts provide spatial, kinesthetic, and aesthetic skills that are the foundation for what it means to be an educated person. Such understandings do not occur spontaneously. They have to be taught.

The process of understanding or creating in the arts is more than unguided play, self-expression, or a tonic for contentment. They can be tools for shattering stereotypes, changing behavior, building a sense of community, and acting as a vehicle for sociopolitical commentary.

In referring to his artwork, Andy Warhol once suggested that he liked to paint boring things. By "boring," he meant everyday items that can be used to find transcendental beauty. An example from the visual arts: Barbara Kruger develops popular imagery that merges words and concepts from other disciplines. Along with other postmodernist artists (like Keith Haring and Jenny Holtzman), she works outside the artistic and the aesthetic frame to harness the formative power of images to affect deep structures of personal and social belief. In a similar manner, artist Alexis Smith combines quotes, flotsam, and jetsam that speak to the artifices and pitfalls of a mythical America. When the right object is connected to the perfect quote, the result can range from the humorous to the toughest and most intriguing social observation.

Moving toward music, storytelling, and dance, Laurie Anderson extends the edges with performance art, combining nearly every basic art form with literary references and video imagery to create theatrical performances. Like many modern artists, she releases possibilities by making use of collaborators across time, media, and subject matter.

MUSIC LESSONS AND SUCCESS ACROSS THE CURRICULUM

Participation in music lessons may lead to higher levels of achievement in other subjects. An edited version of a STEM music lesson developed by Victoria Abbott follows:

The Five Senses Lesson Plan

In kindergarten classrooms across the Maritimes, teachers often teach a unit titled "Exploring the World Using Our Five Senses." The lesson can be linked to a grade 1 unit that is also about the senses: "Exploring Objects and Materials with Our Senses."

Grade Level: Kindergarten or Grade 1

Subject: Science + other subjects.

Unit: "Exploring the World Using Our Five Senses" or "Exploring Objects and Materials with our Senses."

Introduction: To build on multiple ways of knowing (multiple intelligences), Victoria Abbott suggests using two songs that she has rearranged from songs that children may know. "Intelligences" include: musical/rhythm, verbal/linguistic, bodily/kinesthetic, and visual/spatial.

1. The 5 Senses Songs (Note: The square parentheses are suggested actions for you and your students).
   a. "The Senses Family" (Sung to the tune of the first verse of "The Addams Family Theme Song").

I have 5 different* senses [Hold up five fingers]
That help me every day
They help me in many ways
Now sing them all with me.

With my eyes I see, [Point to eyes]
My nose lets me smell, [Point to nose]
My ears help me hear, [Point to ears]
And with my tongue I taste. [Point to tongue]

Now, don't forget the fingers; [Wiggle all your fingers]
They help us to feel
Everything we touch [Gently rub fingers together]
Now let's begin again.

I have 5 different senses [Hold up five fingers]
I see, I smell, I taste, [Point to eyes, then nose, and then stick out tongue]
I hear and I feel. [Point to ears and then rub fingers together]
Thanks for singing them with me.

* *Different* should be pronounced *diff'rent* to help the song flow smoothly.

2. "There Are 5 Senses" [Sung to the tune of "Do Your Ears Hang Low"]
There are 5 senses [Hold up 5 fingers] Can you tell me what they are?
[Shrug shoulders]
Do you use your eyes to see near or far? [Point to your eyes then motion
near or far]
Does your nose tell you if something smells good or bad? [Point to your
nose and then give thumbs up or down]

How many senses do you have?
There are 5 senses [Hold up 5 fingers] Can you tell me what they are?
[Shrug shoulders]
Do you use your tongue to taste a chocolate bar? [Stick out tongue]
Do your fingers tell you if something is soft or hard?
Tell me how many senses there are.

Which sense is left? [Shrug shoulders] Can you tell me what it is?
We know you see and smell, taste and feel, [Point to your eyes, nose,
tongue, and fingers]
We won't forget the last sense, have no fear. [Wag your fingers during
"have no fear"]
We use our ears so we can hear. [Point to ears]

There are 5 senses [Hold up 5 fingers] Yes, we learned them all.
But did you know there are some people who don't have them all.
Some can't see, feel, smell, or taste. Some can't hear me.
But we are all special, and we are unique.

Activity: [The same procedure can be followed with both songs]

1. Create a big poster with the lyrics written or typed on them.
2. Create five smaller posters with each of the senses on them. You can either draw the body parts that are attached to the senses or find pictures on the Internet to use.
3. Read the lyrics to children while doing the actions.
4. Sing the song to the children (You can play an instrumental in the background, sing it without music, or play along with an instrument).
5. Have the children sing the song with you.
6. After the song is done, ask the students to share with a partner what they thought about the song. Depending on the class's reaction, you can decide how often to do the song with the children.

Assessment: An informal assessment can be done by keeping a note on who was able to point to the correct body parts along with the songs.

OPENING UP A SHARED SENSE OF WONDER

There is a connection between productive citizenship, academics, and the arts. For students to make these connections, it will take more than a specialist in the art class for one hour or a week or an inspirational theater troupe visiting the school once a year.

Brief experiences can help and inspire—but it takes more sustained work in the arts to make a real difference. Quick "drive-by teaching" is the equivalent of driving a motorcycle through an art gallery—you might get some blurred notion of color but not much else. Avoiding arts education denies students a vital quality-of-life experience—expression, discovery, and an understanding of the chances for human achievement.

The arts can open up a sense of wonder and provide students with intellectual tools for engaging in a shared search. This won't occur if children are having fewer experiences with the arts at school and in their daily lives. They at least have to know enough to recognize what to notice and what to ignore. This means that some grasp of the discipline is required if the arts are going to awaken anyone to the possibilities of thoughtfulness, collaboration, and life.

There are some excellent models or prototypes of art education. The Minneapolis discipline-based art program is one example. Another is in Augusta, Georgia, where the National Endowment for the Arts (NEA) has supported the development of an exemplary arts education model. This program uses the arts to improve academic achievement, the general learning environment, student self-esteem, attendance, creative thinking, and social equity among students.

ART ACTIVITIES THAT ENCOURAGE REFLECTION

Reflecting is a special kind of thinking. Reflective thinking is both active and controlled. When ideas pass aimlessly through a person's mind, or someone tells a story that triggers a memory, that is not reflecting.

Reflecting means focusing attention. It means weighing, considering, choosing. Suppose you want to drive home. You get the key out of your pocket, put it in the car door, and open the door. Getting into your car does not require reflection. But suppose you reached in your pocket and couldn't find the key. To get into your car requires reflection. You have to think about what you are going to do. You have to consider possibilities and imagine alternatives.

A carefully balanced combination of direct instruction, self-monitoring, and reflective thinking helps meet diverse student needs. The activities suggested here are designed to encourage higher-order thinking and learning and provide a collaborative vehicle for arts education.

1. Looking At the Familiar, Differently
   Students are asked to empty their purses and pockets on a white sheet of paper and create a face using as few of the items as possible. For example, one case might be simply a pair of sunglasses, another a single earring representing a mouth, and a third could be a profile created by a necklace forming a forehead, nose, and chin. It gives students a different way of looking at things. It's also an example of a teaching concept known as aesthetic education.

2. Collage Photo Art
   Students at all levels can become producers as well as consumers of art. We used a videotape of David Hockney's work from *Art in America*. Hockney, one of today's important artists, spoke (on the videotape) about his work and explained his technique. Students, then, used cameras to explore Hockney's photo collage technique in their own environment. Student groups can arrange several sets of their photos differently—telling unique stories with different compositions of the same pictures. They can even add brief captions or poems to make more connections to the language arts, social studies, science, or music. Photographers know the meaning of their pictures depend, to a large extent, on the words that go with them.

   Note: teachers do need to preview any videos before they are used in the classroom because some parts may not be appropriate for elementary school children. Teachers can also select particular elements and transfer them from one device to another so that only the useful segments are present on the tape used in class.

3. Painting with Water Colors and Straws
   In this activity, students simply apply a little suction to a straw that is dipped in tempera paint. Working in pairs, students then gently blow the paint out on a sheet of blank paper to create interesting abstract designs.
4. Creating Paintings with Oil-Based Paints Floating on Water
   Working in groups of three, have students put different colored oil-based paints on a flat dish of water. Apply paper. Watch it soak up the paint and water. Pull it out and let it dry.
   [We sometimes use acrylic paint].
5. Lesson Title: Color Mixing [Version of a lesson plan by Jasmine Roberts]. The goal is to help students understand which two colors need to be mixed to make purple and green.

Question for the teacher before the lesson: When and why might it be important to know about mixing colors?

Student Directions: Show which two colors mix together (to make purple and green) by painting a picture.

Procedures:

1. Have students work in pairs.
2. Allow each pair to have four colors to choose from to make purple and green.
3. Advise each student to paint something that they can take home and put up.
4. Ask each pair to answer the question: *Who might find it important to mix colors?*

Objective: Introducing students to color mixing and establishing the relevance of mixing colors together.

Grade level: K–1.

Materials: paint, canvas or paper, paper towel, paint brushes, and aprons.

EXPANDING SOCIAL AND PERSONAL VISIONS OF THE ARTS

Teachers can create a space for the arts to flourish—a sense of opening—that helps free students from the predicted and the expected. Using the arts to inquire and sense openings results in what Emily Dickinson called "a slow fire lit by the imagination." As America moves toward the new millennium, we need all the imagination we can get.

Advancing the understanding, culture, art, creativity, and human values has everything to do with the life and quality of this nation. Nevertheless, educational decision makers often don't pay much attention to these issues. In the United States, for example, the arts are most often found on the fringes of the curriculum and instruction. This is due in part to not having a long tradition of broadly prizing artistic expression beyond the cute and the comfortable. Little is expected of citizens or leaders when it comes to knowledge about artistic forms.

The arts can open new horizons, enrich the spirit, and help educate students to expand cultural visions. An artistic perspective can color the way we see other aspects of social and educational change. When the arts are viewed as a personal luxury—and not traditionally associated with "real wage earning" occupations—developing or maintaining a good arts education program is more difficult. This is a disappointing portrait of ourselves—a reflection not of human strength and aesthetic vision, but of their absence. Restoring faith in the arts—and arts education—means expanding the margins to restore faith in ourselves as a nation.

Human societies have always depended on the arts to give insight into truths, however painful or unpopular they may be. Today, in many countries, there is wide agreement that the arts can aid children in developing creativity, becoming good citizens, and being productive workers. The basic notion is that the person and the world are poorer without the arts.

A country's richness of knowledge, enlightenment, and enduring resources for thoughtfulness also benefit from artistic endeavors. From Asia to Europe, serious arts education is one of the integrating features of the school curriculum. Such an investment of the arts is seen as an investment in the community—and vice versa. Americans are beginning to take notice.

Inventing the future of arts education means expanding the links within the arts, community, and the schools. There is a world out there that students must explore with the arts if they are to be broadly educated—to say nothing of developing self-examination, critical thinking, and problem-solving skills. All of these qualities can be taught and reinforced through the arts. They can also help children integrate thinking skills by such activities as producing critiques, reflecting on aesthetic concerns, and dealing with the nature of our humanity.

Children and young adults frequently have the innate ability to do creative work in the arts. What is frequently missing are basic artistic understandings and the opportunity for expression and analysis. Experience within a discipline matters because it is hard to do something new unless some of it is automatic.

When students have the chance to express themselves, there is the excitement of producing in their own way—conveying their personal aesthetic experience through the use of figurative language (metaphors, similes, etc.) in their writing and symbolism in their painting. The challenge is to provide the necessary background and opening doors so that meaningful concepts and images will emerge.

INCLUDING ART EDUCATION IN SCHOOL REFORM

In an effort to make arts education part of the national curriculum reform, the Getty Foundation put forward a series of *Discipline-Based Art Education* reports. These reports encouraged the schools to help students go beyond crafts to art criticism, history, and aesthetics.

In some of the small-scale projects, art educators, historians, philosophy professors, and local teachers gathered to collaborate in making aesthetics less mysterious for children and young adults. It was felt that even at early levels, students needed to be grounded in the ability to reflect on art, study the discipline, and test out the skills involved in production.

The United States provides an example of a national effort to make sure that the arts touch every classroom. The NEA has an agreement with the U.S. Office of Education to create an "in-depth arts-in education program" that could be part of the effort to "reinvent" American schools.

The arts are recognized as representing a body of knowledge—as well as a practical study of technique. Isolated school experiments are proving that there are a number of ways of doing this beautifully on a small scale. The question is whether the call for "world-class standards" in the arts will mean real change for a significant number of schools.

Although the connection to a rich artistic tradition is important, no response should be considered *the* "right" one. In fact, seeking the rewards of what some adults see as good creative products often makes their appearance less likely. Instead, teachers can mix modeling intellectual stimulation with the natural rapport and creative production that is such an important part of the mysterious art of good teaching.

Art criticism, history, and aesthetics contribute to production and a child's ability to draw inferences and interpret the powerful ideas. Art (like film, reading, or mathematics) makes use of certain conventions and symbol systems to express figurative meaning. In the visual arts, for example, this may include symbols in its expression through style (the fine detail), composition (arrangement of elements), and creating the possibility for multiple meanings. "Reading" an artist's symbols is as much of a skill as reading print or video images.

Art means going beyond the transient messages that are often over-valued by the culture. Multicultural societies also weave artistic material (visual arts, movement, and music) from other cultures into the curriculum, enabling students to creatively confirm the truth and beauty of their heritage. Art is not limited to specific times or cultures. Greek art was learned from Egypt. Christian art was shaped by ideas from Greece and the East. African, Chinese, Egyptian, and Mexican art have influenced Modernism. A high-quality national culture can provide a unifying frame for a rich multiplicity of cultural influences (Gelineau, 2004).

Exposing children to a variety of artistic forms and materials will make it easier to locate areas of strength and weakness. All students may have a similar range of choices, but it is how these choices are made that count. Choosing from a variety of artistic and intellectual possibilities is beneficial for building both the strength of creativity and basic skills. In addition, the arts can also help to get a dialogue going between groups or disciplines that often ignore each other.

When knowledge from diverse subject matter areas are brought together through art, the result can be a new and valuable way of looking at the world.

Children can be involved in artistic interdisciplinary projects—ranging from illustrating their own books to designing movement, to poetry, to producing videos with camcorders. Process, production, and critical dimensions are all important. To understand literature, for example, children must function as critics. With art experiences, critical analysis is equally important.

The creative effect of questioning, challenging, and aesthetic reflection all contribute to creative habits of mind and set up possibilities for action. It is also important for students to see how the arts can set up possibilities for positive action and take on our world concerns. The Art Institute of Los Angeles, for example, was asked to provide design concepts and tools to help solve problems, like affordable housing, attractive parks, small shopping centers, and ways to make the community more aesthetically pleasing.

CREATING POSSIBILITIES: SOME IDEAS FOR INCORPORATING ART EXPRESSIONS ACROSS SUBJECT AREAS

What if? These are magic words. They add exciting new possibilities to our world and the world of the child. "What if I would drop a rock into this tub of water?" "What if I would make a ship for the rock out of tin foil—would the rock float instead of sink?" Since the beginning of time, people have grappled with similar types of questions. An Italian sailor asked his colleagues

"What if I sailed west across the unknown ocean?" That sailor discovered America! A sixteen-year-old German schoolboy asked himself what would happen if he sent out a beam of light and he could keep up with it. That boy was Albert Einstein, and ten years later, his "what if" led him to create the theory of relativity.

In music, a frequent way of creating new possibilities is to vary a theme. Composers may start with a musical theme and then invent variations by changing it. Sometimes, the melody is speeded up, sometimes slowed down, and many times musicians shift keys, change notes, or add harmony. Jazz, for example, is often based on playing variations on a theme.

Music is not the only area where variations are invented. You can start with anything. For instance, teachers can vary a theme in their science, math, music, literature, history, and social science classes. The way to find variations is easy, and is much the same whether you are working with music, poetry, or mathematical equations. You rearrange the parts of what you began with, looking for new arrangements.

STRATEGIES FOR ARTS-CENTERED COLLABORATION

For teachers: getting students to actively collaborate in thematic lessons that build on the arts requires a depth of planning, modern assessment techniques, and cooperative classroom management skills. Collaborative learning values differences of abilities, talents, and background knowledge. Within a classroom that values teamwork, many conventionally defined "disabilities" integrate naturally into the heterogeneity of expected and anticipated differences among all students.

Organizing an interdisciplinary lesson around a theme can excite and motivate all students to actively carry out projects and tasks in their group. "Disabilities" and "differences" come to constitute part of the fabric of diversity that is celebrated and cherished within cooperative groups. In such an educational climate, no individual is singled out as being difficult, and no one student presents an insurmountable challenge to the teacher when it comes to accommodating a student with special needs.

In a collaborative classroom, no student needs to be stereotyped by others when they realize that there are many and varied "differences" among students. It is easier for the student with special needs to fit in. For some, pupils' "differences" may in fact constitute a "disability," defined as the inability to do a certain life or school-related task. Such a difference, however, need not constitute a handicap, as cooperative learning is a joint enterprise. Some may have a disability or special talent, but all have information and skills to contribute to the learning of others.

The central question is how do individual classroom teachers, already overwhelmed with tasks, find ways to: adapt collaborative techniques, plan thematically, and modify approaches for successfully accommodating all students within their classrooms.

Collaborative group learning is a proven way to learn how to imaginatively solve problems. Adapting techniques and modifying current methods can help—especially when it involves rethinking the structure of the curriculum and seeking different approaches for teaching students in a way that builds on their unique human qualities.

Art flourishes where there is a sense of adventure.

—Alfred North Whitehead

USING THE ARTS TO PROVIDE ACCESS TO EVENTS

The arts can provide openings to other subjects by opening the imagination to other areas of understanding. They fit naturally into language and literacy lessons. Literature, for example, has always connected directly to the arts. So has social studies and the concern about understanding cultural differences.

Ethnic background images must be made available in schools. But good choices are harder to come by. The typical painting of Native Americans, for example, represents a romantic vision of Indian life that obscures the damage done (to them) and the hard realities of their lives. If teachers aren't careful, they will simply add to the mound of sentimental clichés tying non-European cultures to the "cute-sy" in American life.

Aesthetic creativity seems to be deeply rooted in how a child's early symbolic products convey the meaning of their world. Even very young children can describe, interpret, and evaluate their visual and auditory perceptions. Adult creative effort often draws on such early efforts in the arts. Creativity in any realm rarely occurs from scratch. Most often, it is a combination of choices within a particular area.

Prizing imaginative insight and artistic expression in children should be viewed as essential to cognitive competence and effective citizenship. There is an aesthetic world out there that youngsters must explore if they are to be truly educated in any subject.

The arts can motivate the social, civic, cognitive, personal, and aesthetic development of students. They can also provide evidence of a shared national perspective while celebrating multicultural diversity. In spite of differences, we share certain common cultural values that are separate from European, Asian, or African traditions. This multicultural perspective is built upon the premise that human lives are fully real and valuable no matter how far from the engines of power and celebrity they are lived.

To see a really good play forty years ago, you usually had to go to New York. Now, thanks to public support (NEA), you can see world theatrical productions all over the country. Many of the poorest areas in the United States share one characteristic: swift and overwhelming demographic change. Schools *must* take seriously their role as multicultural communities; they are the one place young people from all these different backgrounds come together.

There has to be an open dialogue to honor the cross-section of students found in schools today. This means exhibiting student artistic expression so that their thinking is made public. Many local papers will, for example, devote an occasional section to advertisements designed by students. What an opportunity for artistic design, connection to the mass media, and communication! So is using just about any digital device to create a spin-off of thirty- or sixty-second TV commercials. The next step is placing it online.

The historical record makes it clear that creativity in the arts and other fields can be fueled by the raw stuff of life, big ideas, and a well-informed imagination. The arts are more than pretty pictures or pleasing music. For example, in today's visual art world, digital technology is sometimes used to recycle found personal images into art. From odd arrangements of old mug shots to paintings that are built around public records, privacy protection is an afterthought. We now live in a social media world where it is possible to see images and sounds as they happen, or as they are being created.

Is the future of artistic design going to be guided by benevolent software pieces of distilled mathematics (algorithms)? It's unlikely. Binary digits (bits) will probably not overwhelm the atoms of the physical world. A better guess would be that the digital future will be a marriage with the physical world, rather than a takeover of it.

Placing the arts closer to the heart of school reform is important to civic values and the full functioning of the human mind. They can help convey the notion that we are all one humane world where the arts can't be separated from thinking, dreaming, and social change. There is danger in the belief that the isolated self is the center of the universe and that getting in touch with one's feelings is more important than rational discourse. When it becomes more important to focus on your own problems than on larger social issues, bad things start to happen.

The arts are particularly effective in reducing insecurity. By sharing a commitment to each other and honoring what each individual brings to the process, this gives students many access points to the arts, other subjects, and the world. Solid intercultural friendships and a broad consensus that doesn't accept bigotry can reduce the display of intentional bias and inadvertent discriminatory behavior.

Arts education programs can help the early formation of strong multicultural relationships that can make a major contribution to intergroup understanding.

THE POWER TO DEFINE, CHALLENGE, AND EXPLORE

Even the Eurocentric tradition of art has borrowed from others and the geopolitical circumstances of its time. Influences fly in every direction. Octavio Paz has observed that "every Latin American work is a prolongation and a transgression of the Western tradition." The arts are both an end in themselves and a means to achieve other ends. They have the power to define us, challenge us, and help us explore the frontiers of human existence. The effect goes well beyond the art room or performance space to connect to other domains.

Herbert Read once said that the goal of education is the creation of "artists"—people who can creatively make things with potential social impact. The arts can also make us more aware and more alive. Good art participates in the creation of culture. Malcolm Muggeridge described this process as "a natural cafe of the mind, in which we are all the clientele; a meeting place which can be raucous at times both political assembly and place of entertainment, dance floor and theater with all kinds of rooms off it."

Quality control matters. A few decades ago, editors, directors, and other experts often created something special because they knew something. Now, the Internet has become a forum for an endless supply of unexamined choices.

With today's technology, anyone (with or without talent) can be an artist, writer, or music producer. It may be helpful for students in your classroom to "publish" their classwork. But at the same time, a constant barrage of mediocre work can get in the way of connecting to those who are genuinely talented or deserving.

In the context of invention, everything from science to social studies can be viewed as an art form. The arts can sharpen the imagination by providing openings to the untried. Good teachers play a key role in preparing students for difficult concepts. This is done in much the same way that art critics prepare the public for nonrealistic art.

To generate ideas, we need a rowdy natural cafe of the mind where you can find every discipline, a band, and a dance floor.

Do you have to be good at something before you can do it? No. In the arts—or in anything else—successful practitioners spend much of their time learning from their mistakes. The more successful you are, the more likely you are to get many things wrong before you get a few things right. When you dare to take a risk and get a few things right is when you are most likely to make a positive difference in the world.

CONNECTING TO MODELS OUTSIDE OF SCHOOL

Fostering creativity in the arts means encouraging students to think for them-selves and coming up with different solutions to problems by linking arts edu-cation to their own personal experience. Just as it is in life outside of school, creativity involves innovative answers to questions that can, sometimes, change the very nature of the question itself (Bertram, 2014).

Creating an educational renaissance will require all the community resources educators can connect with. Some schools are experimenting with residencies by area artists. Others have connected to adult models by spon-soring projects on sites (an art gallery, symphony hall, the ballet company). In-depth thematic units can be developed that allow students to work on site to solve real-world and complex problems, understand subject matter in depth, and make connections across disciplines.

Getting students interested in a topic or a problem and interacting with others in an environment that allows thoughtful and creative expression are objectives that few educators will disagree with. Yet how, with today's already cluttered curriculum, testing requirements, and red tape, does a teacher find time to unearth art topics of interdisciplinary interest? Team training can help to share the load, and community resources can free up some teacher time. But to keep reform going, we are going to have to change organizational structures and protect teachers from bureaucratic requirements.

Teachers can supply classroom vignettes about effective teaching: the butterfly that "hatched" from a chrysalis in their classroom, students' creative language experience stories, movement (dance), creative dramatics, and painting murals. Other teachers might recall the newscast of the whale trapped in the ice that spawned an array of activities: research on whales, letters to elected representatives, a bulletin board charting bird migration patterns, and an attitude survey graph. Good teachers know that to be really excited about a subject they must really care about it.

The social forces surrounding a field of study and individual talent are important factors in generating (or inhibiting) creativity. As far as arts educa-tion is concerned, this means: legitimizing its goals by becoming an active force in educational change, assuming a more aggressive role with "at risk" students, and focusing on the potential of the arts to foster thinking skills and problem-solving abilities.

All social and educational institutions convey messages that can affect creativity and artistic development. Deep questions of value are involved in the kind of models we set and our methods for evaluating artistic prod-ucts. Art may belong to everyone, but being literate in the subject means being able to understand, critique, and create in a whole array of symbol systems.

It's best to get high-quality instructional experiences and training early on. As children gain more aesthetic understanding, teachers can think of them as participants in the artistic process. As students paint their own paintings, compose music, and collaborate in arranging their own dances, they come to experience the inner nature of how aesthetic creativity develops.

CLASSROOM ACTIVITIES THAT INVITE THOUGHTFULNESS: IDEAS FOR TEACHERS ON HOW TO CREATE WRITING PARTNERSHIPS

A common collaborative learning strategy is to divide the partnership into a "thinker" and a "writer." One partner reads a short concept or question out loud and tells what he or she thinks the answer should be. The writer writes it down if they agree. If not, they try to convince the "thinker" that there is a better answer. If agreement cannot be reached, they write two answers and initial one.

Literature and Movement

Some poems, stories, myths, and ballads are particularly suited to interpretation through movement. Choose one or two students to read while the others respond to the reading with creative movements. Create a magical atmosphere with poetry. Use penlights in a darkened classroom or use colorful ribbons for creative movement that requires group effort and harmony. While the teacher or one of the children reads, have the other children reflect on or enact the poem in movement. Each child can hold a penlight or ribbon to help create an effect.

Improvise Short, Original Music Pieces

Students can improvise music pieces and variations on existing pieces, using voices or instruments (e.g., traditional, nontraditional, jazz, rock, electronic).

Working with a Partner in the Art Museum

In an art museum, students might focus on a few paintings or pieces of sculpture. Have students make up a question or two about some aspect of the art they wish to explore further—and respond to five or six questions from the list in a notebook or writing pad they take with them.

Possible Questions for Reflection:

- Compare and contrast technology and art as ways for viewing the past, present, or future differently.
- How is the artwork put together?
- How are pictures, pottery, and music used to communicate?
- How did the creator of the visual art image expect the viewer to react or respond? Is the content or subject of the artwork the most important part of it? What else might the artist have wished to produce?
- How does your background affect how you view the message?
- Visuals are authored in much the same way print communication is authored. How does the author of a picture or piece of sculpture guide the viewer through such things as point of view, size, distortion, or lighting?
- What are the largest or smallest artistic designs of the work?
- What is the main idea, mood, or feeling of the work?
- When you close your eyes and think about the visual, what pictures do you see? What sounds do you hear? Does it remind you of anything—a book, a dream, TV, something from your life?
- How successful is the sculpture or artwork? What is your response to it?
- Where did the artist place important ideas?
- How do combinations or the organization of things make you feel?
- Does the artwork tell us about big ideas such as courage, freedom, or war?
- How does it fit in with the history of art?
- What does the work say about present conflicts concerning art standards, multiculturalism, and American culture?
- How did the work make you feel inside?
- Was the artistic work easy or hard to understand?
- Why do you think it was made? What would you like to change about it?

PRODUCTIVE CREATIVITY

Creativity is more than originality. There is a strong connection between creativity (including originality and novelty) and basic academic skills. The two feed on each other. Developing a unique clarity, style, and focus is as essential as any skill area. The rote drill approach of educational fundamentalists represents narrow thinking patterns that can hinder comprehension and creativity. To flesh out dry facts with substance, it is necessary to build on elements of basic skills to open up a multiplicity of images that can be creatively tapped and explored.

The traditional notion of educators is that if fluency, flexibility, and originality were systematically taught, true creativity would follow. Unfortunately, it isn't that simple. To begin with, teachers didn't know how to teach it or model these concepts. Secondly, fluency doesn't count for much if all the ideas generated are trivial. Even "originality" as it's understood in this context is sometimes simple social accommodation, rather than intuitive boundary pushing or barrier breaking.

Traditionally, common school practice encouraged children to be plodders who saw the rules as conduits for action, rather than as springboards for changing realities. In the real world, we learn a lot about creativity from our failures, accidents, and the personal restructuring of our reality in the face of uncertainty.

Taking risks, dealing with failure, the desire to be surprised, and enjoying ambiguity are all essential elements in creative behavior. All are difficult for teachers to teach and model *and* for many students to accept. However, both students and teachers profit from undergoing the fatigue of figuring things out for themselves.

The research suggests one way to fuse creative thinking to basic skills is to provide a rich arts environment and enough structure for a student to search out interesting material (Herz, 2010). Skillful teachers, then, examine the quality of the thought that has gone into student productions and helps with critical analysis and self-cultivation.

Some schools have proven that they can design learning experiences that in the arts are optimal for a diversity of student dispositions. They do this by assisting students in developing both disciplined basic skills and genuine creativity, thus providing multiple paths for student development (Opitz & Ford, 2014).

Gaining creative observational skills seems to help students develop distinctive styles and gain familiarity with a wide range of artistic approaches.

Without the arts, students would be denied the opportunity to develop the mental skills that makes art possible. Art is more than some abstract notion of beauty. Good art helps us rethink our conception of reality and alters our perspective. The creativity engendered can be a catalyst for information, change, and the enrichment of our intellectual, cultural, and civic life.

Artistic production, particularly for younger children, can play an important role as students produce in different artistic media. But even at early levels, students need to be grounded in the ability to reflect on art and be able to think about the thinking skills involved. Seeking the rewards of what adults see as good creative products makes their appearance less likely. No student response should be considered *the* "right" one. The mix of modeling intellectual stimulation and natural rapport is part of the mysterious art of good teaching.

Criticism, history, and aesthetics all contribute to production and a student's ability to draw inferences and interpret the powerful ideas. The arts make use of certain conventions and symbol systems to express figurative meaning. This can include symbols in its expression through style (the fine detail), composition (arrangement of elements), and by creating the possibility for multiple meanings. "Reading" an artist's symbols is as much of a skill as reading print. This means going beyond the transient messages that may be overvalued by the culture.

The playful invention of a young child may be closer to the way an innovative scientist or an artist works than that of a more "sophisticated" older student. Both good artists and good scientists have a highly developed sense of wonder and skepticism. They share a world of complex options and multiple paths that require flexibility and the energy to negotiate.

Neither the art nor the science world is well understood by many Americans. Even the well educated have barely enough understanding of art to act effectively on aesthetic, scientific, or political matters that they encounter in their personal, professional, or civic lives.

To paraphrase Aristotle, being an educated good person is more than looking at things from multiple perspectives or knowing moral rules that are informed by the arts and the sciences. It is about actually performing social roles (like student, teacher, or friend) as well. In other words, thinking, knowing, and action must somehow come together.

ESTABLISHING A COLLABORATIVE ARTS COMMUNITY

Valuing a range of contributions within a supportive and collaborative community can make the difference between a competent self-image and the devastating belief that nothing can be done "right." Recasting the teacher's role from authority figure dispensing knowledge to that of a collaborative team leader (coaching mixed-ability teams) is a major ingredient of collaborative learning.

Making students active participants in deciding what and how they should learn doesn't diminish the need for informed decision makers. But without these—and other changes—in the power relationships within schools and within the schoolroom, educational reform will be stymied. This process is particularly important with some media (like video) because it often takes a small group to do much of the production.

In a collaborative setting, the teacher helps students gain confidence in their ability and the group's ability to work through problems and consequently rely less on the teacher for validating their thinking. This involves a conceptual reexamination of today's student population, the learning process, decision-making relationships, and classroom organizational structure. Challenges for the professional teacher in this new environment are:

• taking a more active role in serving students of multicultural backgrounds and "at risk" students. In many cases this means addressing non-Western artistic formats.

- focusing and taking advantage of cooperative learning teams to foster students' thinking, reasoning, and problem-solving abilities.
- making use of cooperative learning strategies, peer tutoring, and new technology to reach a range of learners and learning styles.
- working to professionalize arts education and legitimatize the arts in the schools. This includes assessment of student knowledge, ability, and performance.
- developing exemplary materials supportive of cooperative learning. This development will have to be done with particular attention to: the promotion of thinking skills; the needs of "at risk" students; the needs of teacher professionalism; and assessment, accountability, and the advent of new technologies.

Although children are capable of both imitation and figuring out structure on their own, they can use mechanisms for thinking and digging deeply into subject matter and themselves. They also need structures for analyzing works of art, music, dance, and drama—frameworks for sorting out what is real in the environment. Children have widely divergent talents and interpretations that they derive from their own perceptions and ways they filter the world.

It is difficult to consider products of the imagination apart from the system of values brought to it. Good exercises in art education involve students in altering familiar or unfamiliar images along lines they feel are promising. Students need the chance to try things out, reflect on what they have done, and try again. Most teachers know how to encourage or reorient students if they are getting nowhere.

Good teachers believe all children will learn and recognize the need for high expectations as they strive to reach every individual. Successful instructors are also able to facilitate, probe, and draw on additional information, examples, and alternative approaches for those students who were unable to connect with the information initially. This requires knowing enough about the subject to feel comfortable with it.

All of our students possess the capacity to absorb knowledge—but it takes intelligent teaching to use that knowledge to reason effectively. Curriculum development requires staff development. It is often adult models (like teachers) and family support that make the difference between a commitment to the arts or dismissing them as irrelevant.

Effective teachers strive to ensure that what's being learned is a center of interest for students. This often means walking a fine line as they engage students as active thinkers—without interfering when children are working well on their own. Creative experiences in the arts are a blend of informed adult encouragement and opportunities for creative exploration.

A flexible arts curriculum requires not only knowledge about each child, but judgment about when to intervene, recognizing (like Emerson) that sometimes it is best to "let the bird sing without deciphering the song."

A COLLABORATIVE ARTS CURRICULUM MEANS:

1. *Active learning*
   Students exchange ideas when they are involved in well-organized tasks, with materials they can manipulate. Active learning is enhanced when students can collaboratively make predictions, find patterns, and explore and construct ideas, models, and stories.
2. *Interesting activities*
   Lessons should include activities that are designed to develop higher-level thinking skills, rather than quick, right answers. Problems on diverse topics, which encourage speculation or estimation, are more likely to motivate and encourage students to work together on the lesson.
3. *Chances for student interaction*
   Students need to develop the ability to work together and to become sensitive and responsive to group members and group needs. There is a need for activities that involve all group members as well as a need to sensitize the group to include all members in active involvement.
4. *Opportunities for thinking*
   Students should be given opportunities to explore diverse ideas emphasizing concepts and relationships. Challenging tasks and opportunities for interaction with peers can lead to more advanced thinking and creative discussions.
5. *Teachers as advisors and curriculum developers*
   Textbooks and teacher's manuals need to be altered or replaced by teacher ideas, materials, and activities that arouse student interest and encourage cooperation. The teacher's role becomes that of a consultant, advisor, and learner who interacts with teaching peers.
6. *Lesson structure and accountability*
   Opportunities should be provided for group- or teacher-led summaries of important aspects of the tasks. Students need to discuss what they have learned with the teacher and other students in order to understand and explain the activities they have worked on.

Students are encouraged to take an active role in planning what they will study and how they will do it. One way to divide the class is to have students self-select into cooperative groups based on common interests in a topic. Students decide on what specifically they wish to find out, divide up the work among themselves, summarize, and present their findings to the class.

There is much freer communication and greater involvement when students share in the planning and decision making and carry out *their* plan. Students achieve more through discussing, investigating, and working in mixed-ability groups than if working alone. The arts are used to create a broad perspective in a way that amplifies basic subject matter and help those involved become better cooperative thinkers and decision makers (Eisner, 2005).

Like any concept for organizing learning, the value of interdisciplinary curriculum lies in the quality of the implementation. It always comes back to teachers and their knowledge of their discipline—*the characteristics of effective instruction.* Like E. B. White, who wrote that he wanted to keep the notes of his own meeting, teachers must learn to script their own daily life in the classroom.

FOSTERING CREATIVITY WITH THE ARTS

Mass media, social, and educational institutions convey messages that can affect creativity and artistic development. Deep questions of value are involved in the kind of models we set and our methods for evaluating artistic products. An important twenty-first-century educational goal involves making sure that students are able to understand, critique, and create in a wide range of symbols, pictures, and sounds.

It seems desirable to have some basic skill training early on. The arts without imagination is sterile. But the arts without at least some technical skill and understanding aborts its image. As children gain more aesthetic understanding, it makes sense to think of them as participants in the artistic process. Children can paint their own paintings, jointly compose music, and collaborate in making the video and arranging their own dances. This way, they can experience the general nature and specific possibilities of aesthetic creativity.

By the middle school level, there is often some division of labor, with specialists in core subjects. But at the primary level, teachers often have dozens of subjects to teach; in many cases, they don't have arts education specialists. So, if the arts are going to be influential across the curriculum—or covered at all—the regular classroom teacher has to be involved. And that teacher has to have enough artistic knowledge and skill to teach things like painting, music, drama, and the use of digital technology.

It is as important to get students to understand the arts as to worry about the end product or the performance. Yes, helping students explore the broad philosophical dimensions of the arts is at least as difficult as teaching students to actually do art. But like most subjects, just teaching the subskills involved in producing art won't get it done.

Techniques and bits of knowledge are most useful if they are integrated into a larger whole. With inspired teaching and hard work, students can develop artistic sensitivity and reasoning skills in ways that touch other subjects.

Distinctive modes of human intelligence can manifest themselves in surprising circumstances. The arts are natural to the way children learn. Making schools really responsible for the different ways students learn involves changing institutional structure and power relationships.

Since digital technology is one of the major inventions of our age, it is bound to change our approach to various art forms. Computers, microchips, and online networks are innovations that now generate compelling visions and inventions. A background in the STEM subjects (science, technology, engineering, and mathematics) certainly helps. But some understanding of the arts and humanities is required to gain a more integrated, broader view of things when many of the jobs today are changing quickly—or didn't even exist five years ago.

THE ARTS AS A FRAMEWORK FOR
INQUIRY AND INVENTION

There was a time when you could look to artists, musicians, poets, dramatists, and other creators in the arts to arrange things in a way that would enlighten human understanding. Is something missing in the twenty-first century?

STEM-related activities can help students integrate the arts in a way that provides students with opportunities to apply the design processes of invention and innovation. Along the way, the arts can help put scientific, social, and political conditions into a creative framework and bring multiple dimensions of problems into view.

Along with integrative art investigations in the classroom, it is important to make sure that all students become confident and competent with the arts. This includes making sure that every child has access to a rigorous arts curriculum in a climate of reasoned thoughtfulness and high expectations. In addition, tomorrow's instruction in the arts will be more discipline-based and pay more attention to developing sophisticated consumers of the arts.

Improving education has as much to do with improving cultural quality as it does with increasing productivity. Much of what students have to do in the world outside of school involves the ability to work in groups, self-regulate, plan, execute, and complete various kinds of work.

When the arts are used as a framework for inquiry across the curriculum, they also serve as a productive way for both teachers and students to rethink and better understand basic real-world issues (Barone & Eisner, 2012). As teachers help their students learn to identify artistic themes, develop questions, and examine works of art, new and exciting pathways can be opened for examining all kinds of topics.

Arts education can be an agent of social change, in general, and education, in particular. If visual artwork, music, dance, and drama are not found in the public schools, then the chances for thoughtfulness, self-expression, and aesthetic appreciation are bound to be diminished. On a broader plane, the arts can help counter the tendency for standardization in the school reform process.

Imaginative behavior involves breaking out of established patterns and looking at things in different ways. The possibilities the arts offer for a unique opening up of new spaces will be sorely missed if they are relegated to the margins of educational restructuring.

Whether it is in the arts or other subjects, fostering creativity in the classroom has a lot to do with encouraging students to make something original, pose significant questions, and solve problems of consequence. The basic idea is to help learners deal with different solutions to problems, build on personal experience, and think for themselves.

The arts can positively influence the understanding of many topics. As a bridge to other subjects—or on their own—the arts can help us all reach out for new ideas that challenge and inspire. Like any other subject worth studying, they should be taught and learned for their own sake.

The current efforts to pay more attention to arts education are partly the result of adding the arts to the national educational goals. Activities in the arts are clearly viewed as crucial to developing and using analytical thinking skills to ask deeper questions.

Topical understanding and pleasure seeking lie at the root of the aesthetic experience. Whether it is in the arts or the sciences, an important goal has always been to gain insights that give those involved a greater appreciation of the human experience and a better understanding of the natural world.

> *Innovations usually begin life as an attempt to solve a particular problem, but once they get into circulation, they end up triggering changes that would have been extremely difficult to predict.*

> —Steven Johnson

SUMMARY, CONCLUSION, AND LOOKING AHEAD

Whether it is in the arts or anyplace else, innovation goes hand in hand with collaborative environments that encourage experimentation, risk taking,

diversity, and the combining of skills from many fields. Technology is a powerful lever that changes the context of all media. It has also created new forms
of modernity that inherently involves more uncertainty and risk.

At school and in life, the arts can refine and mediate risk taking, intellectual
curiosity, and continuous learning. In addition, they can aid the search for
new ideas by enhancing the ability to make thought-provoking intellectual
connections (Holmes, 2014).

As an integral part of perception, expression, problem solving, thought,
and action, the arts can offer all kinds of insights. They enrich and burnish
learning with wisdom by opening up spaces and that help us see beyond what
is. This includes clearing away the mental clutter in a way that helps us reach
beyond the mundane to something new.

It is important for students to understand how art forms interconnect with
each other and other subjects. Discipline-based arts education also pays close
attention to the analysis, history, and culture of the various art forms. But
whether on their own or as part of an interdisciplinary unit, the visual arts,
music, dance, and theater (drama) all have a place in the classroom.

New ideas are not created in a vacuum; they are networks built on the
ideas of others. It doesn't happen in a vacuum. Art is but one example of
work that is created in response to ideas and culture. Like real artists, it's
fine for students to collaborate, borrow ideas, and get feedback from peers
(Thornton, 2014).

In most areas, innovation is sparked by putting together creative teams in
an environment that values experimentation and accepts mistakes as part of
the process.

Some have suggested that the arts can help students move beyond pop
culture's common assumption that the past is our only future (Gurche, 2013).
There are always plenty of new ways to say, compose, paint, and construct.
And you do not have to paint like Matisse or compose music like Stravinsky
to make worthwhile art. All of us can learn to appreciate and be inspired by
the arts.

What about building on the arts to influence the future in a positive way?
Do we have any concrete ideas—or do we even know where to look or what
questions to ask? In 1910, for example, not Picasso, Einstein, Marconi, or
anyone else could envision what a visually intensive global communication
device (iPhone) would look like.

Something inventive and new is likely to involve many creators who are
involved in constant collaboration. From the light bulb to the devices of the
digital age, new products usually don't have a single inventor. Thomas Edison
and Steve Jobs may have been the first to bring some of their ideas to the
masses, but neither one was the first to experiment with artificial light or
design MP3 music players.

Innovation and the working out of the details require individual genius and cooperative teamwork. The same can be said for getting people to buy something new that they didn't know they needed (Johnson, 2014). Imaginative new approaches, especially in tech companies and startups, often require mixing heads-down engineers with people who are good at seeing beyond the immediate task.

One of the reasons that many workplaces strive for a balanced work culture is because the step-by-step engineering mentality has its limitations. The arts and humanities tend to prepare people with broader horizons. And both engineering and artistic tendencies are needed when future problems are not known and need to be discovered or defined in a new way.

The understandings sparked by analysis, mastery, and values inherent in arts have a lot to do with getting ready for the world we cannot yet know. As far as the classroom is concerned, informed encounters with the arts are a proven way for helping the young look outside today's reality and cooperatively construct alternate views of what the future might look like.

The years' doors open like those of language to the unknown.
Last night you told me to think up signs
Sketch a landscape,
Fabricate a plan on the double page of day and paper.
Tomorrow we shall have to invent once again the reality of this world.

—Elizabeth Bishop

REFERENCES

Barone, T., & Eisner, E. (2012). *Arts based research.* Thousand Oaks, CA: SAGE Publications.

Bishop, E. (1968). *Brazil.* West Sussex, UK: Littlehampton Book Series.

Brown, V., & Pleydell, S. (1999). *The dramatic difference.* Portsmouth, NH: Heinemann.

Bertram, V. (2014). *One nation under taught.* New York: Beaufort Books [Examines how to help American students who are falling behind in the STEM subjects].

Chatterjee, A. (2013). *The aesthetic brain: How we evolved to desire beauty and enjoy art.* Oxford, UK: Oxford University Press.

Crawford, M. B. (2015). *The world beyond your head: On becoming an individual in an age of distraction.* New York: Farrar, Straus and Giroux (MacMillan).

Cooper, M., & Sjostrom, L. (2006). *Making art together: How collaborative art-making can transform kids, classrooms, and communities.* Boston, MA: Beacon Press.

Cornett, C. (1999). *The arts as meaning makers: Integrating literature and the arts.* New Jersey: Prentice Hall.

Davis, J. (2008). *Why our schools need the arts.* New York: Teachers College Press.

Donahue, D., & Stuart, J. (Eds.). (2010). *Artful teaching: Integrating the arts for understanding across the curriculum.* New York: Teachers College Press.

Eisner, E. (2005). *Reimagining schools: The selected works of Elliott Eisner.* New York: Routledge.

Gardner, H. (2011). *Truth, beauty, and goodness reframed: Educating for virtues in the twenty-first century.* New York: Basic Books.

Gelineau, R. P. (2004). *Integrating the arts across the elementary school curriculum.* Belmont, CA: Wadsworth/Thompson Learning.

Gurche, J. (2013). *Shaping humanity: How science, art, and imagination help us understand our origins.* New Haven, CT: Yale University Press.

Herz, R. (2010). *Looking at art in the classroom: Art investigations from the Guggenheim Museum.* New York: Teachers College Press.

Holmes, R. (2014). *The age of wonder: The romantic generation and the discovery of the beauty and terror of science.* New York: Vintage.

Johnson, S. (2014). *How we got to now: Six innovations that made the modern world.* New York: Riverhead Books (Penguin Group).

National Standards for Arts Education. (1994). *What every young American should know and be able to do in the arts.* Reston, VA. Developed by the Consortium of National Arts Education Associations.

National Standards for Education in the Arts. (1994). *The arts and education reform goals 2000.* Washington, DC: U.S. Office of Education.

Opitz, M., & Ford, M. (2014). *Engaging minds in the classroom: The surprising power of joy.* Alexandria, VA: ASCD.

Sinclair, C., Jeanneret, N., & O'Toole, J. (Eds.). (2008). *Education in the arts: teaching and learning in the contemporary curriculum.* Oxford, UK: Oxford University Press.

Thornton, S. (2014). *33 artists in 3 acts.* New York: Norton.